Painting Childhood

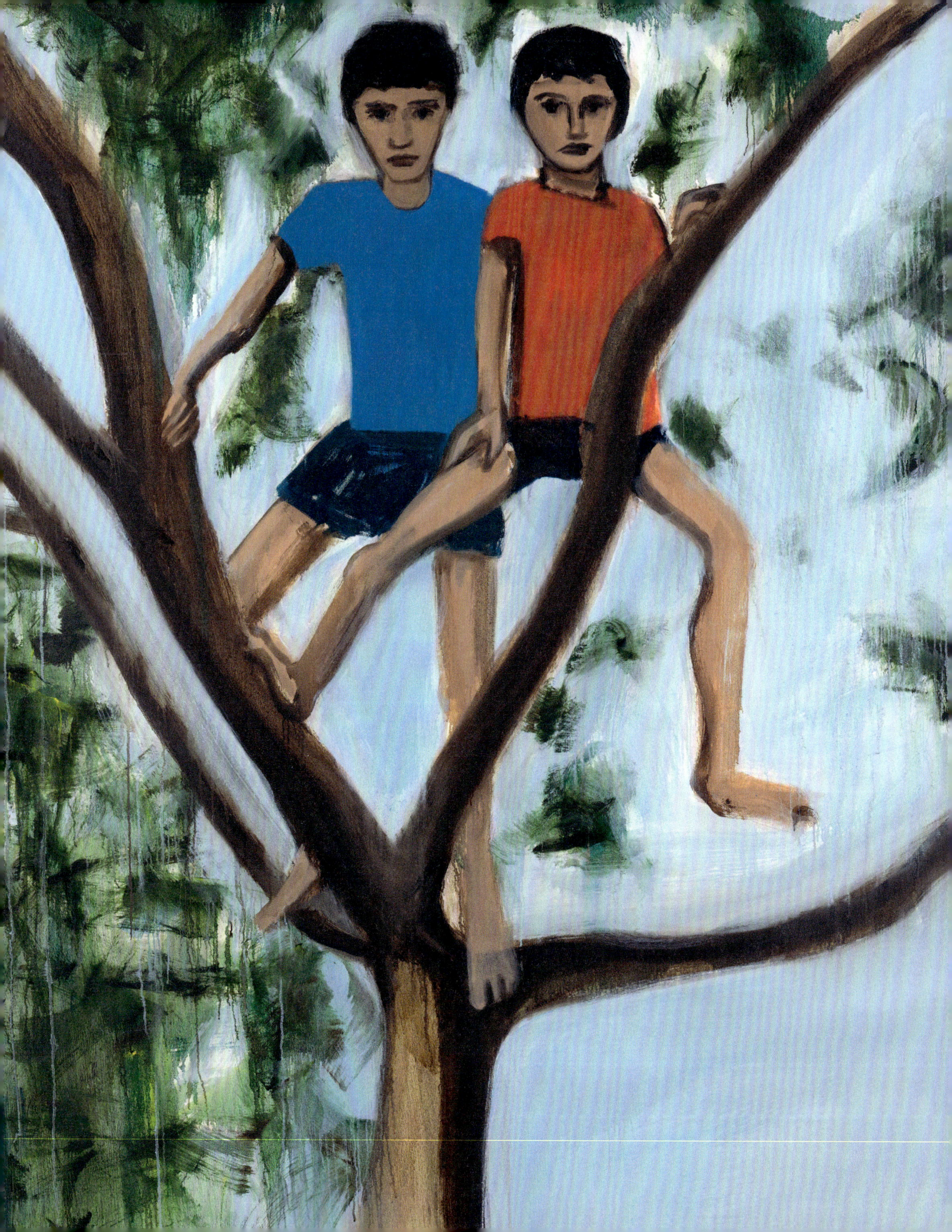

Painting Childhood

EDITED BY
Amy Orrock

CONTRIBUTIONS BY
Emily Knight, Amy Orrock, Martin Postle and Jill Seaton

COMPTON VERNEY
in association with
PAUL HOLBERTON PUBLISHING

Published to accompany the exhibitions

Painting Childhood: From Holbein to Freud

AND

Childhood Now

Compton Verney Art Gallery & Park, Warwickshire
16 March – 16 June 2019

ISBN 978-1-911300-56-4

British Library Catalogue in Publishing Data

A CIP record of this publication is available from the British Library

Produced by Paul Holberton Publishing
89 Borough High St, London SE1 1NL
WWW.PAULHOLBERTON.COM

Designed by Laura Parker
Printed by Gomer, Llandysul

FRONT COVER Frans Xaver Winterhalter, *Albert Edward, Prince of Wales, later Edward VII* (fig. 12, detail)

BACK COVER Winifred Nicholson, *The Artist's Children* (fig. 56, detail)

FRONTISPIECE Matthew Krishanu, *Limbs* (detail), 2014, oil on canvas, 180 × 140 cm

Contents

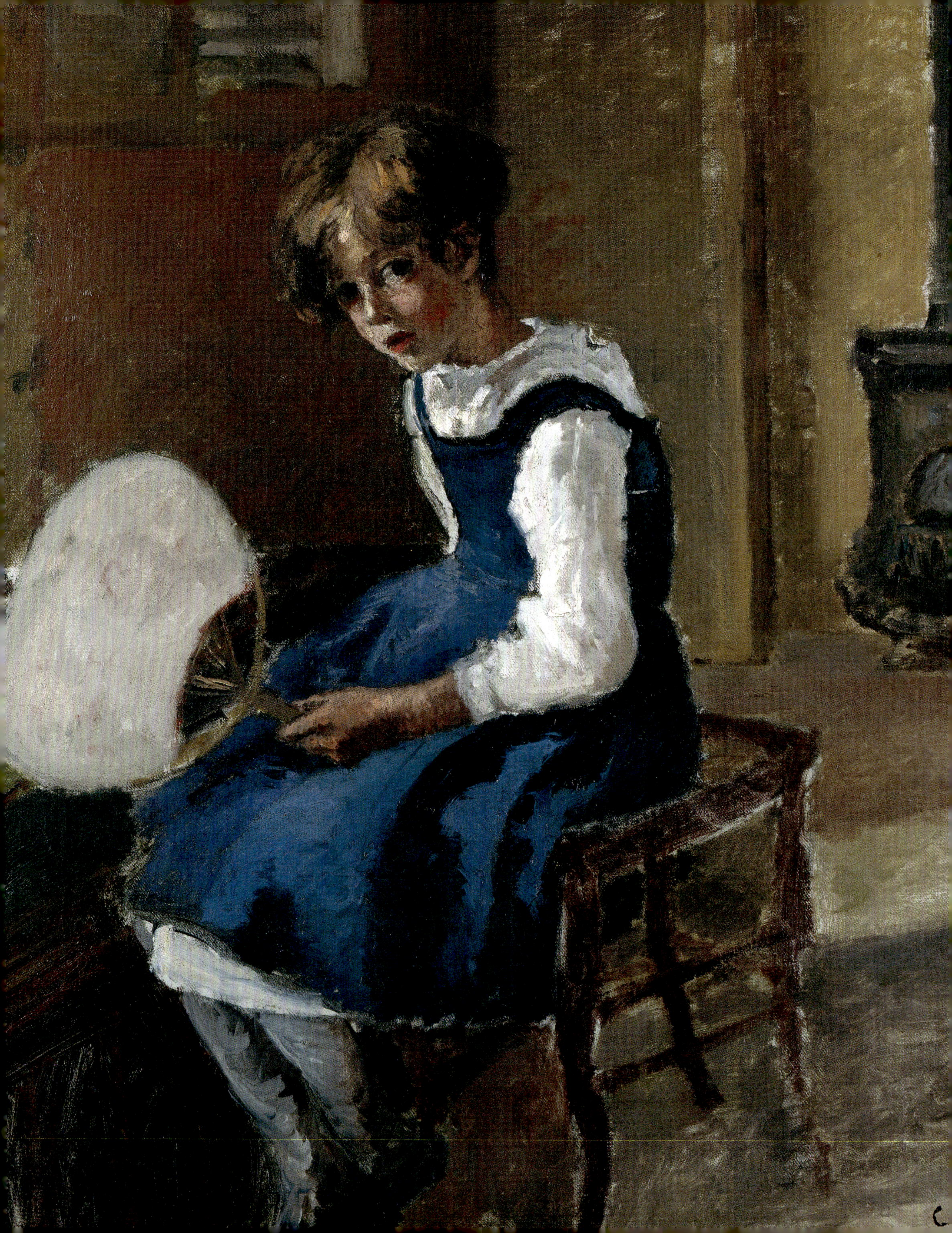

Foreword

Now more than ever, we are anxious about the state of childhood – its very existence threatened by the speed of contemporary society and the technological innovations that have come with it. An exploration of the hopes and fears of adults and children, examined through the lens of centuries' worth of paintings, is thus timely and illuminating.

The exhibition was inspired by three portraits from Compton Verney's own collection: two likenesses of Henry VIII's son, Edward VI (1537–1553), and a portrayal of a child by Marcus Gheeraerts the Younger (c.1561/2–1636). Hung beside works from the past five hundred years, it is the similarities rather than the differences that strike us, irrespective of the societal changes and artistic styles that have come and gone. Universal themes and common concerns of innocence, play and learning underpin them all.

We are hugely grateful to the lenders who have generously allowed us to exhibit their works. Without their support, ambitious projects like this would not be possible. It has been a joy to work with living artists to create a partner exhibition, *Childhood Now*. We are grateful to Chantal Joffe, Mark Fairnington and Matthew Krishanu for embracing this project with passion, and for their bold responses to the subject. *Childhood Now* provides a stimulating counterbalance to the historic exhibition, and offers more personal reflections on the theme.

I would like to thank all collaborators who have contributed to this project, particularly Dr Amy Orrock, who conceived both exhibitions and the book. The contributing authors, Emily Knight, Dr Martin Postle and Dr Jill Seaton, have given time and considerable expertise, enabling this publication to reflect both the content of the exhibitions and to capture new research. Several years in the making, the exhibitions have been made possible through funding from a Jonathan Ruffer Curatorial Grant and the Charlotte Bonham Carter Charitable Trust. Guidance and support has come from many people, but particular gratitude is due to Compton Verney's previous Director, Professor Steven Parissien. Thanks also to Paul Holberton Publishing, and the team at Compton Verney, who have worked tirelessly to deliver this outstanding exploration of a familiar theme in a bold new light.

AMY BANKS
Director of Creative and Engagement, Compton Verney

Camille Pissarro, *Jeanne Holding a Fan*, c.1873, oil on canvas, 56 x 46.5 cm, Ashmolean Museum, Oxford

Introduction
Painting Childhood

AMY ORROCK

The unique power of a painting to capture and preserve youth is intensified by the passage of time, with subjects remaining forever children despite the passing centuries – fixed like flies in amber. The starting point for an exhibition about paintings of children was three early portraits in the collection at Compton Verney – two likenesses of Henry VIII's son, Edward VI (1537–1553), and a portrait of a child by Marcus Gheeraerts the Younger (c. 1561/62–1636). The history of the child and the family is one of the most emotive and contested areas of modern history, and using images as evidence of childhood remains problematic.[1] Children do not commission paintings, and images made of them invariably reflect the interests and wishes of their governing adults, who include the paying patrons and in some cases the artists themselves.

The pictures gathered here reveal childhood to be a contradictory state – at once robust and fragile, unguarded and highly constructed. Common themes that emerge when looking at the contexts in which paintings of children have been produced and displayed include the responsibilities of dynasty, the moralities of play, the idealization and commercialization of youth, and the hopes and fears engendered by family ties. These four topics have been used to organize the pictures on loan from British collections for the exhibition of historic works at Compton Verney, *Painting Childhood: From Holbein to Freud*. A second exhibition at Compton Verney, *Childhood Now*, provides a fascinating opportunity to reflect on the place of children as artistic subjects today, through a focused display of works by three contemporary figurative painters, Chantal Joffe, Mark Fairnington and Matthew Krishanu. The material is combined from both exhibitions in this book, with chapters focusing on royal portraits, memorial portraits, 'fancy pictures' and artists' paintings of their own children. Such a survey can never be comprehensive, but it is hoped that the exhibitions and publication will provide a sense of the many remarkable and intriguing images of children that have been made over the centuries.

Marcus Gheeraerts the Younger's portrait of *A Boy Aged Two* is one of the earliest in the exhibition (fig. 1). With dark eyes in a pale face, the child wears a green velvet doublet and skirt over a hooped frame. At first glance the sitter could be mistaken for a girl, but is a boy, his gender signified by his short hairstyle, his front-fastening doublet and the dagger worn at his waist. In the sixteenth and seventeenth centuries, young boys typically wore skirts until between the ages of six and seven, when they were removed from the care of their mothers and 'breeched' – a public sign that they had entered the world of men. The impression given by the portrait is one of wealth: the boy's outfit is encrusted with silver embroidery and 'spangles', an early form of sequins, and the lace of his cuffs and collar are finely painted. Red is used as an accent colour throughout the painting, from his bright crimson shoes peeping below the hem of his skirt to the coral bracelets at his wrists, worn to protect children from misfortune.[2] A painted inscription at the top of the painting tells us that the boy is aged two and the year is 1608, but, as so often in portraits of children from this period, the sitter's identity and the reason why the painting was made have been lost. Gheeraerts's portrait captures a moment in time and the posy of wild pansies and robin tied to a cord also indicate time arrested. At any moment the bird could flutter up, scattering the carefully grasped flowers. While children typically kept birds as pets,

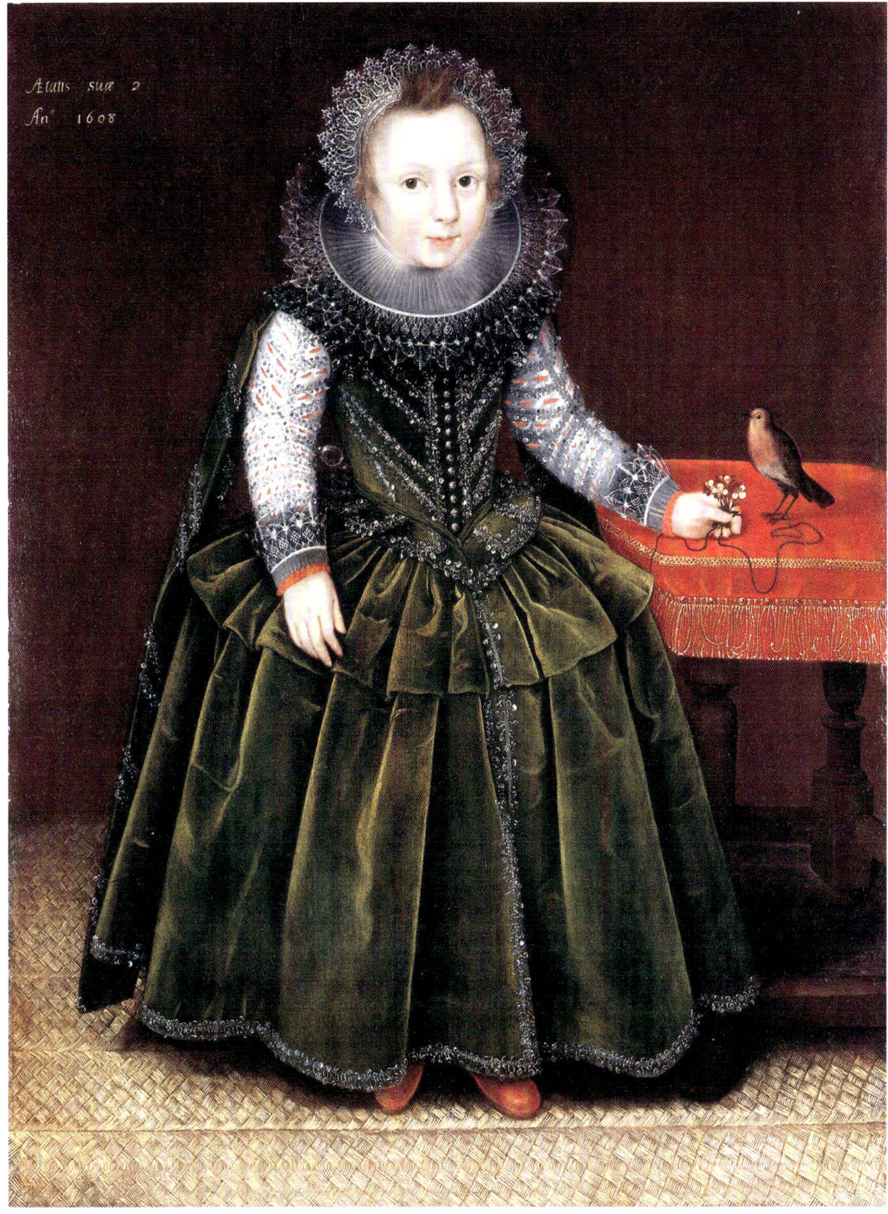

1
Marcus Gheeraerts the Younger, *A Boy Aged Two*, 1608, oil on panel, 114.3 x 85.7 cm, Compton Verney Art Gallery & Park

the combination of bird and flowers here may symbolize the transience of life, and it is indeed possible that this lively portrait of a young boy was made after his death.[3]

The middle of the sixteenth century was marked by a growth in portraits of children produced for the nobility, the gentry and the 'middling sort', who began to record the ages and appearances of their children for posterity.[4] It was also the period when numerous portraits were made of Edward VI, both as Prince of Wales and as a young King. On the Continent, children's portraiture developed rapidly, and depictions of anonymous children also became more common, as seen in the works of Pieter Bruegel the Elder (c. 1525–1569), who transformed the representations of cavorting children found in the margins of illuminated manuscripts into large-scale panel paintings. The production of images of children increased during the seventeenth century, and is represented in this exhibition through paintings by Anthony van Dyck

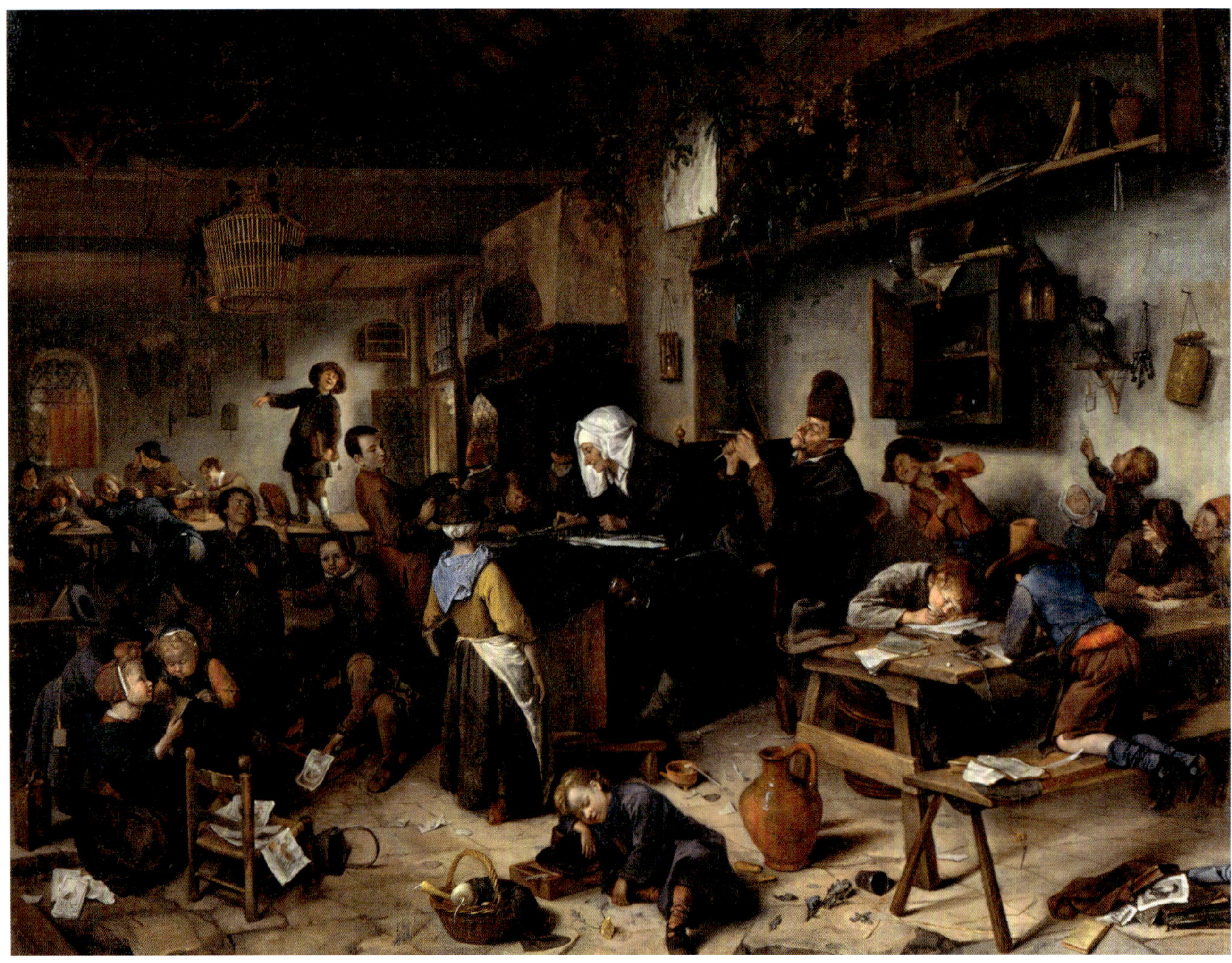

(1599–1641), Bartolomé Esteban Murillo (1617–1682), Judith Leyster (1609–1660) and Jan Steen (c. 1626–1679). Working independently of each other and in very different cultural milieus, these painters would exert a considerable influence over artistic representations of children for centuries to come. Recent exhibitions on the theme of childhood have focused fruitfully on the eighteenth century as a period of transition in both the status of the child in society and the development of child portraiture in Britain.[5] Building on these, the scope here extends through the nineteenth and twentieth centuries and up to the present day, providing further opportunity to reflect on the changing face of childhood and on the relationships that pictures of children have to one another.

The paintings exhibited and discussed here operate on two levels. They belong to a strong visual tradition, and illuminate examples of artistic exchange, appropriation and transformation across the centuries. Yet they are also each culturally specific objects, products of a particular time, place and set of circumstances. This is demonstrated by Jan Steen's chaotic classroom in *A School for Boys and Girls* (fig. 2), a painting that both documents and satirizes seventeenth-century teaching practices. Education was important in the Dutch Republic and its children were among the most literate in Europe, with even poor children able to attend school in classes that sometimes numbered over one hundred pupils.[6] The children in Steen's schoolroom wear patched clothes and holey stockings,

2
Jan Steen, *A School for Boys and Girls*, c. 1670, oil on canvas, 81.7 x 108.6 cm, National Galleries of Scotland

3
Judith Leyster, *A Boy and a Girl with a Cat and an Eel*, c. 1635, oil on panel, 59.4 x 48.8 cm, National Gallery, London

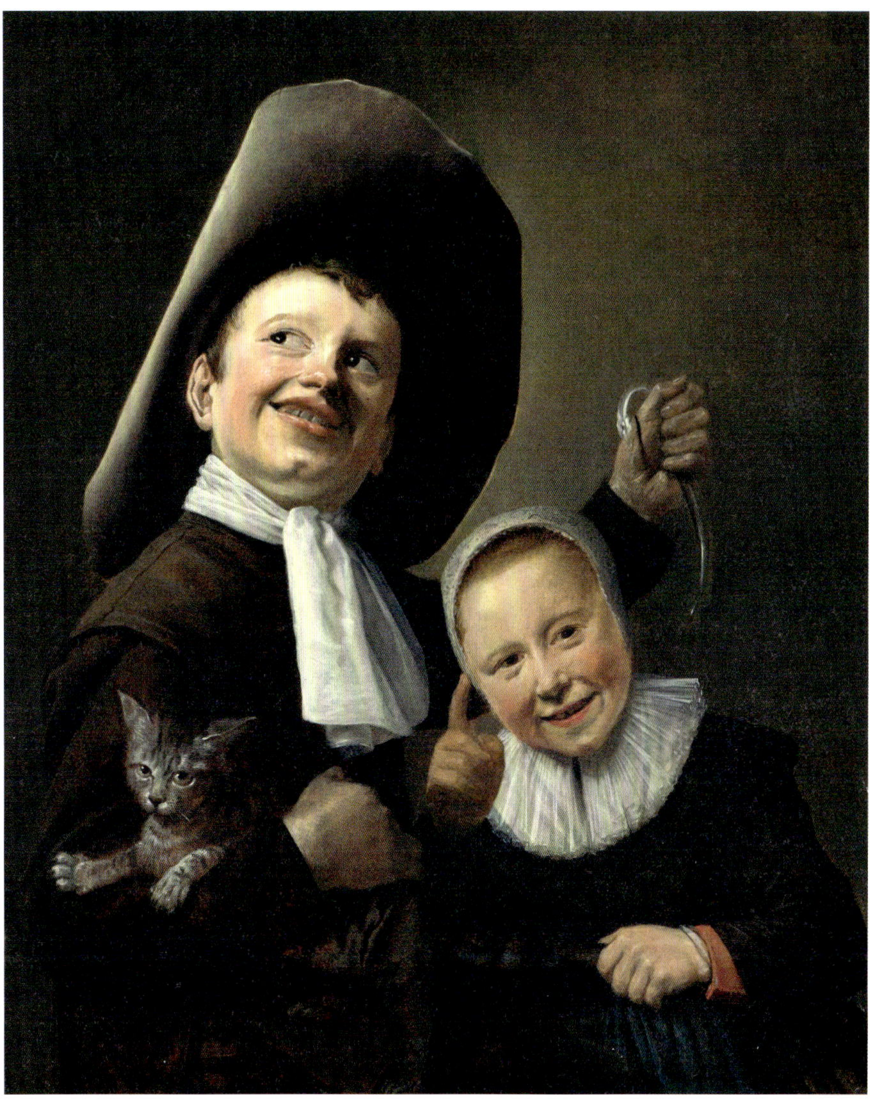

but several are actively engaged in learning, and one child has a simple *ABC* hornbook hanging from his waist. The scene also contains jokes that reference artistic traditions and contemporary culture, and these would have been apparent to its original audience. The composition is loosely based on Raphael's gathering of philosophers, *The School of Athens*, and amongst the detritus of schoolbags and half-eaten vegetables on the floor is a portrait print of the great sixteenth-century educationalist Erasmus.[7] Steen delights in painting the behaviour of the rowdy schoolchildren, who fight, leap on the table, or sleep in the foreground, and depicts the schoolmaster as lazy and inattentive, as he leans back and sharpens his quill, his spectacles balanced on the end of his nose. Behind the schoolmaster a cheeky boy pulls a face while another offers spectacles up to an owl, which is perched beside a lantern. Wise owls traditionally symbolize learning, but here the bird's appearance is ironic, expressing the popular proverb 'what use are glasses if the owl cannot see?'[8]

The protagonists in Judith Leyster's *A Boy and a Girl with a Cat and an Eel* similarly embody popular wisdom to poke fun at the behaviour of both adults and children (fig. 3). Smiling knowingly, the little girl wags her finger as she tugs on the cat's tail. Beside her, the grinning boy is unaware of

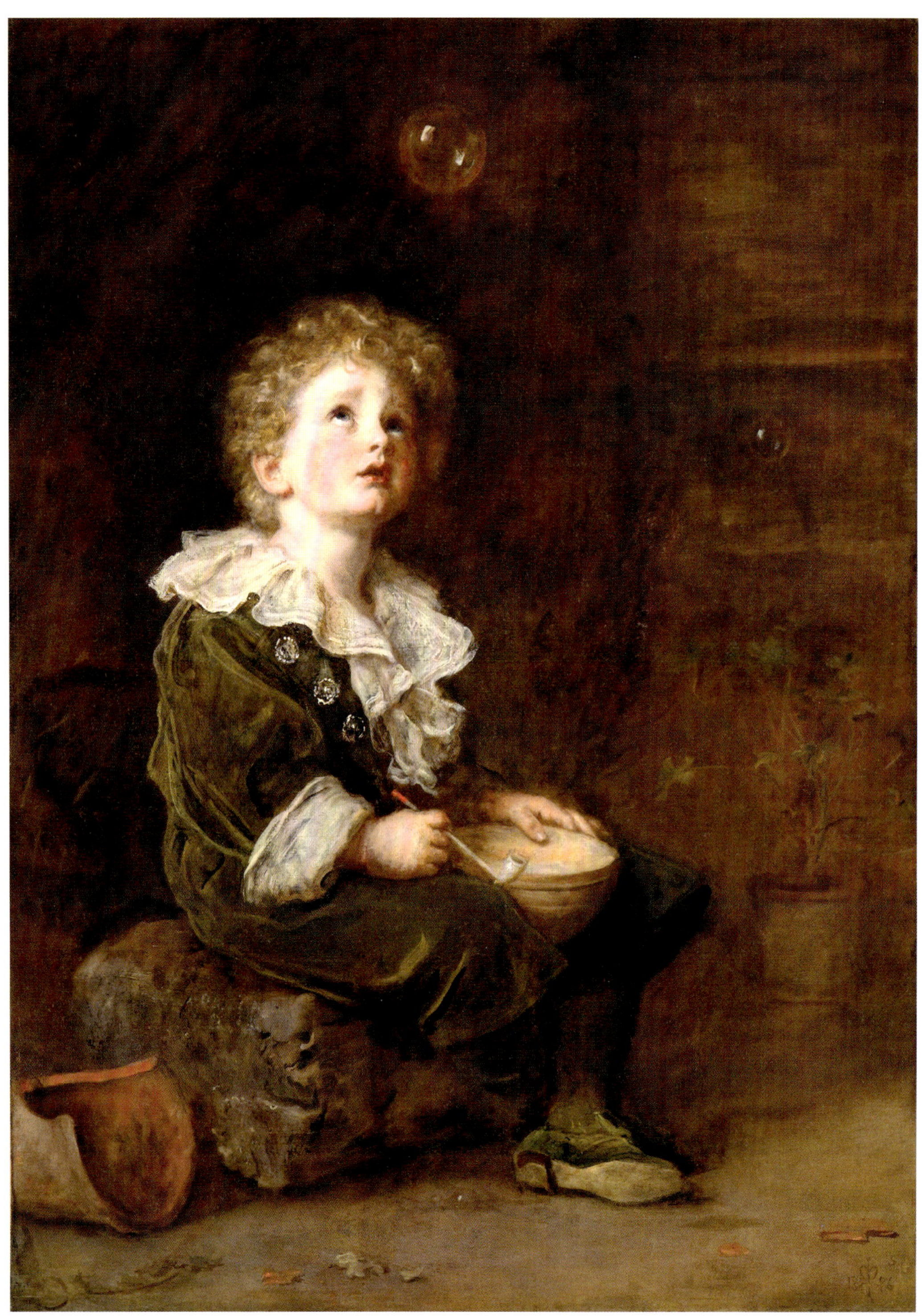

4
John Everett Millais, *Bubbles*, 1886, oil on canvas, 107.5 x 77.5 cm, National Museums of Liverpool, Lady Lever Art Gallery

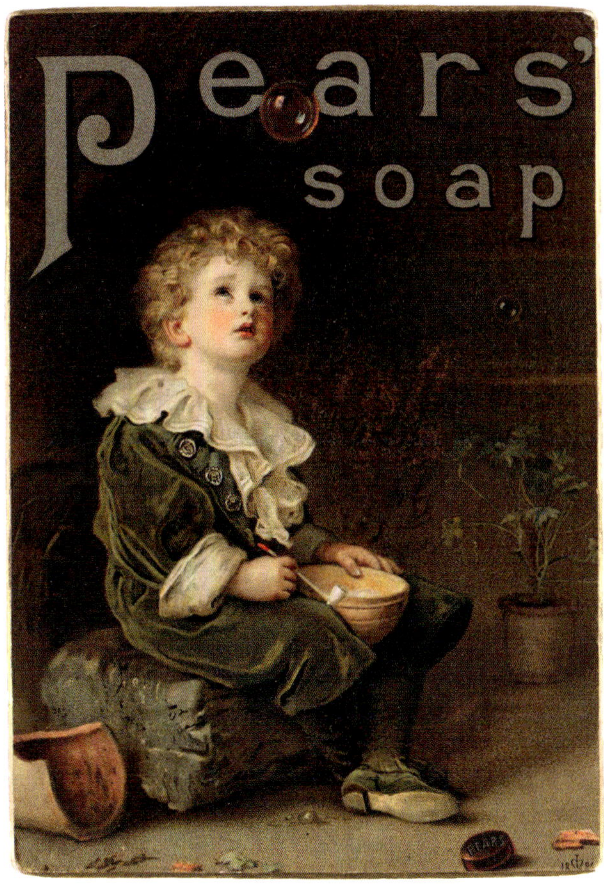

5
John Everett Millais (artist);
A.F Pears Ltd (publisher)
Bubbles, c. 1888–89,
chromolithograph on paper,
16.5 x 11.6 cm, Victoria and
Albert Museum

this development, but is complicit in the mischief – he has lured the cat into his grasp using an eel or a slow worm as bait.[9] The painting appears to depict the popular saying 'play with a cat and get scratched' (look for trouble and you will get it), and the genders of the children may be read as a warning about the predatory sexuality of women. In *Girl Teasing a Cat*, c. 1630, by Jan van Bijlert (1598–1671; Walters Art Gallery, Baltimore), the young girl is naked from the waist up, suggesting an erotic dimension. This is also felt in the painting by Joseph Wright of Derby (1734–1797) of *Two Girls Dressing a Kitten by Candlelight*, c. 1768–70, discussed later in this book (fig. 46). A different mood is conveyed in Thomas Gainsborough's (1727–1788) double portrait of his daughters in *The Painter's Daughters with a Cat*, c. 1760–61, National Gallery, London. The appearance of a snarling cat with its tail being pulled in this otherwise tender portrait is somewhat incongruous. It demonstrates both the longevity of visual traditions and cautions against drawing straightforward conclusions from motifs found in paintings of children.

Blowing bubbles is another example of a common children's pastime that was widely depicted by artists in the seventeenth century, including Frans Hals (1582/83–1666), Jan Miense Molenaer (1610–1668), Caspar Netscher (1639–1684) and David Teniers the Younger (1610–1690). In these works the game of blowing bubbles becomes an established artistic motif, emblematic of both the fleeting nature of childhood and the transience of life itself.[10] Two centuries later, the Victorian artist John Everett Millais (1829–1896) appropriated this iconography and posed his four-year-old grandson Willie James blowing bubbles, suspending a glass bauble in his studio in order to portray accurately light falling on the bubble (fig. 4). The boy's archaic outfit, pose and wistful gaze all hark back to earlier images, and the original title of the painting – *A Child's World* – suggests a quiet moment of private reflection. The painting was to enjoy a very public reception, however, when it was purchased for reproduction in the *Illustrated London News* and was subsequently used in an advertisement for Pears Soap (fig. 5).[11]

The paintings that the Spanish artist Bartolome Esteban Murillo (1617–1682) produced of beggar boys are another example of the longevity enjoyed by certain images of childhood. In *Three Boys* (fig. 6) a black servant boy pauses on his errand to fetch water and begs for a piece of tart from a white street urchin. Much like the boy pulling a face behind the schoolmaster in Steen's scene, here only the viewer is able to observe that the servant boy is being pickpocketed. Around twenty such anecdotal paintings of children by Murillo survive. Feted for their 'great charm', the children remain picturesquely poor despite their dirty feet.[12] All of the protagonists in the *Three Boys* are well fed, and may be modelled on children known personally to Murillo, possibly his sons Gabriel (born 1657) and Gaspar

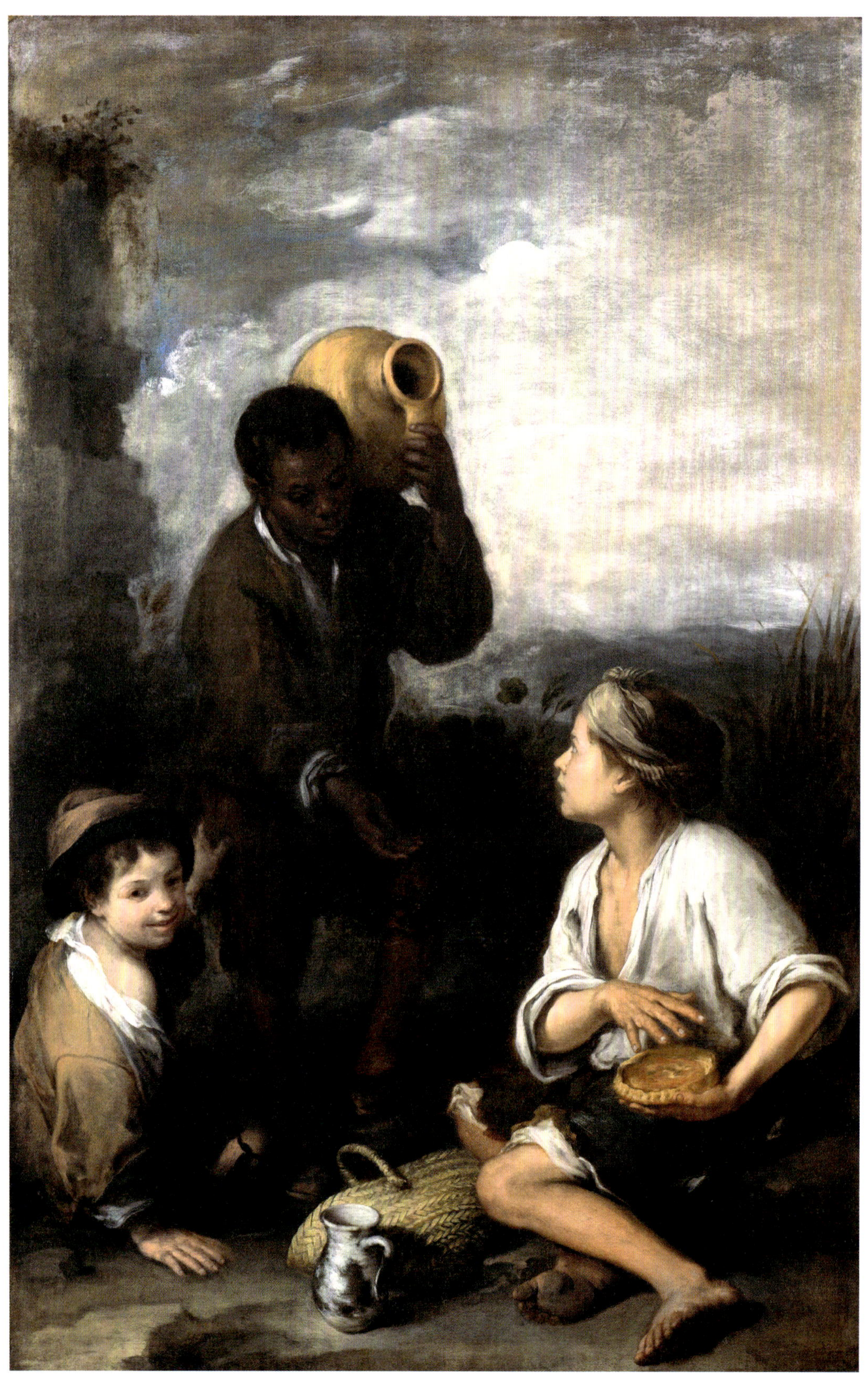

6
Bartolomé Esteban Murillo, *Three Boys*, c. 1670, oil on canvas, 168.3 x 109.8 cm, Dulwich Picture Gallery

(born 1661) and Felipe, the son of his black household slave girl, Juana de Santiago.[13]

Murillo's paintings of beggar boys were popular within the artist's lifetime, when they were copied and reproduced in tapestries, and exported to Northern Europe by visiting merchants. The *Three Boys* was first recorded in Britain in 1690 along with Murillo's *Invitation to a Game of Argolla* (c. 1665–70). Both paintings made a considerable impression on the British art scene, and were among the founding works in the collection of Dulwich Picture Gallery when it opened to the public in 1817. Here they were seen and copied by artists and even inspired a special edition of wallpaper, exhibited at the Great Exhibition in 1851.[14] Gainsborough owned three paintings by Murillo, and his *Peasant Girl Gathering Faggots in a Wood* (fig. 50) recalls many aspects of Murillo's work.[15] Like Murillo's boys, Gainsborough's girl is artfully dishevelled. Paused midway through her task of collecting sticks, she appears entirely at one with the rural landscape in which she is pictured. Both Gainsborough and his contemporary, Sir Joshua Reynolds (1723–1792), made use of orphans and beggar children as models. Perhaps as a result of this direct connection with their models, their paintings have been read as showing some sympathy for the plight of poor children.[16] The urchins in eighteenth-century paintings certainly look more melancholy, although, as with Murillo's beggar children, the harsh realities of poverty were often played down in order to create a painting that would please the buying public.

Challenges and Processes

Painting children has never been an easy task, and anecdotes reveal some of the responses of painters faced with the practical requirement to keep a young child entertained during a portrait sitting. When Lucas Cranach the Elder (1472–1533) painted the Emperor Charles V as a boy of eight, he took the tutor's advice and hung a polished weapon on the wall, which held Charles's attention for the necessary period of time.[17] A century later, Queen Henrietta-Maria wrote of her three-year-old daughter's impatience with sitting for a portrait by Van Dyck.[18] Eighteenth-century accounts describe how Reynolds, a childless bachelor himself, would entertain children during portrait sittings by telling them fairy tales and playing with them:

> Grand rackets there used to be at Sir Joshua's when the children were with him! He used to romp and play with them, and talk to them in their own way; and, whilst all this was going on, he actually snatched those exquisite touches of expression which make his portraits of children so captivating.[19]

Works by artists as varied as Domenichino (1581–1641), Van Dyck, Reynolds and Millais all demonstrate that it was often easiest to depict a young sitter after they had fallen asleep.[20]

It is surely no coincidence that many of the most successful painters of children have been those with an ability to work quickly, recording a likeness from life in a brief preparatory sketch that could then form the basis of a painted portrait. This is exemplified in the exhibition by pairing finished paintings with preparatory sketches by Hans Holbein the Younger (1497/98–1543), Van Dyck and William Hogarth (1697–1764).[21] An early and remarkably lifelike study of a child is *The head and shoulders of a swaddled baby, lying down* by Federico Barocci (c. 1533–1612), which informed the depiction of the Christ Child in a painted *Nativity* now in the Prado (fig. 7).[22]
Made with pastels on blue paper, the sketch shows the artist using rapid, searching lines to denote the shape of the baby's head, the colour of its skin, and the effects of light and shade. Such preparatory sketches were often

7
Federico Barocci, *The head and shoulders of a swaddled baby, lying down*, c. 1595, pastels on blue paper, 16 x 22.1 cm, Royal Collection Trust

8
Titian, *Ranuccio Farnese* (detail), 1541–42, oil on canvas, 89.7 x 73.6 cm, National Gallery of Art, Washington

integral to a painter's working process, and are discussed here along with other types of media to which paintings inevitably relate, including prints, ephemera, photographs and decorative objects.

When is a young sitter no longer a child? The point at which children are considered grown is highly culturally specific, and in the case of the children of the elite it is even more complex. During the sixteenth century the legal age of marriage was twelve for girls and fourteen for boys, but royal children were frequently matched in dynastic marriages or assumed power from a much younger age than this.[23] Edward VI was crowned King in 1547 aged nine, providing portraitists with an interesting challenge. In Venice, Titian (c. 1488/90–1576) produced an impressive response to the challenge of portraying an important child. To modern eyes, his portrait of *Ranuccio Farnese* (fig. 8) remains a brilliantly sensitive depiction of a twelve-year-old boy, his expression thoughtful and his narrow frame swamped by his heavy robe. Ranuccio was the grandson of Pope Paul III, and the Maltese Cross on his robe denotes his important new role as Prior of a property belonging to the Knights of Malta. The portrait of Ranuccio was commissioned for his mother, Girolama Orsini, by his tutor, Gianfrancesco Leoni, and appears to capture the moment at which the boy left his childhood behind.[24] Van Dyck's pocketbook contains a sketch of Titian's *Ranuccio Farnese*, suggesting that this portrait made an impression on the Flemish painter when he encountered it on his travels in Italy.[25] Titian's influence can be felt in Van Dyck's tender depictions of the children of Charles I, which have often been praised as the first paintings to show royal children looking convincingly 'childlike'.

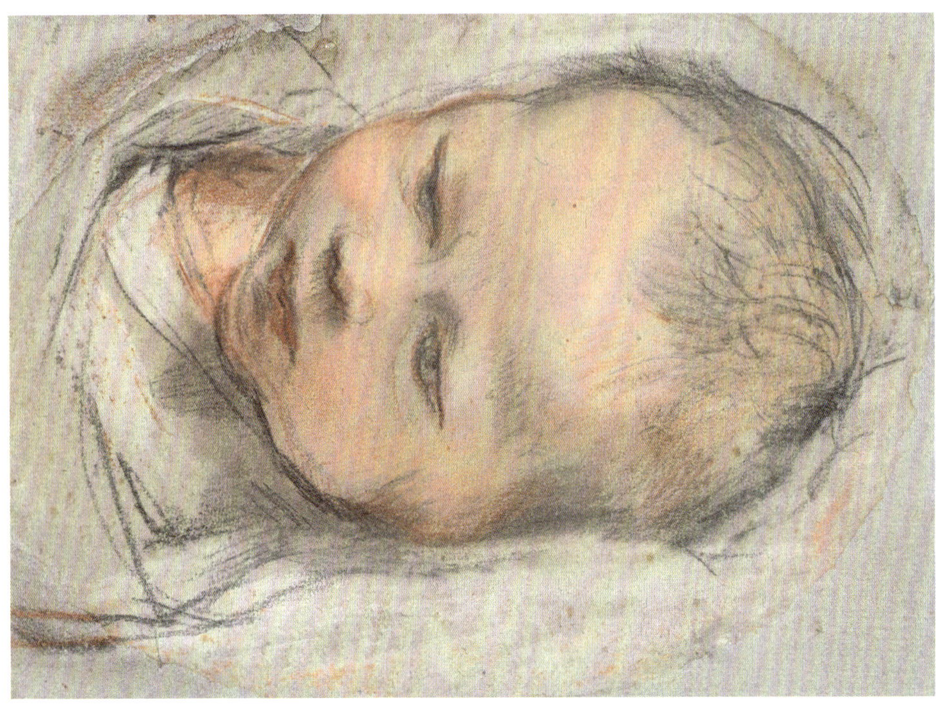

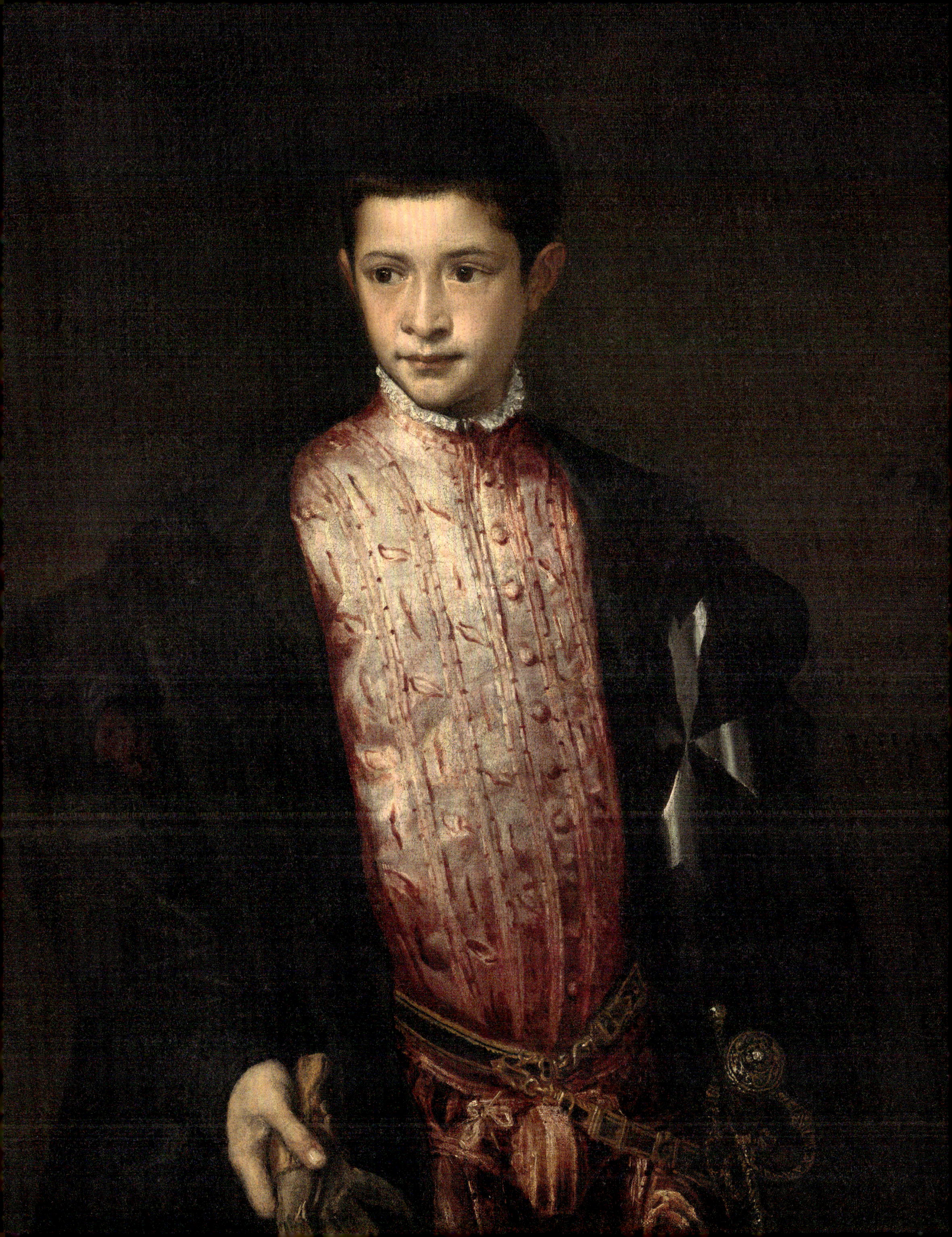

Van Dyck's masterful painting of *The Five Eldest Children of Charles I* (fig. 21) is one of a number of works discussed in Chapter 2, which considers the evolution of the royal portrait in Britain from the sixteenth century to the nineteenth century. Painting royal children brought specific challenges: the small, fragile bodies of princes and princesses represented the future of an entire dynasty, and they needed to be depicted appropriately. Royal portraits have been widely circulated and emulated, as demonstrated by Frans Xaver Winterhalter's likeness of Albert Edward, Prince of Wales (fig. 12), which led to a fashion for children's sailor suits. On occasion, portrait painters have caught royal attention following commissions they have undertaken outside the court. An attractive pair of portraits of the children of John, 3rd Earl of Bute were among the first works executed by the German painter Johan Zoffany (1733–1810) on his arrival in England. Both works are set outdoors, in the grounds of the family estate. The elegantly dressed figures are arranged in a pyramid and are engaged in gender-appropriate activities – the boys have abandoned their archery to raid a bird's nest, while the girls play with pet squirrels (fig. 9). Bute was a close advisor to George III, and it was through this introduction that Zoffany began to paint the royal family.[26]

It is a sad truth that some of the most powerful images of children have been produced in response to their death, and this is discussed by Emily Knight in Chapter 3. In England childhood mortality (defined as deaths before the age of nine) sat at 26.5% between 1650 and 1750, peaking at 28.8% in the nineteenth century.[27] A number of postmortem portraits of children were made in the Netherlands, and this may be the context in which the portrait of *Cornelia Burch, Aged Two Months* (1581, Ferens Art Gallery, Hull) should be understood. In this painting a partially swaddled baby is shown with her eyes open, surrounded by luxurious objects including a gold cross and shark's tooth teething rattle. The portraits and memorials discussed in Chapter 3 were all made in England during the eighteenth century, and they are examined in terms of the circumstances of their production and the essential function that they performed for grieving parents. It can be surprising to find that a lively portrait of a child was in fact produced after their death, as exemplified by the portrait of Thomas Graham, the youngest child in Hogarth's *The Graham Children* (fig. 33). In other examples, such as Pissarro's portrait of *Jeanne Holding a Fan* (see page 6), the sitter's illness is evident in her flushed cheeks and listless expression.

Chapter 4 is again rooted in the eighteenth century. Here Martin Postle explores the transmission of picture types in the evolution of the childhood 'fancy picture' in Britain. This developed from seventeenth-century paintings produced in Spain and Holland, and was closely associated with the print trade. Soon found to be commercially successful, the childhood fancy picture became a favoured mode of expression for artists such as Joseph Wright of Derby (1734–1797), John Singleton Copley (1738–1815) and Joshua Reynolds, with the boundaries between child portraiture and fancy pictures becoming increasingly permeable. Revived in the mid to late nineteenth century in the paintings of Millais, the fancy picture is a genre of painting that refuses to be ignored; found in everything from advertising and cinema to toffee boxes.

A final and important category of images is the intimate likenesses that artists produced of their own children, and these are discussed by Jill Seaton in Chapter 5. Freed from the traditional constraints of an artist-patron relationship, the dynamic within these paintings shifts. A painting of an artist's children, observed within the familiar surroundings of the home, can feel more spontaneous

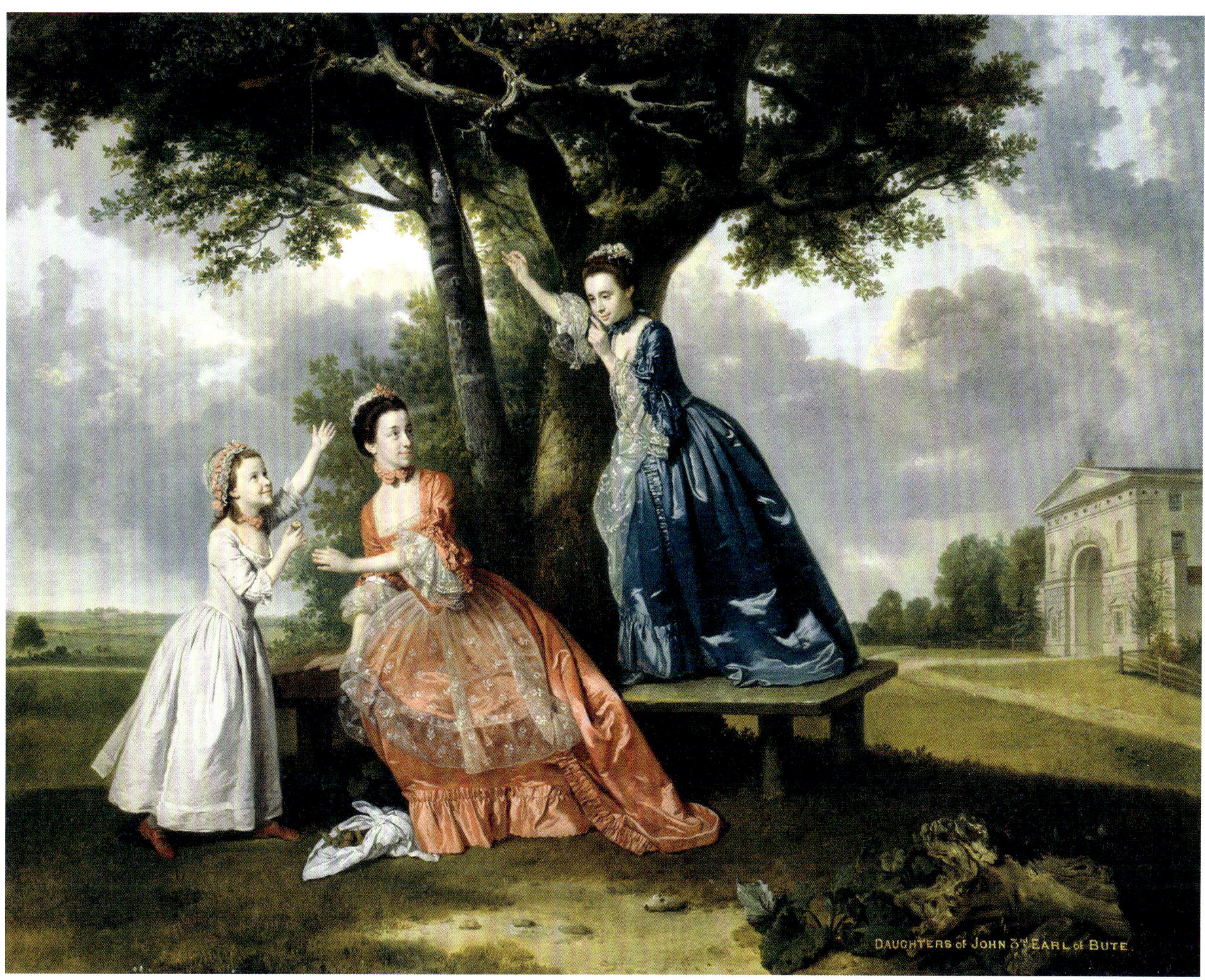

9
Johan Joseph Zoffany, *Three Daughters of John, 3rd Earl of Bute*, c. 1763–64, oil on canvas, 101.2 x 126.5 cm, Tate

and personal than a commissioned portrait, with the children often captured at their most natural and relaxed, whether eating, bathing or playing. Such paintings are more likely to have been left unfinished, adding to their sense of intimacy, and offering interesting insights into an artist's methodology. Mary Beale (1633–1699), one of the most prolific female artists working in the seventeenth century, painted her sons 'for study and improvement', while, for Gainsborough, depicting his daughters chasing a butterfly outdoors provided an opportunity to experiment with scale and technique outside the constraints of a commission.[28] Other painters, including Stanley Spencer (1891–1959) and Winifred Nicholson (1893–1981), have depicted their children at moments when their family lives were fracturing, the resulting paintings seeming to offer insights into their personal lives. For Louise Bourgeois (1911–2010), the experiences of motherhood, childbirth and family life were a recurrent source of inspiration for her artistic practice. By contrast, Lucian Freud (1922–2011) eschewed sentiment when portraying his own children, but courted controversy by painting them naked.

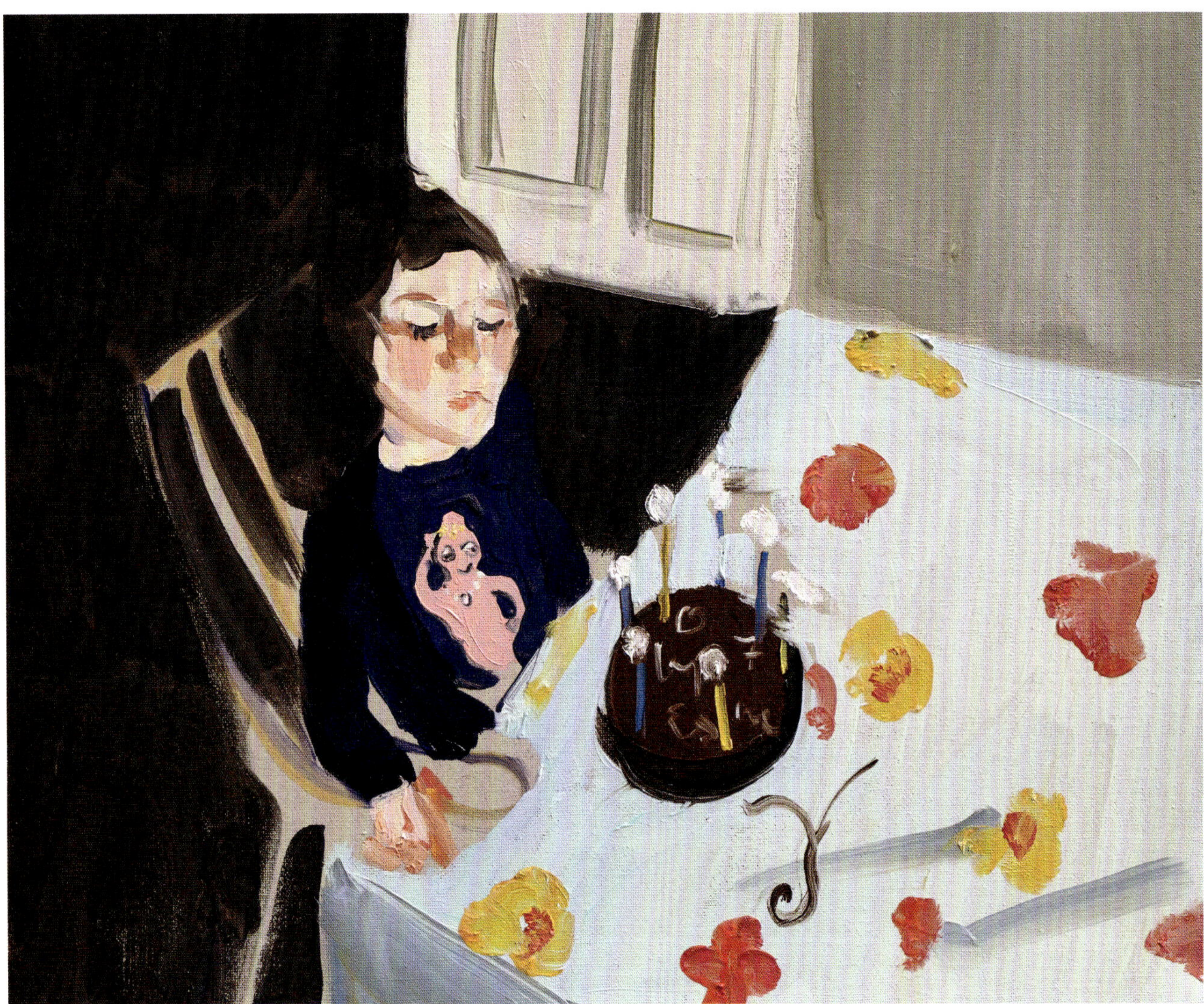

10
Chantal Joffe, *Esme's 7th Birthday*, 2011,
oil on canvas, 38 x 46 cm

Artists working today remain challenged and excited by both the medium of paint and the subject matter of children. For contemporary painters the processes involved are more fluid than ever. Matthew Krishanu is a rare example of an artist who has chosen to paint himself as a child, using family photographs to reimagine his youthful adventures growing up with his brother in Bangladesh (see frontispiece, p. 2). Replaying adult memories of lived childhood experiences, the 'two boys' in Krishanu's luminous paintings become characters, somewhat removed from the artist, despite their shared histories. Mark Fairnington's paintings of his twin sons Lee and Jason are also made with the aid of photographs, which function as the starting point for paintings that record the boys' similarities and differences with microscopic precision. Referencing past painting traditions, such as 'lover's eye' miniatures, these works invite us to question the limits of what a painted portrait can represent. Like Fairnington, Chantal Joffe paints her own child (fig. 10). The works exhibited at Compton Verney are all of her daughter Esme, and chronicle her development from newborn to teenager. Joffe both records significant birthdays and the typically uncharted moments of everyday life (watching TV on the sofa) with equal vigour. What emerges is an intimate portrait of a relationship between a mother and her daughter – colourful, tender and constantly evolving.

As viewers, we are privileged to enjoy a wealth of paintings of children today, both historic and contemporary. Childhood is a universal experience, shared by us all. Yet these images are unique in the places that they transport us to and the insights they provide. Whether in the palace or the schoolroom, the painter's studio or the family home, the intimate encounter between a painter and their young subject remains as elusive and fascinating as ever.

Amy Orrock *is the curator of the exhibitions* Painting Childhood: From Holbein to Freud *and* Childhood Now *at Compton Verney. She completed her PhD on Pieter Bruegel the Elder's* Children's Games, *and has worked on projects at the Holburne Museum, Bath, the Royal Collection Trust and the National Portrait Gallery, London.*

Notes

1 Philippe Ariès's *L'enfant et la vie familiale sous l'ancien régime* (1960), first published in English as *Centuries of Childhood* (1962), initiated much debate among historians about the existence of parental affection and the concept of childhood in the past. For a summary of Ariès's thesis and responses to it see Dekker and Groenendijk 1991, pp. 317–35. On the use of visual material as evidence by historians of childhood, see Pointon, 1993, pp. 177–78 and Berkeley/Memphis/Omaha 1995–96, p. 13.

2 Huggett and Mikhaila 2013, p. 28, and Haarlem/Antwerp 2000, cat. nos. 8 and 24.

3 During the Renaissance violas or pansies symbolized thought, their name deriving from the French *'pensée'*. They often appear alongside other vanitas motifs, as in the portrait of *A Man with Pansies and a Skull*, attributed to a follower of Jan van Scorel, c. 1535, National Gallery, London. Fisher 2011, p. 139.

4 The portrait of *Lady Arabella Stuart (Aged 23 months)*, 1577, Hardwick Hall, is another example of this type of portrait; for more examples see London 2013–14, cat. nos. 29, 31, 32, and Strong 1969, nos. 25, 39, 47, 58, 60, 82, 99, 198, 212, 215, 263, 289. There has been no comprehensive study of the portraits of children produced in Britain during the sixteenth century. An important exhibition and catalogue focusing on Netherlandish examples is *Pride and Joy: Children's Portraits in the Netherlands 1500–1700* (Haarlem/Antwerp 2000). Here the authors assert that the wealth of portraits 'testify to the pride and affection in which parents held their offspring.' Haarlem/Antwerp 2000, p. 28.

5 These include *The Changing Face of Childhood: British Children's Portraits and their Influence in Europe* (London/Frankfurt 2007), *Pictures of Innocence, Portraits of Children from Hogarth to Lawrence* (Bath/Kendal 2005) and *The New Child: British Art and the Origins of Modern Childhood, 1730–1830* (Berkeley/Memphis/Omaha 1995–96).

6 Figures from Amsterdam in 1650 suggest that around 70% of men and 50% of women could write, an unprecedented number for the period. Frijhoff and Spies 2004, vol. 1, p. 240, and Durantini 1983.

7 Steen and his contemporaries would have known Raphael's composition from engravings. Smith 1981.

8 The painting continues a Netherlandish tradition of comedic 'unruly schoolrooms' that has precedents in prints such as Pieter Bruegel the Elder's *The Ass in School*, Pieter van der Borcht's *The Cobbler and his Wife as a Teacher* and the paintings of the Van Ostade brothers. Washington/Amsterdam 1996, cat. 41, pp. 231–34.

9 The animal in the boy's hand was traditionally identified as an eel, suggesting that the proverb 'to hold an eel by the tail does not mean you have caught it' would be applicable to the scene. Recently it has been suggested that the creature is a slow worm (*anguis fragilis*), a legless lizard which is common in Europe and can be kept as a pet. See Hofrichter 1989, p. 64, and MacLaren and Brown 1991, p. 227.

10 The Latin maxim *homo bulla* ('man the bubble') was revived by Erasmus in 1500. See Langmuir 2006, pp. 216–30 and Schama 1987, pp. 512–15.

11 Ibid., and London/Amsterdam/Fukuoka/Tokyo 2007–08, cat. 107.

12 Gombrich 1950, p. 18.

13 London/Munich 2001, p. 124.

14 On the history and availability of the Dulwich paintings as models see Bray 2013, pp. 21–31.

15 Gainsborough seems to have known the Dulwich beggar boys – a direct borrowing of the pose of the seated boy in the *Invitation to a Game of Argolla* is discernible in the engraving made after Gainsborough's painting of *A Shepherd*, which was exhibited at the Royal Academy in 1781 but destroyed by a fire at Exton Park in 1810. See Nottingham/London 1998, p. 59, and Žakula 2011.

16 Crown 1984. One of the street children that Reynolds invited into his studio became a favourite and appears in at least four paintings, including *The Schoolboy* and *The Infant Samuel*. Paris/London 1986, pp. 60–61 and cat. 105, p. 277.

17 Campbell 1990, p. 180.

18 Letter quoted in Barnes et al. 2004, p. 477.

19 Whitley 1928, vol. 1, p. 369.

20 See figs. 18, 36, 37 and 38 in this publication. Millais painted his daughters Effie and Alice asleep in *My Second Sermon*, 1864, Guildhall Art Gallery, London, and *Sleeping*, 1865–66, private collection. London/Amsterdam/Fukuoka/Tokyo 2007–08, pp. 174–75.

21 See figs. 14, 18, 22, 23 and 35 in this publication.

22 Saint Louis/London 2012, pp. 262–71.

23 Orme 2001, p. 329 and 334–37.

24 London 2003, cat. 25.

25 Italian Sketchbook, fol. 108r, British Museum. See Antwerp/London 1999, p.169. Van Dyck eventually owned 19 works by Titian.

26 Shawe-Taylor 2009, pp.102–03.

27 Pollock 1987, p. 12.

28 London 2018, p. 20 and cat. 9.

Born to Rule
The Evolving Image of Royal Childhood

AMY ORROCK

There is a striking contrast between the sixteenth-century Compton Verney portrait of Edward VI as a child, painted after a design by Hans Holbein the Younger (fig. 11), and Frans Xaver Winterhalter's nineteenth-century portrait of Edward VII as a boy (fig. 12). Separated by three hundred years, images of these two princes bookend developments in royal portraiture that saw the formal and heavily coded Tudor portrait type softened to a picture of Victorian sentimentality. Many portraits were made of Henry VIII's longed-for son, and most frame him in the square and recognizable image of his father – presciently, given that Edward VI (1537–1553) would be crowned King at the tender age of nine. In place of Holbein's studied boy king, Winterhalter presents the future Edward VII (1841–1910), eldest son of Queen Victoria (1819–1901), as a carefree child, safely ensconced within his mother's long reign. By the Victorian era, black and white photography was available to capture the likenesses of royal children, but Winterhalter's portrait exploits the colourful potency of paint. Albert Edward – or 'Bertie' as he was known – is posed in bright sunlight before the seashore. Curls peep from below his wide-brimmed hat, and his childish proportions are enhanced by the miniature sailor suit that he wears.

The changes that took place in depictions of royal children between the sixteenth and the nineteenth century are indicative of wider developments in portraiture, and tracing the evolution of royal portraits over this period involves engaging with everything from princes poised ready for battle to 'conversation pieces' that include beloved family pets. In turn, portraits of monarchs influenced portrait fashions for non-royal

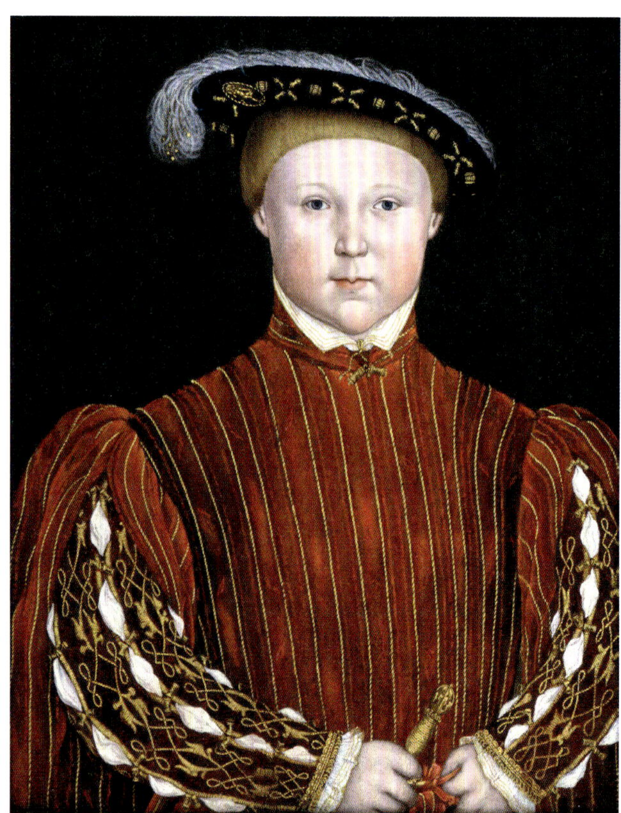

11
Follower of Hans Holbein the Younger, *Edward, Prince of Wales, later Edward VI*, c. 1542, oil on panel, 53 x 41.5 cm, Compton Verney Art Gallery & Park

12
Frans Xaver Winterhalter, *Albert Edward, Prince of Wales, later Edward VII*, signed and dated 1846, oil on canvas, 127.1 x 88 cm, Royal Collection Trust

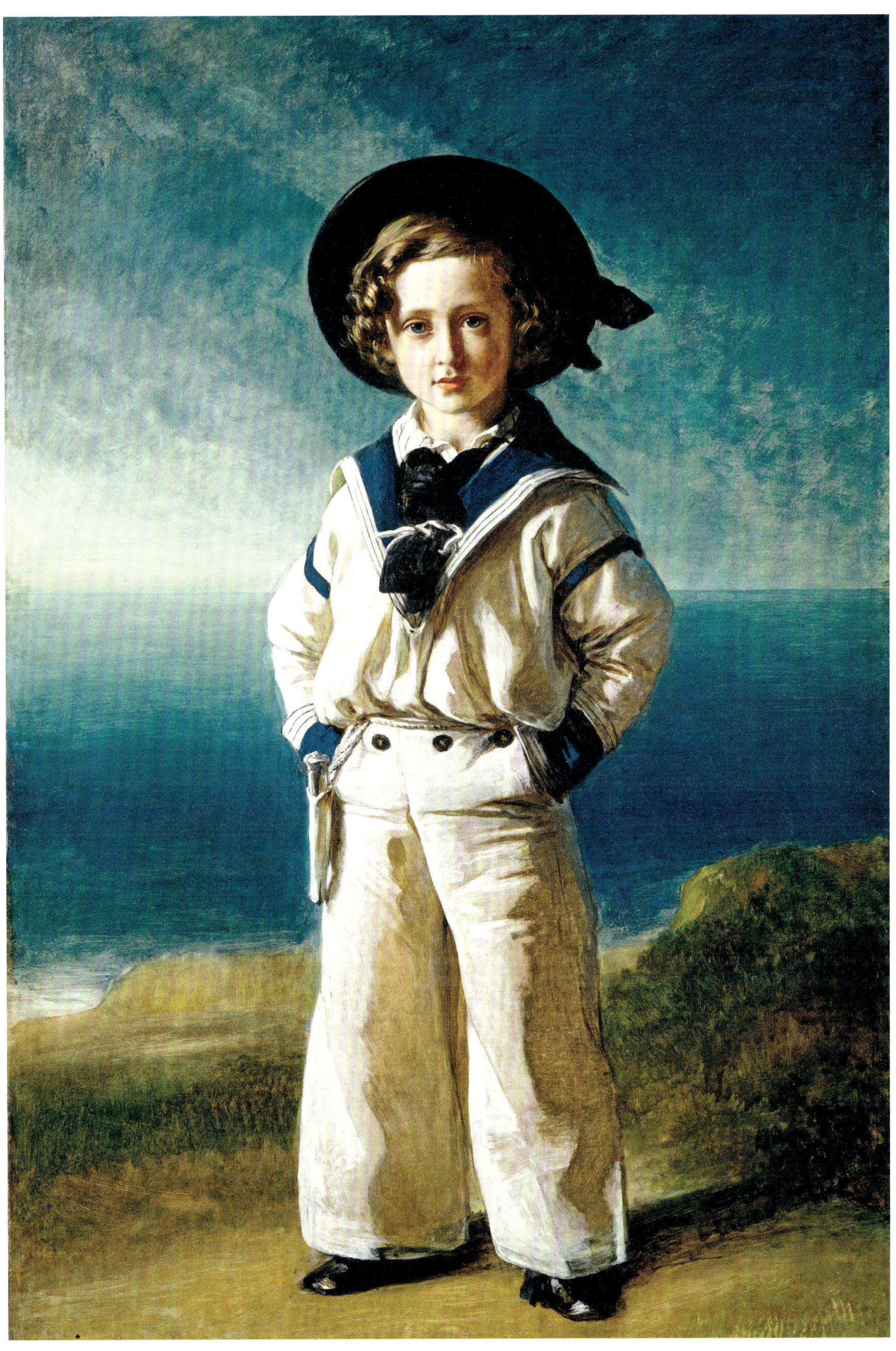

13
Hans Holbein the Younger, *Edward VI as a Child*, 1538, oil on panel, 56.8 x 44 cm, National Gallery of Art, Washington

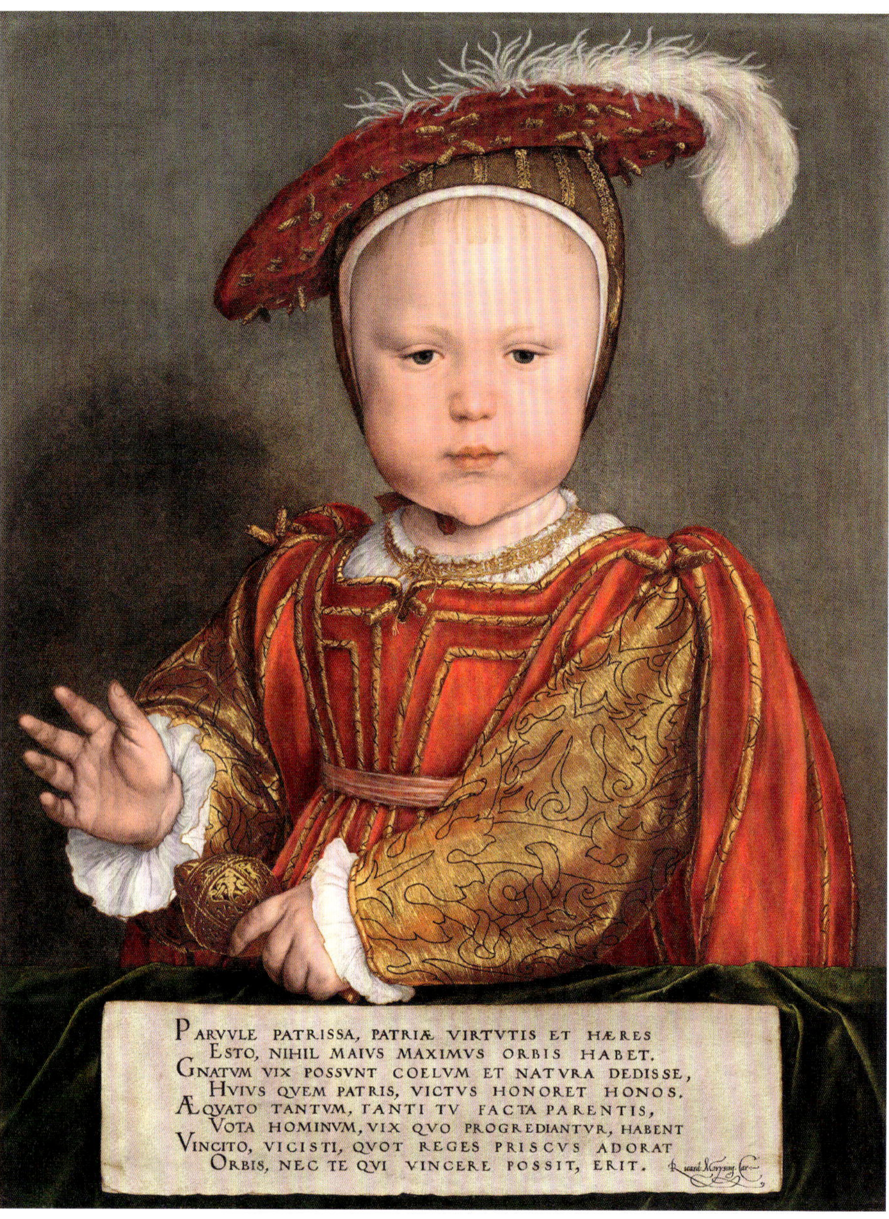

sitters, as images of royal children came to be widely disseminated through copies and engravings. But paintings of royal children also have a distinct narrative of their own – one closely connected to the vagaries of power and court culture. However young they were, many royal sitters had been born to rule, amplifying the challenge already present for any artist painting a child of elevated social status. Relationships like those that arose between Hans Holbein the Younger (c. 1497–1543) and Henry VIII, or between Anthony van Dyck (1599–1641) and Charles I demonstrate the formative role that an individual artist could play in crafting the royal image, once they had gained their patron's confidence. Henry VIII described his young son as 'our most most noble and most precious jewel'.[1] Such a sentiment embodies the notion that the fragile little bodies of princes and princesses were cherished vessels – flesh and blood containing the future of an entire dynasty.

To be successful, a royal portrait needed to express both the inherent potential of the young sitter and the power and glories of their parents. This is amply demonstrated by Holbein's only surviving painted portrait of Prince Edward, now in Washington (fig. 13). This imposing image is thought to be the 'table of the prince's grace' that Holbein presented to the King as a New Year gift in 1539, and as such may be an example of a royal portrait initiated by the artist, rather than the ruler, in an attempt to win favour.[2] Aged beyond his fourteen months, the prince wears a close-fitting cap, or 'biggin', upon which rests a miniature version of an adult cap with a white ostrich feather, a detail also found in many later portraits of Edward. Edward's white feathered hat references both contemporary fashion for boys and the heraldic badge of the Prince of Wales, which was formed of three white ostrich feathers. Grasping a gold filigree rattle in place of a sceptre, he raises his small right hand in a gesture of blessing. The parapet beneath bears a Latin inscription that neatly flatters both the sitter and his father: 'Little one, emulate thy father and be the heir of his virtue; the world contains nothing greater. Heaven and earth could scarcely produce a son whose glory would surpass that of a father ....'[3]

Doomed Youths: Edward VI and Henry Prince of Wales

As the only son of Henry VIII and his third wife, Jane Seymour, Edward's arrival was greeted with great rejoicing. Jane died twelve days after the baby's birth but the prince enjoyed a stable early childhood at Hampton Court, where he grew to be a healthy child with a love of learning. Edward was to become the sovereign far sooner than anticipated: Henry's death in January 1547 saw nine-year-old Edward crowned King, with chroniclers recalling that the ceremony was shortened in case the 'tedious length' might 'weary and be hurtsome peradventure to the Kinges Majestie, being yet of tendre age'.[4] The intention was that Edward would rule by minority with the support of a regency council until he reached the age of eighteen, but after seven years Edward too fell ill, dying in July 1553 aged just fifteen. History repeated itself in 1612 when the athletic and talented Prince Henry Frederick (1594–1612), eldest son and brightest hope of James I and his queen, Anne of Denmark, died unexpectedly from typhoid fever, aged eighteen. Knowing the tragic fates of Henry Prince of Wales and Edward VI lends images of both youths a sense of poignancy. However, the portraits of the princes that were created during their lifetimes in fact present them as children who appear commanding and full of promise.

The important role that an artist could play in shaping the public image of a monarch had been firmly established with the arrival of Holbein at the court of Henry VIII. Holbein's iconic depiction of the King, with broad shoulders and an equally wide stance, was devised for a dynastic wall painting often known as the 'Whitehall Mural'. Commissioned in 1537 (the year of Edward's birth), this large mural decorated the Privy Chamber at Whitehall Palace. Although it was destroyed in a fire in 1698, the image of Henry VIII in it was widely disseminated and influenced depictions of his son, as seen in two drawings of Edward now in the Royal Collection.[5] One of these was the basis for Edward's likeness in the Washington portrait, while a second drawing shows Edward aged five or six, and demonstrates the face pattern on which the Compton Verney portrait is based (fig. 14).[6] Drawings such as this were typically how Holbein began a portrait, and evidence taken from his corpus of over eighty surviving portrait drawings suggests that his method of working would have been well suited to the challenge of capturing the likeness of a very young child from life. Holbein's use of pink prepared paper meant that the flesh tone of the sitter was already established and a drawing could be

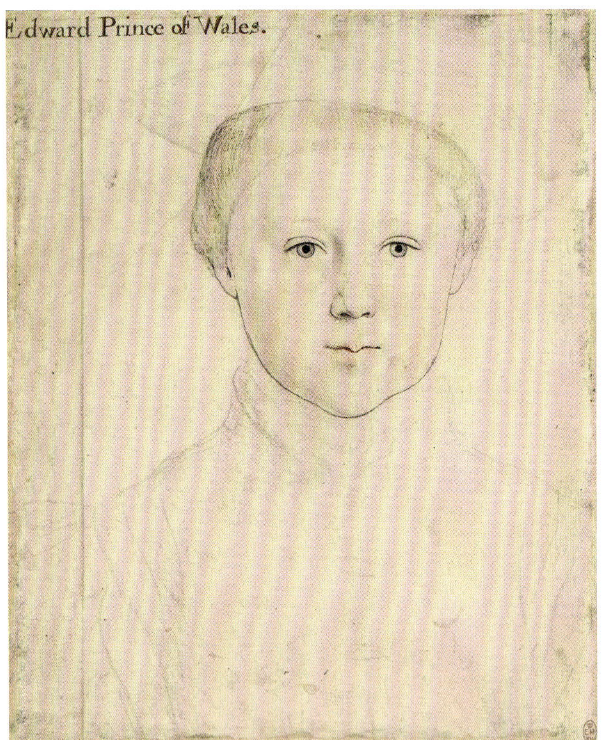

14
Hans Holbein the Younger, *Edward, Prince of Wales, later Edward VI*, c. 1540–43, black and coloured chalks, and pen and ink on pale pink prepared paper, 27.3 x 22.7 cm, Royal Collection Trust

executed quickly, with metalpoint or pen and ink used to outline the sitter's features, and white and coloured chalk to denote highlights. Some of Holbein's portrait drawings contain notations relating to the sitter's jewellery and colouring, indicating that they were made from life in the sitter's presence.[7] These would be worked into the finished painting later, while the features established in the drawing were usually transferred directly on to a prepared panel using a tracing method.

Compton Verney's portrait of *Edward, Prince of Wales, later Edward VI* (fig. 11) is one of several painted portraits which seem to relate to the 'face pattern' established in the second Windsor drawing (fig. 14).[8] It is not clear how such paintings were generated: questions of whether Holbein ran a workshop and what happened to his collection of portrait drawings immediately after his death in 1543 are unresolved. According to the 1590 inventory of Lord Lumley's collection the drawings had been owned by Edward VI, but there is also evidence of artists making additional face patterns from Holbein's painted portraits and from replica portraits.[9] Portraits of Edward were sought throughout the sixteenth century for a number of reasons. Owning an image of Edward as Prince of Wales or as King was a way for courtiers to demonstrate their allegiance, and this significance was revived later in the sixteenth century under Edward's half-sister, Elizabeth I, by which time Edward was venerated as a Protestant martyr. Paintings such as the Compton Verney work could therefore have been produced either during Edward's life or after his death, and could have been based on an original pattern by Holbein or on a replica painted portrait.

As is typical, the portrait drawing in the Royal Collection records a direct encounter with the prince, and focuses chiefly on the details of his face, with his jawline, lips, nose and eyes, which are outlined firmly. Edward's collar, cap and sleeves are described only faintly in the original drawing, but in the Compton Verney painting the unknown artist has paid particular attention to extending these areas, depicting Edward's feathered hat, his broad chest and shoulders, and his lavish clothing. These additions quote elements of the pose and costume of previous full-length portraits of Henry VIII, and help to further the illusion of five-year-old Edward as a capable and fearless leader, the very model of his father. They also appear to be accurate: an inventory of the Wardrobe of the Robes made in July 1600 includes a section that records the 'Robes late Kinge Edwarde the vjth'.[10] This lists a doublet which resembles the red coat he wears in the Compton Verney portrait: 'one Dublet of Crimson Satten allover embroidered with venice gold cut and pulled out with the tincell Sarceonet.'[11] Also listed are a number of different types of buttons and gold 'aglets' (ornamental tags), and in the Compton Verney portrait gold aglets can been seen holding together the slashes in his embroidered undersleeves, finishing his collar and decorating his cap.

A second portrait of Edward in Compton Verney's collection adopts a multi-layered approach to present the

15
William Scrots, *Edward VI*,
c. 1550, oil on panel, 58 x 68 cm,
Compton Verney Art Gallery & Park

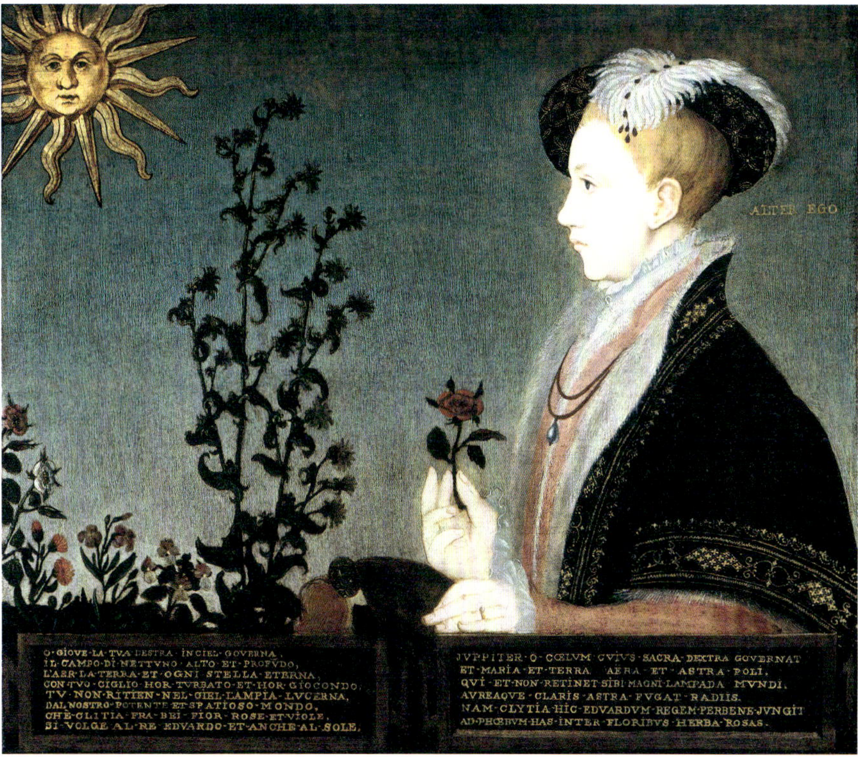

young King during his reign, and uses a profile format (fig. 15).[12] The profile portrait format was revived during the Renaissance, and was considered particularly suited to depicting rulers, given its origins in the coinage of ancient Greece and Rome. Examination of Compton Verney's painting in raking light and with infrared confirms that Edward's profile is inscribed in a continuous line, suggesting a method of transfer whereby a sheet of blackened paper was laid on the panel and the pattern traced through using a stylus, leaving a 'carbon copy' behind. The same profile forms the basis of several other paintings, including the unusual anamorphic portrait now in the National Portrait Gallery. Designed to amaze the viewer, in this painting Edward's face at first appears distorted, and only becomes visible when viewed from a particular angle, similar to the skull in the foreground of Holbein's portrait of *The Ambassadors* (dated 1533, National Gallery, London).[13] Although comparable to Holbein's work, the anamorphic portrait of Edward bears the inscription *Guilhelmus pingebat* (Guilhelmus painted it) on the frame, leading to the identification of the artist as William Scrots (active 1537–1553), Holbein's successor at court. Several of the surviving profile portraits of Edward are extended to bust length and show his hand holding a flower, as in the Compton Verney painting.[14] This painting is unique, however, in pairing the profile of Edward on the right with a selection of flowering plants at the left of the composition. The background of the portrait has been painted in smalt, a pigment that has discoloured over time but would originally have been a striking blue. Gold inscriptions in Italian and Latin on wooden signboards below Edward enhance the lavish appearance of the painting and also tell us something about its iconography. The verses describe the Greek myth in which Clytie was spurned by the sun-god Helios and transformed into a heliotropic flower, condemned always to follow the sun. The legend highlights that the flowers and herbs opposite Edward turn towards him. Edward had previously been conflated with the sun, in an emblem designed by Lucas Horenbout when he was still a prince.[15] In the Compton Verney painting he outdoes the sun, which is shown at the top left of the composition. Edward's left hand rests

16
Robert Peake the Elder, *Henry Prince of Wales with Robert Devereux, 3rd Earl of Essex in the Hunting Field* (detail), c. 1605, oil on canvas, 190.5 x 165.1 cm, Royal Collection Trust

on a tasselled cushion, while in his right he holds a rose. Ignoring the sun and turning towards the young King are the red Lancastrian rose and white Yorkist rose of his ancestors, as well as several heliotropic flowers, including an orange marigold and a tall chicory plant. The plants between these flowers resemble the 'Wilde Pansies' (*violatricolor syluestris*) and 'Hearts-ease' (*viola tricolor*) illustrated in several of the new 'herbals' published in the sixteenth century.[16] These flowers may symbolize romantic love or remembrance, both sentiments that would have been applicable to the young King, who had lost his father and was soliciting a bride.[17] Such esoteric iconography suited a depiction of the scholarly young King, who was well versed in Greek, Latin and French, played the lute and enjoyed astronomy. It also reveals something of the interests of the painting's patron, suggesting someone who was keen to show off both their classical interests and their devotion to the promising young King.[18]

A young heir to the throne is cast in a more active role in Peake's dynamic portrait of Henry, Prince of Wales (fig. 16). As an official court painter Robert Peake the Elder (c. 1551–1619) regularly portrayed the Stuart children, but rarely with such dramatic invention. Henry stands at the centre of the picture, legs planted confidently apart, sheathing his sword. He has just slit the throat of the deer at his feet – a ritual moment in a royal hunt. Kneeling beside Henry and grasping the deer's antlers is one of the prince's favourite companions, Robert Devereux, 3rd Earl of Essex (1591–1646). Both boys are dressed in green finery, a common colour for hunting attire. Prince Henry's elevated status is suggested by the additional detailing on his outfit, including the lace edge to his collar, the gold embroidery on his doublet and hose, his feathered hat and the pendant of St George on horseback hanging at his waist.[19] As the heir to the throne it was fitting to show Prince Henry as a capable hunter and horseman, adept at wielding a weapon. The radical nature of Peake's composition is particularly notable when it is compared to a more conventional portrait that he painted of Henry's younger brother, Charles, around the same time. Charles was a sickly child, and Peake's portrait of *Charles I when Duke of York* in Bristol Museum and Art Gallery shows him aged about five, wearing skirts and posed indoors, with a thin and pallid face. When Henry unexpectedly succumbed to typhoid fever aged eighteen the nation mourned, but it was Charles's moment: the sickly second son would become a powerful ruler and formidable art patron.

'The Perfect Artlessness of Childhood': Van Dyck's Royal Sitters

The now iconic paintings that Anthony van Dyck produced of Charles I and his family celebrate dynasty at a moment when the King was secure in his reign and surrounded by a growing brood of healthy offspring. The star of Rubens's studio, Van Dyck had briefly visited England during the reign of James I, then spent several years in Italy painting the Genoese aristocracy, before returning to Antwerp to work on religious commissions and portraits. On his second visit to London in 1632 Van Dyck was warmly welcomed by Charles I, who already owned at least one work by him, and on 5 July Van Dyck was knighted and appointed 'principalle Paynter in Ordinary to their Majesties'.[20] By 1635 the King had provided the artist with a property in Blackfriars, with a specially constructed staircase down to the Thames that enabled him to visit, arriving by boat from Whitehall.

In his painterly ability Van Dyck was unrivalled, bringing a flash of Flemish brilliance to the English court. Where native artists such as Robert Peake had been concerned with detail and outline, producing visually rich but flat-looking paintings, Van Dyck drew on his experiences in Flanders and Italy to model his sitters confidently in a

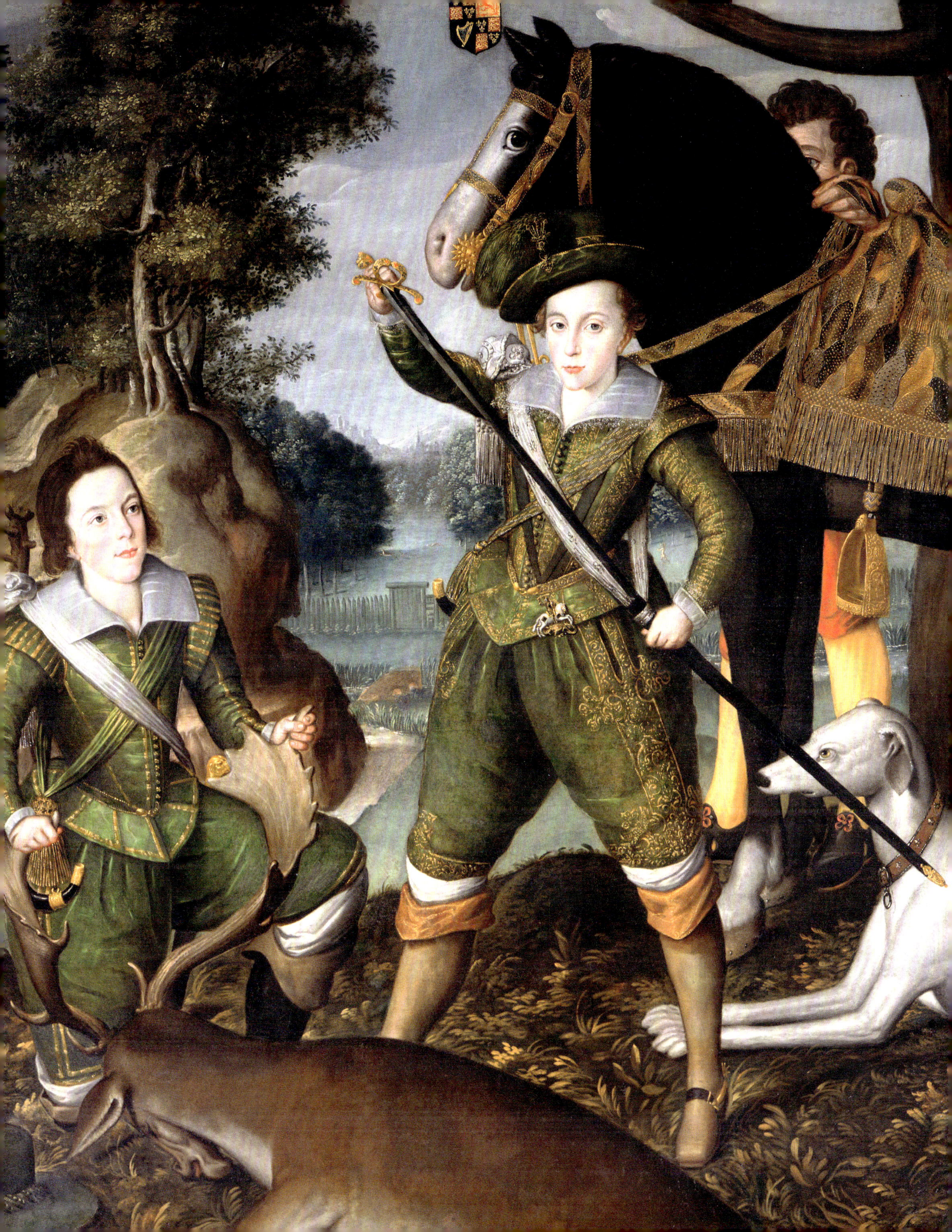

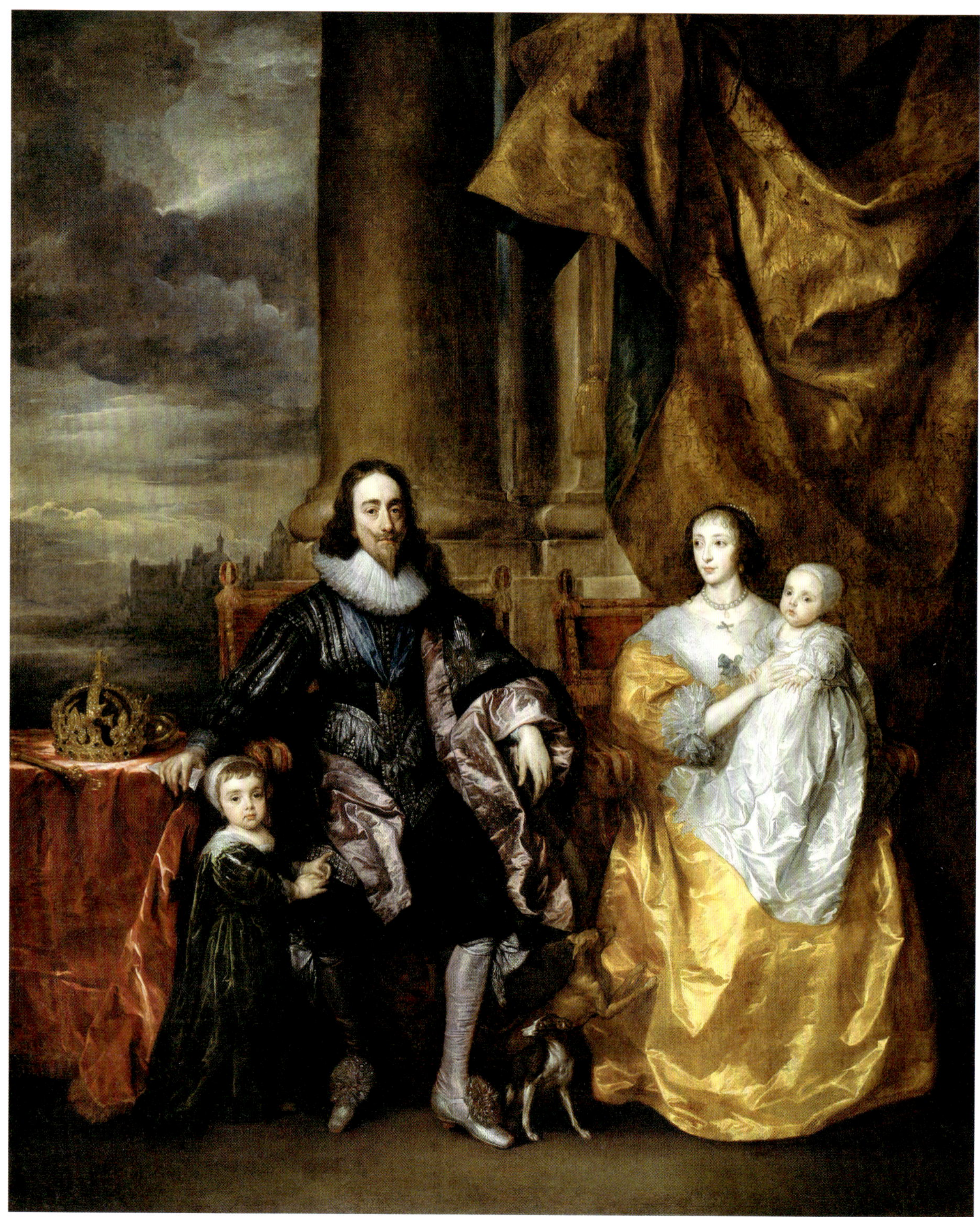

17
Sir Anthony van Dyck, *Charles I with Henrietta Maria and their Two Eldest Children, Prince Charles and Princess Mary,* (*The Greate Peece*), 1631–32, oil on canvas, 303.8 x 256.5 cm, Royal Collection Trust

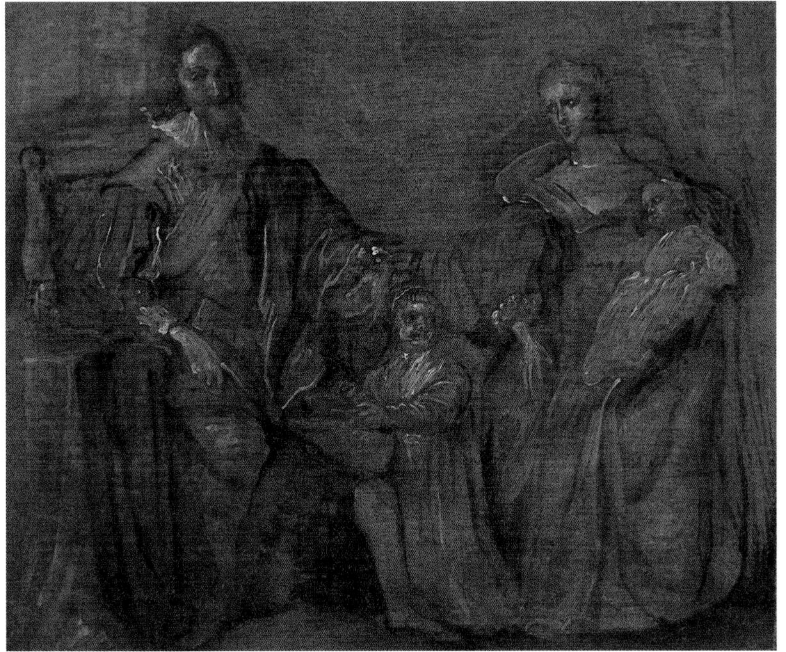

18
Sir Anthony van Dyck, *Sketch of Charles I and Queen Henrietta Maria with their Two Eldest Children, Prince Charles and Princess Mary* (*The Greate Peece*), 1632, oil on oak panel, 19.7 x 23.5 cm, Royal Collection Trust

Continental style, glorying in capturing the dimpled flesh and twisting limbs of his youngest sitters with accuracy. His ambitious portrait style is evident in the first commission he undertook for the King, the monumental family portrait of *Charles I and Henrietta Maria with their Two Eldest Children, Prince Charles and Princess Mary* (fig. 17). Commissioned for the Long Gallery at Whitehall, the painting both responded to existing images of the Tudor dynasty displayed in the Palace, such as the Whitehall Mural, and eclipsed them, bringing a new sense of scale and informal grandeur to the royal portrait. Known as 'The Greate Peece', the portrait was an unequivocal depiction of Charles's power, but it also presented the King as a family man. Queen Henrietta Maria gazes across at him, and both parents are physically supporting their young children, lending intimacy to the scene.

The Greate Peece was followed by a series of paintings of the royal children without their parents, demonstrating Van Dyck's supreme ability as a painter of children and cementing a mode of representation that would be referenced by future generations of artists. For Marcel Proust Van Dyck's painting of the royal children was 'magnificent and grave', while Sir David Wilkie described how Van Dyck was able to combine the sitters' rank and stateliness with inexperience and 'the perfect artlessness of childhood'. William Hogarth praised the physiognomy of the faces of Van Dyck's children in his treatise *On Beauty* (1753) and the influence of Van Dyck's monumental young figures can be felt in Hogarth's eighteenth-century portrait of *The Graham Children* (fig. 33). Van Dyck had studied Titian's portrait of *Ranuccio Farnese* (fig. 8) while in Rome, and recorded an impression of it in his Italian sketchbook.[21] Its influence can be felt in the formula that he developed for painting portraits of children without their parents while he was in Genoa, exemplified by portraits like *Filippo Cattaneo* and *Maddalena Cattaneo* (both 1623, National Gallery of Art, Washington) and *The Balbi Children* (c. 1625–27, National Gallery, London). The children are typically painted at life size, framed by formal architectural features such as steps and pillars, and are dressed in exquisitely sumptuous clothes. The portraits are enlivened by the inclusion of small animals, which provide a sense of scale and a pertinent parallel, with pets such as dogs and birds evoking the classical theory that with the right instruction children can be trained.[22] Body language is important: with their casually crossed legs and

19
Sir Anthony van Dyck, *The Three Eldest Children of Charles I*, 1635, oil on canvas, 151 x 154 cm, Galleria Sabauda, Turin

20
Sir Anthony van Dyck, *The Three Eldest Children of Charles I*, 1635–36, oil on canvas, 133.8 x 151.7 cm, Royal Collection Trust

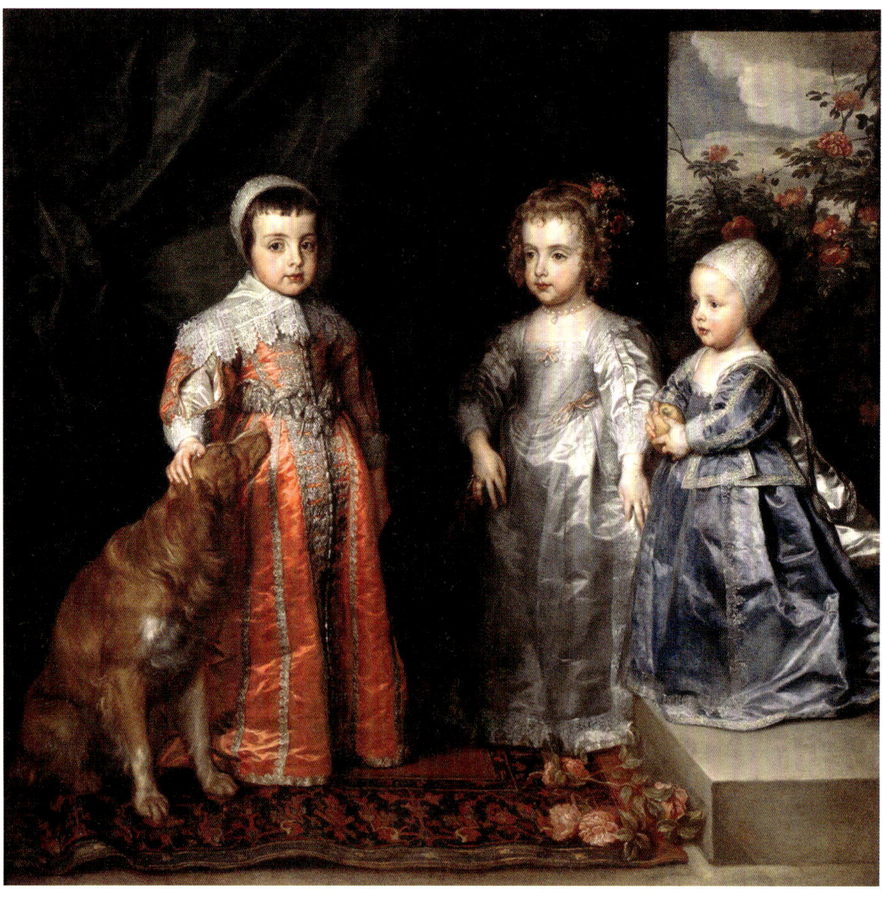

draped arms the the elder children in Van Dyck's paintings often convey a sense of studied, adult nonchalance, while the younger children appear somewhat more hesitant and childlike. Elegant informality is perhaps the defining feature of Van Dyck's portraiture, and the glamorous, illusionistic and flattering likenesses that he created breathed fresh air into English portrait traditions, with one scholar describing how with Van Dyck 'a breeze moves through the room, draperies move in it and the light itself seems to stream with it'.[23]

Van Dyck's portraits of the royal children may appear artfully natural but they were the result of careful negotiations between the artist, the King and his Queen. The earliest painting of the children shows *The Three Eldest Children of Charles I* and is now in Turin (fig. 19). At a time of high infant mortality, one of the chief functions of portraits of children was to reassure distant relatives of a child's size, appearance and health, and this seems to have been the purpose of this painting. The group portrait of the Prince of Wales (1630–1685, the future Charles II), his younger brother the Duke of York (1633–1701; the future James II) and their sister Mary (1631–1660) was made to be sent to Queen Henrietta Maria's sister Christina, Duchess of Savoy, in exchange for portraits of the Duchess's children. In July 1635 Henrietta Maria wrote to her sister stating that the portrait would be sent in a week, adding that her daughter did not have much patience for the sitting.[24] The picture was not dispatched to Turin until October or November, however, and in a letter of 29 November 1635 the Savoy Ambassador in London reported that the King had been angry with Van Dyck for not having painted the children in the *tablié* (aprons) which they customarily wore.[25] The painting shows that Van Dyck had painted near-transparent aprons on the two

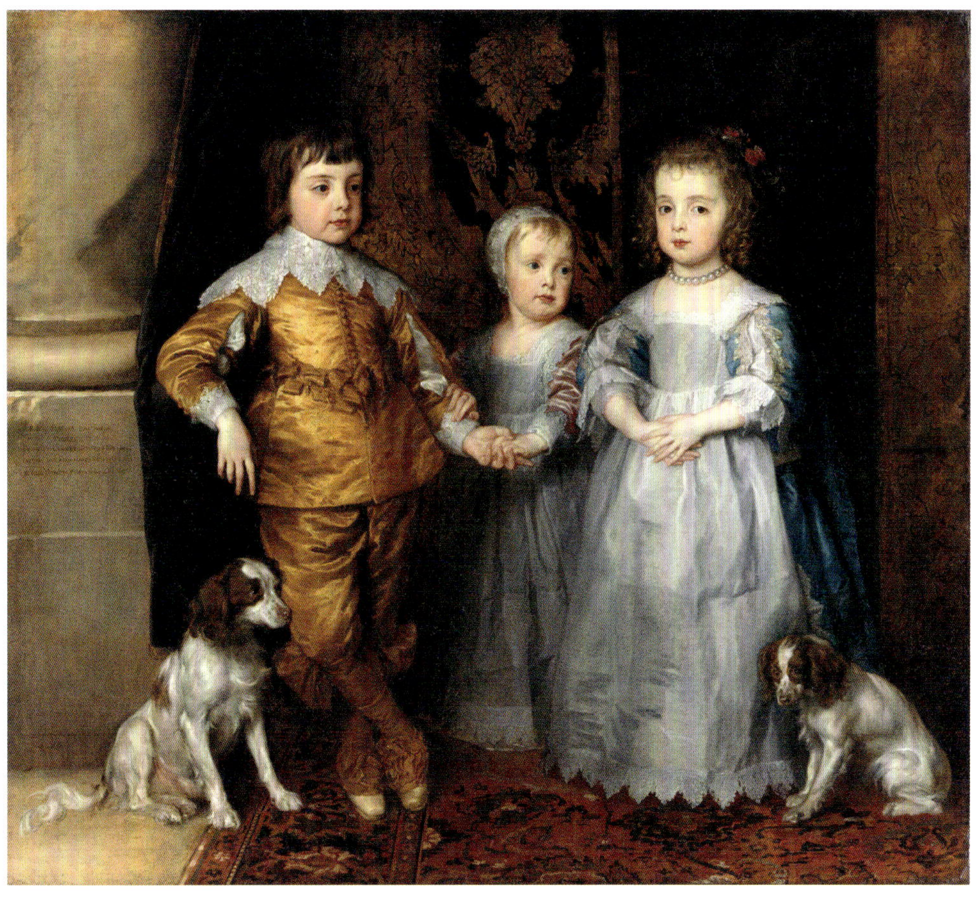

younger children, and, not having seen the picture, the minister may have misunderstood the Queen's account – the King may have disliked how the aprons were painted, but he was probably also displeased by the fact that Van Dyck had depicted the Prince of Wales unbreeched and still in skirts.[26] Both of these elements were corrected in a second portrait of the three children made the following year (fig. 20). In this portrait the aprons are more visible on James and Mary, and Charles wears yellow silk breeches and adopts a more adult pose, leaning against a column, with his legs crossed at the ankles. A sense of the Prince as a benevolent future ruler is expressed by his tenderly extended arm, which supports his younger brother. In this portrait four-year-old Mary's hair has been dressed with flowers according to the adult fashion, but her bodice includes hanging sleeves or leading strings made from the same fabric as her dress, attached at her shoulders and hanging down her back.[27] Hanging sleeves were a Spanish fashion popular with the elite; they would have functioned like modern reins for toddlers, but were often retained once children could walk, indicating that they were a fashion feature.[28] It is thought that this picture was painted for the Queen, who must have been fond of it. Although it was sold during the Commonwealth it was recorded hanging in Henrietta Maria's Presence Chamber at her French house, Colombes, at her death in 1669.[29]

Van Dyck depicted the three children again a year later, this time with their younger siblings Elizabeth and Anne, in *The Five Eldest Children of Charles I* (fig. 21). This painting was hung in the King's Breakfast Chamber, suggesting that again it was made primarily for private contemplation, although as with *The Three Eldest Children of Charles I* numerous copies were made.[30] Although they are absent from the image, the painting implicitly

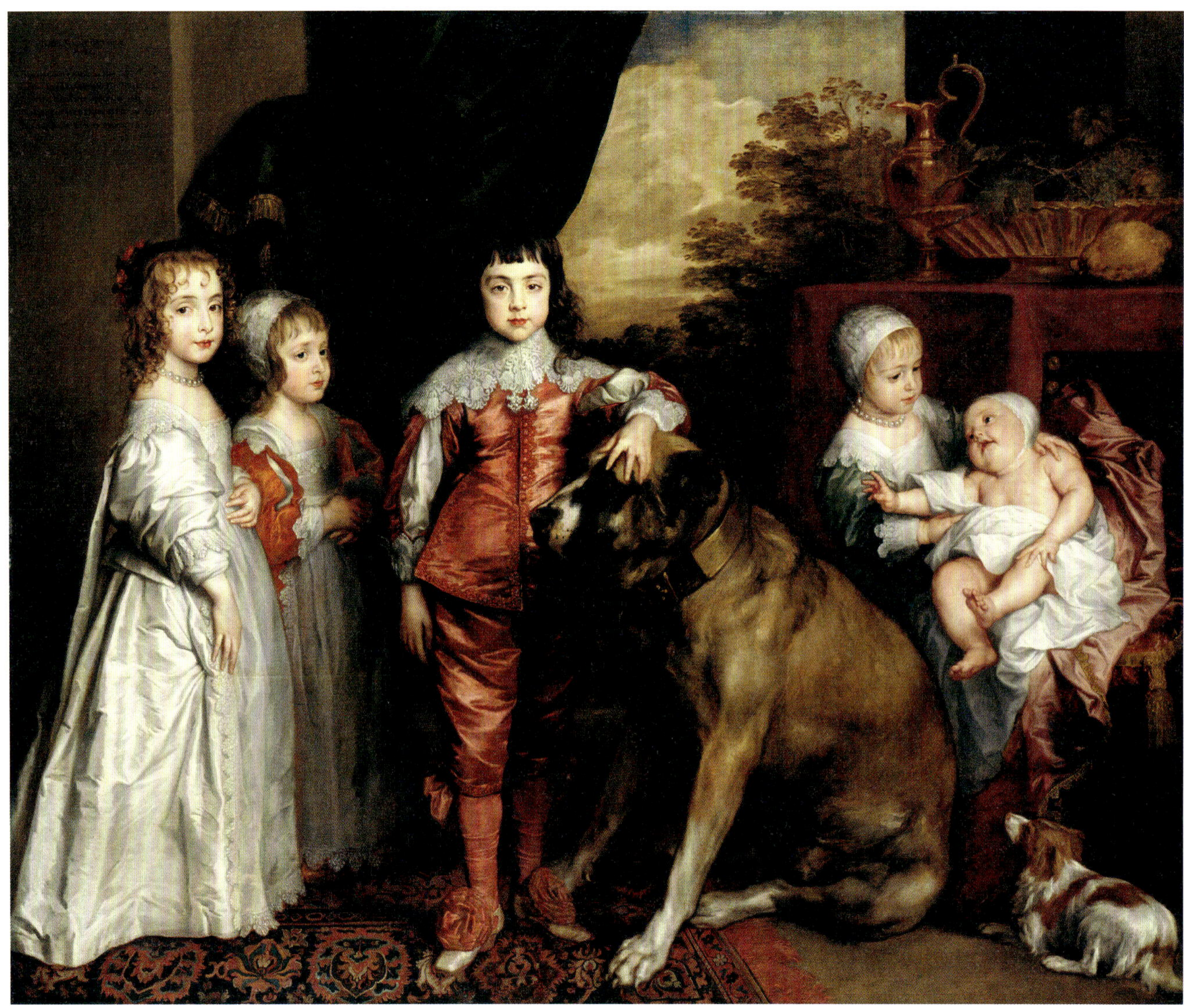

21
Sir Anthony van Dyck, *The Five Eldest Children of Charles I*, signed and dated 1637, oil on canvas, 163.2 x 198.8 cm, Royal Collection Trust

flatters Charles I and his queen, with the jug and bowl of fruit on the table behind the children emphasizing the bounty of their assembled offspring. A notable feature of the painting is the huge mastiff that sits amongst the siblings – seven-year-old Prince Charles, unruffled by its presence, places his left hand on the dog's head and faces the viewer squarely. The boy's innate mastery of the dog is comparable to his father's command of great horses in Van Dyck's equestrian portraits of Charles I. The King was a short man, but in portraits Van Dyck established that he could be made to look imposing when mounted on horseback. Conversely, the large mastiff in *The Five Eldest Children* playfully emphasizes the small stature of the children. As in the earlier portrait of the three siblings, James – still wearing skirts – is cast into Charles's shadow and his infancy helps to enhance his brother's strength. Mary is dressed in a white silk gown with a lace-trimmed apron and is beautifully composed. Shown from the

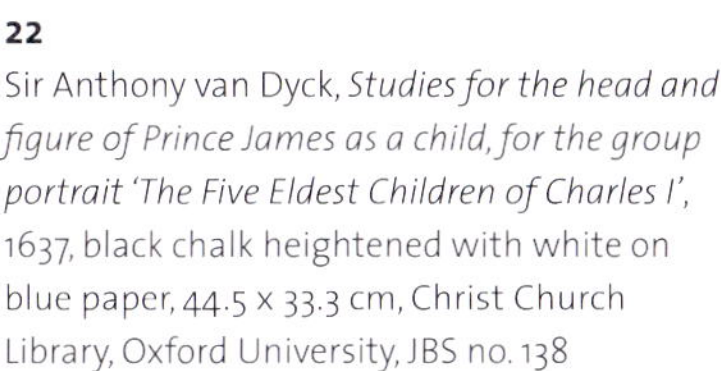

22
Sir Anthony van Dyck, *Studies for the head and figure of Prince James as a child, for the group portrait 'The Five Eldest Children of Charles I'*, 1637, black chalk heightened with white on blue paper, 44.5 x 33.3 cm, Christ Church Library, Oxford University, JBS no. 138

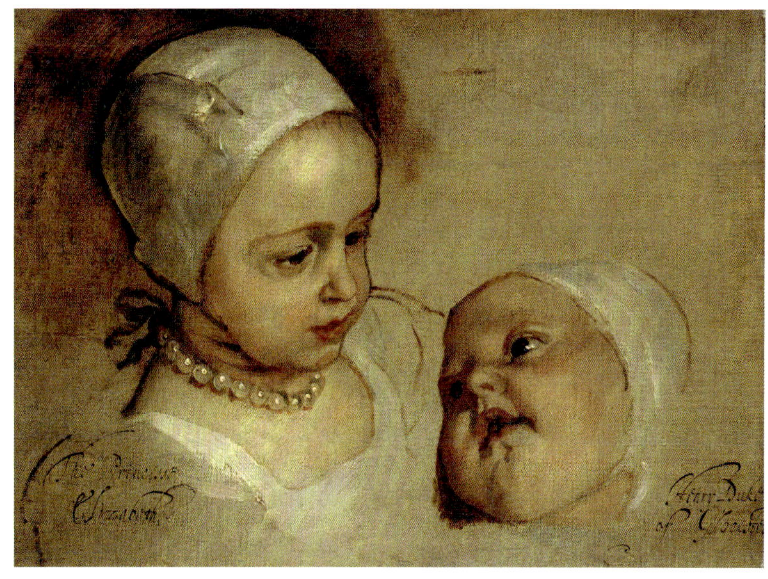

23
Sir Anthony van Dyck, *Princess Elizabeth, and Princess Anne, Daughters of Charles I*, 1637, oil on canvas, 29.8 x 41.8 cm, National Galleries of Scotland

side with her head turned to face the viewer, her pose is reminiscent of that used by Van Dyck to depict adult female sitters of the period. Mary's childhood was indeed short-lived – she was married to the thirteen-year-old Prince William of Orange in 1641, when she was aged just nine, with the occasion recorded by Van Dyck in a double portrait now in the Rijksmuseum. It is the younger sisters, Elizabeth (1635–1650) and Anne (1636–1640), who inject some childish energy into the group portrait. Elizabeth places her arms around her baby sister, Anne, who is swathed in white, but has squirmed enough to release her chubby legs and arms as she reaches for the dog.

Surviving preparatory works for *The Greate Peece* and *The Five Eldest Children* provide insights into Van Dyck's technique for capturing the royal children's likenesses. An oil sketch for *The Great Peece*, executed in oil on panel, shows Van Dyck working quickly and seemingly from life (see fig. 18). In this initial sketch the positioning of the figures is quite different, with Charles on the opposite side of his father, Henrietta Maria inclined more towards her husband, and baby Mary asleep in her mother's arms. Nevertheless, the sketch establishes a sense of compositional hierarchy – for Van Dyck, the recording of an individual's posture and physique in 'sudden lines' was often the starting point for a painting.[31] Rapid sketches in chalk were similarly used to establish the poses and dress of both Charles and James in *The Five Eldest Children of Charles I*. These appear to have been made from life and aided by studio props – a chalk sketch in the Royal Collection depicts the solitary figure of Charles, with his hand resting on a cushion in place of the dog.[32] A separate study for the figure of Prince James is in Oxford, and includes two sketches of the young prince, one at full length and a head study (fig. 22). In Edinburgh a third preparatory work, in the form of a lively oil sketch, demonstrates the artist capturing the moment

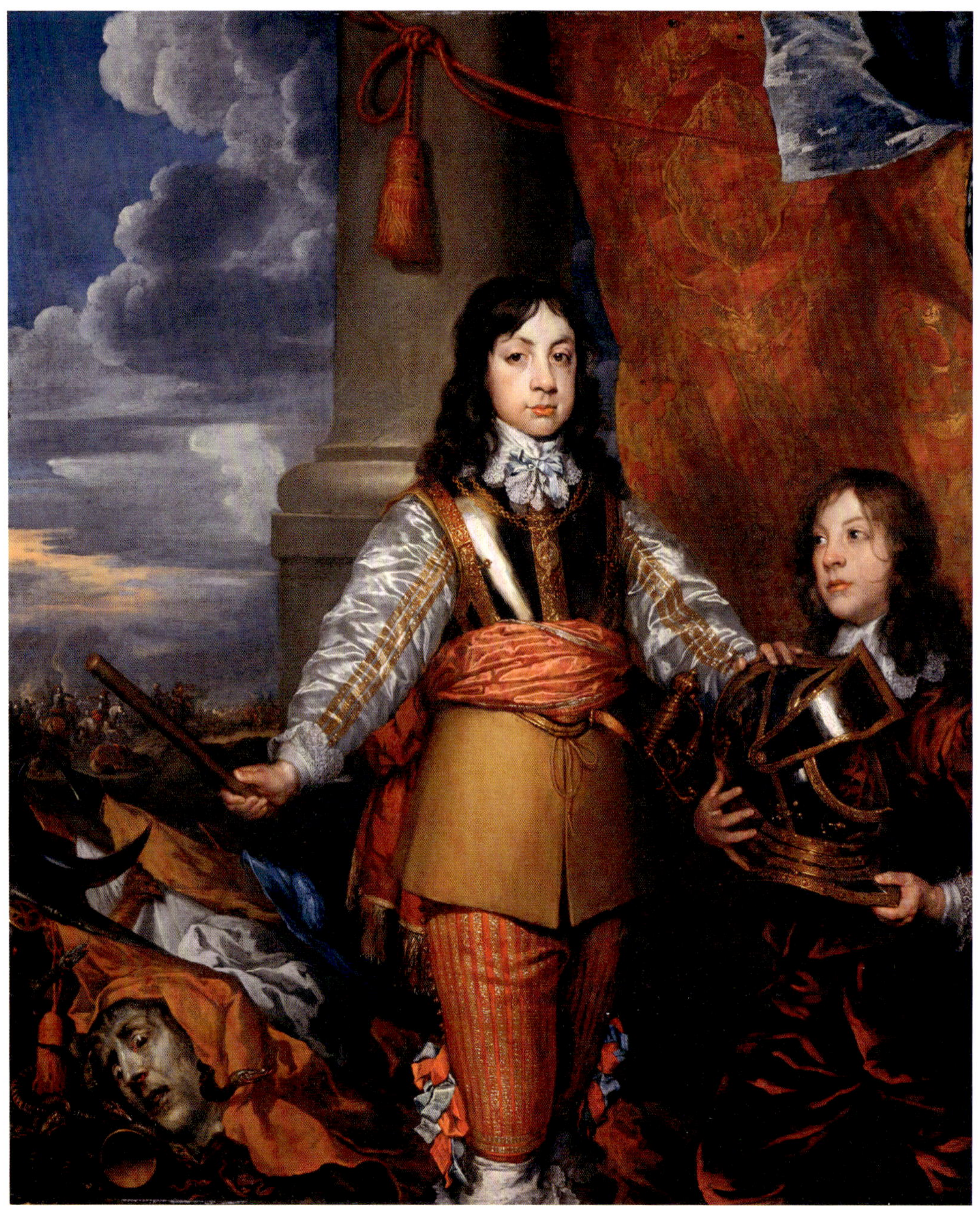

of interaction between the two youngest daughters (fig. 23). This work is less detailed than the finished painting – Elizabeth's fringe and pearl earring are not recorded – but its immediacy and fluency suggest that it was done from life, probably to prevent the need for further sittings for young sitters.[33] Van Dyck is known to have employed male and female studio models to inform the less important details of his portraits, such as the sitter's hands, and also to model clothes after an initial sitting.[34] A composite approach to a complex commission such as a group portrait of the royal children would certainly seem logical; Van Dyck's skill lay in his ability to carry the charming spontaneity of his oil sketches into his finished paintings.

24
William Dobson, *Charles, Prince of Wales, later Charles II, with a page*, c. 1642, oil on canvas, 153.6 x 129.8 cm, National Galleries of Scotland

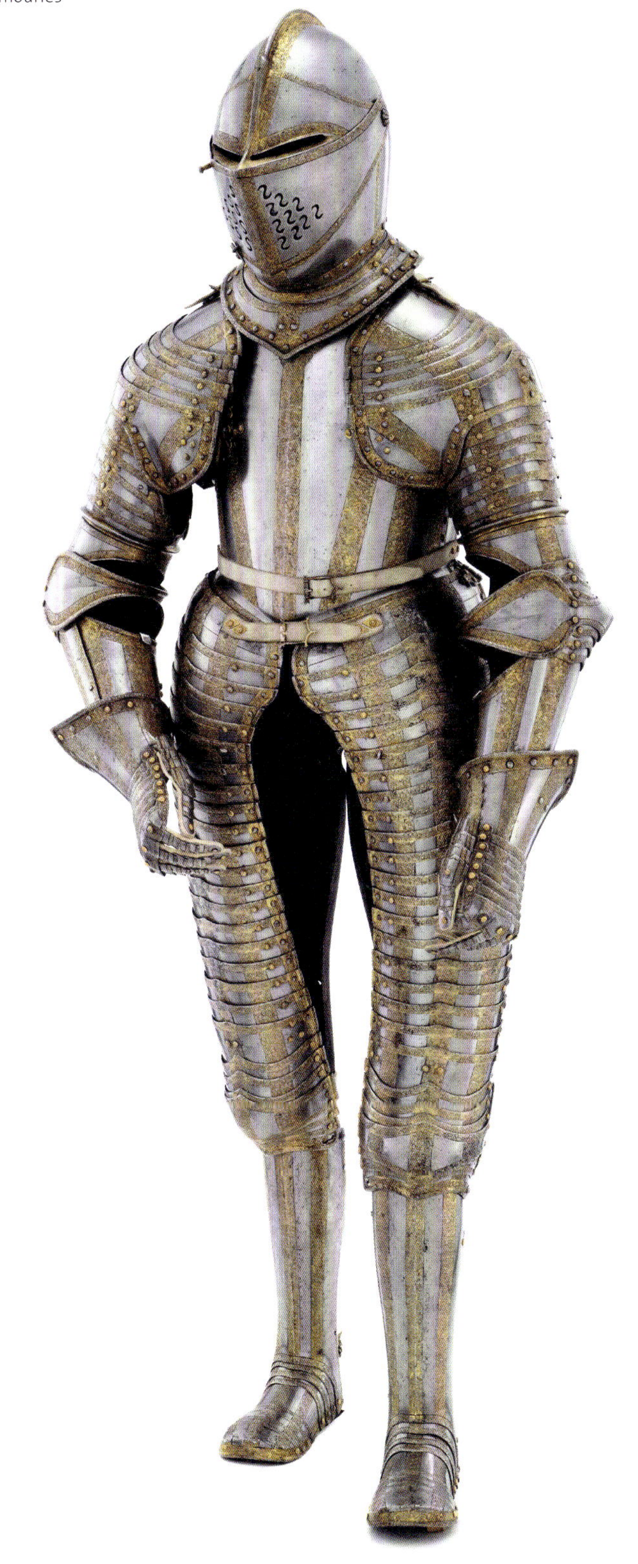

25
Armour of King Charles I as a boy, Dutch, c. 1616, steel, Royal Armouries Museum, 11.90, 144.8 cm

Van Dyck died in London in December 1641 and shortly after this Charles I also fled Whitehall. It was left to the Englishman William Dobson (1611–1646) to record the next turbulent chapter of the reign, as painter to the King in Oxford during the English Civil War. Dobson's portrait of Charles II on the battlefield presents a different image of the Prince of Wales from that evoked by Van Dyck's intimate family groups (fig. 24). In place of the mastiff here the Prince, now twelve years old, rests his left hand on a helmet. His other hand holds a commander's baton and over his satin finery he wears a leather buff coat and the breastplate of a suit of armour. This is probably the 'very curious gilt armour' that the prince was recorded as wearing when he was given nominal command of a troop at York in 1642.[35] The exact armour that Charles wears in Dobson's portrait survives in the Royal Armouries today (fig. 25). Decorated with narrow gold bands of scrolling foliage, it weighs the same as an adult armour (19.5kg) but is clearly proportioned for a youth, and was worn by three generations of princes (Charles I, Charles II and William III).[36] Charles and James were both present at the Battle of Edgehill later in 1642, where they performed an important, if dangerous, symbolic role. The depiction of Charles in armour in Dobson's portrait serves a similar symbolic purpose. It connects the portrait to a long history of leaders shown in military outfits, and speaks to a desperate need to assert the power of a royal dynasty in the face of grave opposition.

Tried and executed in 1649, Charles fell from power even more dramatically than he had ascended. Despite this, the sophisticated iconography associated with the court of Charles I continued to hold sway over future generations of rulers and artists. Sold during the Commonwealth, the painting of *The Five Eldest Children of Charles I* was purchased in 1765 by George III (1738–1820) and was one of several paintings by Van Dyck to

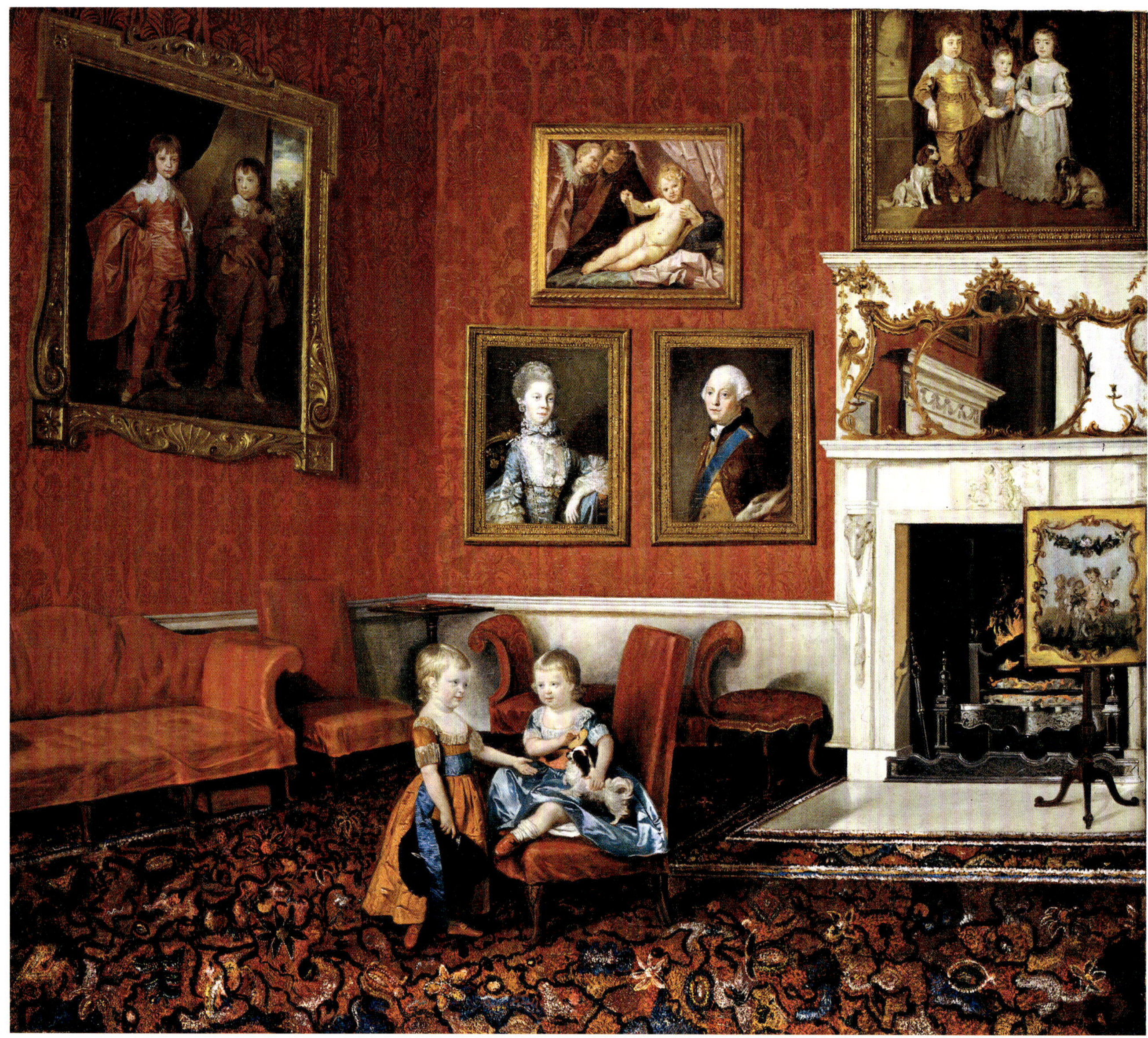

26
Johan Joseph Zoffany, *George, Prince of Wales and Frederick, later Duke of York, at Buckingham House*, 1765, oil on canvas, 111.9 x 127.9 cm, Royal Collection Trust

influence the royal portraitist Johann Zoffany (1733-1810). George III and his wife, Queen Charlotte, had fifteen children, and the children's wet-nurse recorded how the King 'at times would shed the dignity of the monarch in the natural impulse of the parent' and crawl about with the children.[37] The eldest two children are pictured by Zoffany playing with a dog in the newly decorated Second Drawing Room of Buckingham Palace in *George, Prince of Wales, and Frederick, later Duke of York, at Buckingham House* (fig. 26). Small figures on a richly patterned carpet, the two boys are not yet breeched and are dwarfed by their surroundings, which include walls decorated with red damask and hung with paintings by Van Dyck. The historical portraits literally 'look down' on the children at

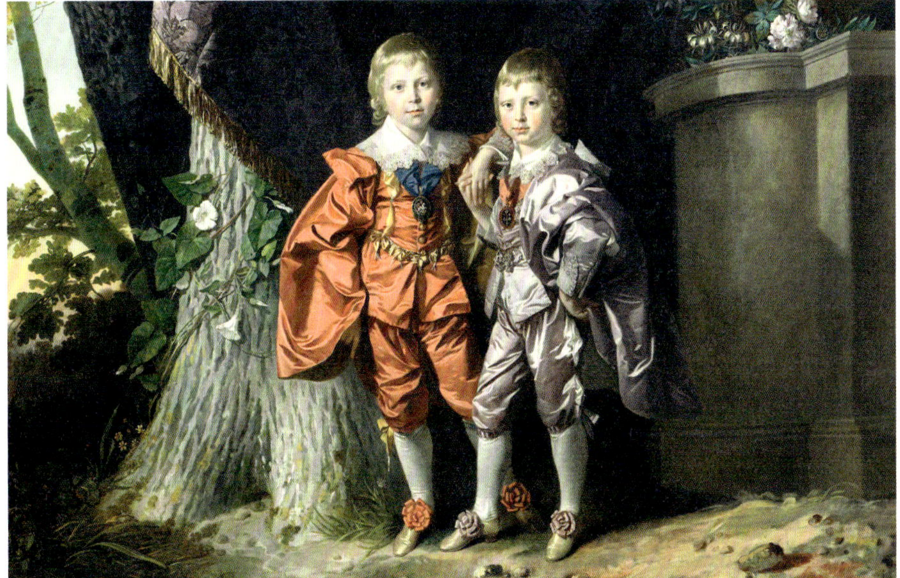

27
Johan Joseph Zoffany, *George, Prince of Wales, later George IV, with Prince Frederick, later Frederick, Duke of York*, c. 1770, oil on canvas, 131 x 202 cm, Royal Collection Trust

play, suggesting dynasties of both royal children and royal portraitists.

Zoffany paid homage to Van Dyck again in his portrait of *George, Prince of Wales, later George IV, with Prince Frederick, later Frederick, Duke of York* (fig. 27). Although separated by over one hundred years, the paired boys are posed in a similar manner to the two brothers in Van Dyck's *George Villiers, 2nd Duke of Buckingham and Lord Francis Villiers* (painted in 1635 and visible on the left-hand wall in fig. 26). The mood of Zoffany's double portrait is lighter than that of Van Dyck's and shows a greater degree of intimacy between the boys than its precedent: George leans on Frederick, their legs intertwine and they link hands. While the background contains a heavy draped curtain like the earlier portrait, in Zoffany's scene George and Frederick are clearly situated outdoors, in a sunlit wooded glade. This reflects recommendations made in contemporary treatises on childrearing, such as John Locke's best-selling treatise *Some Thoughts Concerning Education* (1693) and Jean-Jacques Rousseau's *Émile, ou de l'éducation* (1762), both of which stated the benefits of the outdoors for children.[38] One of the most striking parallels between the two paintings is that George and Frederick are wearing 'Vandyke' dress – outfits of contrasting, brightly coloured satin, with lace falling collars and shoes decorated with rosettes. This historic style of fancy dress, which was based on the clothing depicted in portraits by Van Dyck, became popular for masquerade balls and portrait sittings between 1730 and 1790.[39] It had a variety of connotations, but was considered particularly appropriate for sitters wishing to express their artistic or antiquarian interests, or for portraits of children, where it was thought to impart a sense of timeless elegance. The two boys appear again with linked arms in the public 'conversation piece' *George III, Queen Charlotte and their Six Eldest Children* (1770), and here the entire family wear Vandyke dress.[40] Although Horace Walpole found the outfits 'ridiculous' when he saw the painting in 1771, Zoffany had evidently found a mode of representing the royal children that pleased his patron, by both embracing past glories and playing to modern sensibilities.

Doting Parents: Victoria and Albert

The image of royal childhood underwent a further evolution with the arrival of a family for Queen Victoria (1819–1901) and Prince Albert (1819–1861). The Queen gave birth to nine children, and surviving pictures of the burgeoning family provide evidence of Victoria and Albert's loving marriage. Many of the images were commissioned privately by the couple, to be exchanged as tokens between them on

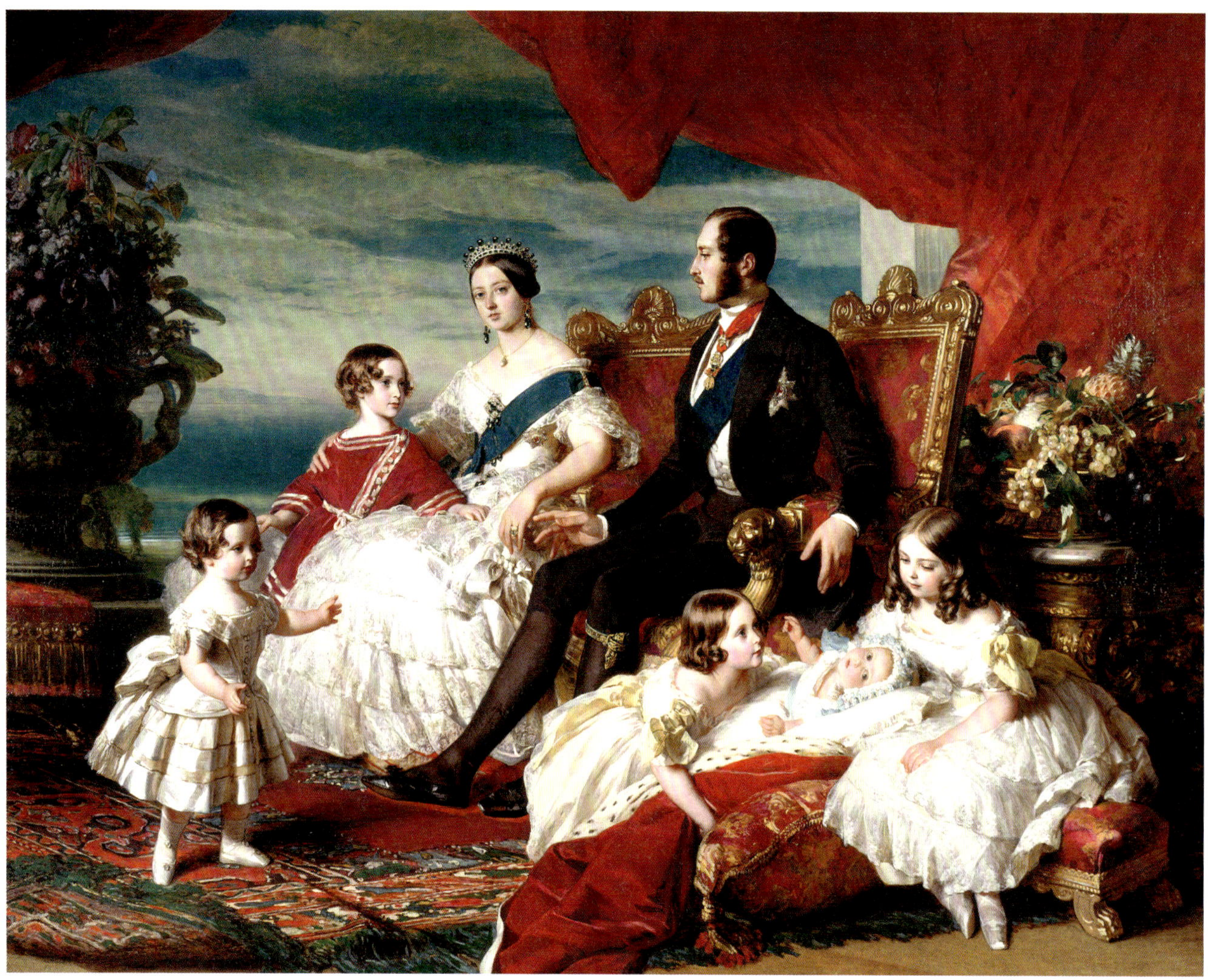

28
Frans Xaver Winterhalter, *The Royal Family in 1846*, 1846, oil on canvas, 250.5 x 317.3 cm, Royal Collection Trust

birthdays and anniversaries. Most intimate of all are the many depictions of the royal children that were executed by Victoria and Albert themselves, both of whom were enthusiastic amateur artists. For an official image of her family Queen Victoria turned to another émigré painter, the German Frans Xaver Winterhalter (1805–1873). His painting of *The Royal Family in 1846* (fig. 28) captures the family at life size, in a majestic manner which recalls Van Dyck's *Greate Peece*. Just as Henrietta Maria gazed across at Charles I in the earlier painting, here Albert turns his head to look at his eldest child, allowing the viewer's focus to fall on the sovereign, who calmly returns our gaze. The royal couple wear elegant evening dress, and gathered around them their five children provide both comforting dynastic ballast and a sense of playfulness. The most formally posed child is Prince Albert (Bertie), who leans against his mother as he receives instruction from his father. In the foreground Princess Victoria and Princess Alice concern themselves with the baby Helena, whose twisting posture recalls that of baby Anne in *The Five Eldest Children of Charles I*. Prince Alfred, still in skirts, totters across the carpet towards this trio, his action suggesting the lively

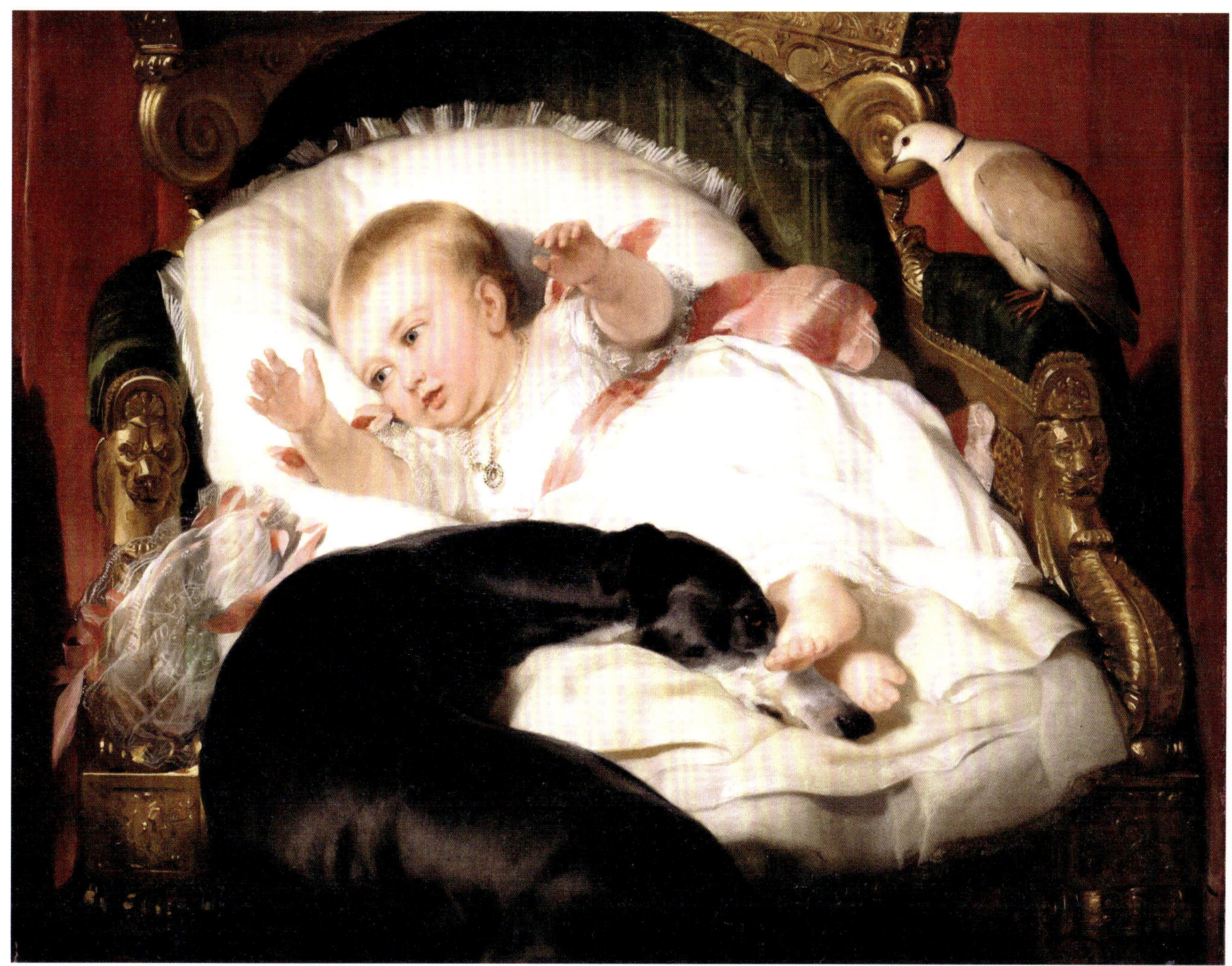

29
Sir Edwin Landseer, *Victoria, Princess Royal, with Eos*, 1841, oil on canvas, 71.8 x 91.8 cm, Royal Collection Trust

unpredictability of domestic life. The children's unguarded behaviour both references and loosens the conventions of earlier royal portraits, with the busy scene showing the influence of the 'conversation piece', a more informal mode of group portraiture that had become fashionable in England during the eighteenth century.[41] The painting was hung in the Dining Room at Osbourne House, the Queen's private residence on the Isle of Wight, but not before it was publicly exhibited. Although it was criticized in the press for displaying a 'want of taste' and for being by a foreign artist, the Queen declared that she was 'enchanted' by the painting. She made her own informal pen-and-ink sketch of the picture and in 1850 the painting was engraved for public circulation.[42]

The individual painted portraits of Victoria's children result from a more private desire to chart their growth and please her husband. In 1841 the Queen commissioned a portrait of their first child, Victoria, nicknamed 'Pussy', as a birthday gift for Albert. The resulting painting, *Victoria, Princess Royal, with Eos* (fig. 29) shows the eight-month-old posed with Albert's favourite dog. Dressed in a white robe with a pink sash around her waist and a pendant

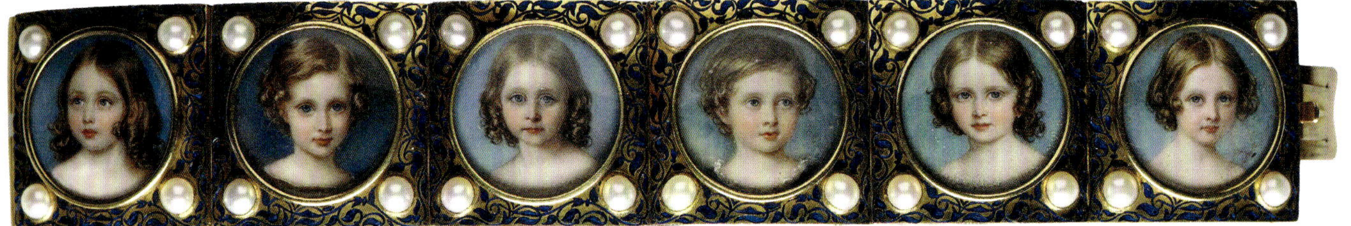

30
Bracelet with miniatures of the Royal children by William Essex, c. 1845–50, Gold and blue champlevé enamel, pearls, enamel, hair, 18 x 3 x 0.8 cm, Royal Collection Trust

around her neck, the Princess Royal's bare feet touch the nose of the greyhound, who was her frequent playmate. Albert is recorded as having been 'quite delighted' with the portrait. The inspiration for Winterhalter's painting of the couple's second child, *Albert Edward, Prince of Wales* (fig. 12), arose during a sailing trip around the Channel Islands in 1846 on board the Royal Yacht. As a surprise for Albert, Victoria requested that the naval tailor make up a miniature sailor suit to fit their four-year-old son. Her Journal describes how Bertie emerged on deck to the delight of everyone, including his father. Bertie's original sailor suit still survives in the National Maritime Museum, but it was immortalized when Prince Albert commissioned the portrait of his son as a Christmas present for Victoria. Winterhalter's painting went on display at St James's Palace in 1847, where it was seen by over 100,000 members of the public. Described by the Prime Minister, Sir Robert Peel, as 'the prettiest picture I have ever seen', the lively portrait sparked a fashion for children's sailor suits that lasted for much of the century. With its timeless connotations of status, adventure and patriotism, the sailor suit was the ideal outfit for a little boy, and remains a popular choice for many occasions today, influencing everything from Japanese school uniforms to page boys at Christian weddings and outfits worn by the children of the current Royal Family.[43]

Images of Victoria and Albert's children adorn other tokens exchanged between them. On her twenty-sixth birthday Albert presented Victoria with a bracelet set with pearls and containing a miniature by William Essex of their eldest child, Princess Victoria, aged four. This was subsequently added to: featuring portrait miniatures of each of the six eldest children when they reached the age of four (fig. 30), the bracelet is engraved on the reverse with the sitters' birthdates and inset with locks of their hair. In another example, a gold box is decorated with thirteen miniature enamel studs depicting portraits of the royal children. Painted by William Essex and William Charles Bell, the studs were presented by the Queen to Prince Albert on the occasion of their wedding anniversary, 10 February, and her birthday, 24 May, and were probably mounted together following Albert's death.

The 224 drawings of the royal children pasted into the thick volume of 'Sketches of the Royal Children by V.R. from 1841–9' tell an even more intimate story of family life. Executed by the Queen herself, the assembled images capture the royal children off-duty – playing with toys, bathing, being fed, and posed wearing fancy-dress costumes or special new outfits. Victoria's interest in her children's appearances, natures and relationships is evident – each sketch is carefully captioned with the date and nickname of the child, sometimes with additional personal observations, recorded for posterity, such as 'Pussy with Bertie in the dresses they wore on little Alice's christening day June 2 1843'. As the Queen's firstborn, Victoria Princess Royal features most frequently in the album, with an early drawing showing Pussy asleep, aged three weeks (fig. 31). In other sketches Pussy is depicted with Bertie surrounded by toys (fig. 32). Here Albert has used a lively sketch by Victoria as the basis for an etching;

the couple enjoyed working on etchings together, and received lessons from the artists George Hayter and Edwin Landseer, even installing a printing press in Buckingham Palace in 1840.[44] It has been argued that Victoria's record of domestic bliss owes much to Albert, who organized the children's schedules and whom the Queen described as 'wonderfully handy and gentle'.[45] Certainly the images of happy family life end in 1861, with Albert's death. Victoria seems to have derived more joy from her role as a wife than from her duties as a mother. Her writings repeatedly assert the wish that her children will grow up to be as handsome and talented as their father, and in 1857 Victoria

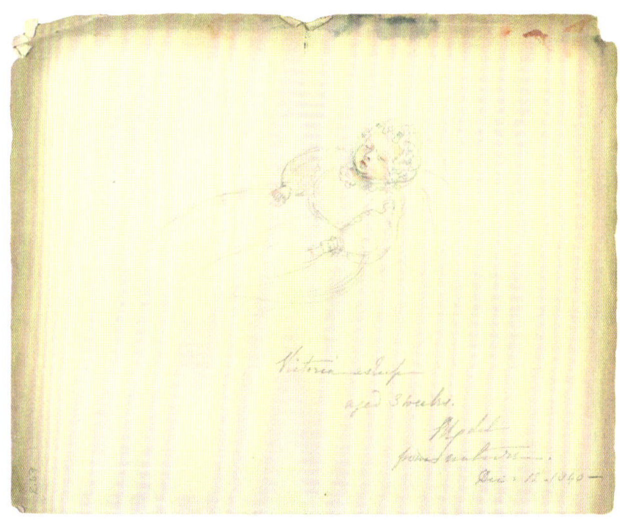

31
Queen Victoria, *Victoria asleep aged 3 weeks*, dated 12 December 1840, pencil with touches of watercolour, 22.3 x 27.5 cm, Royal Collection Trust

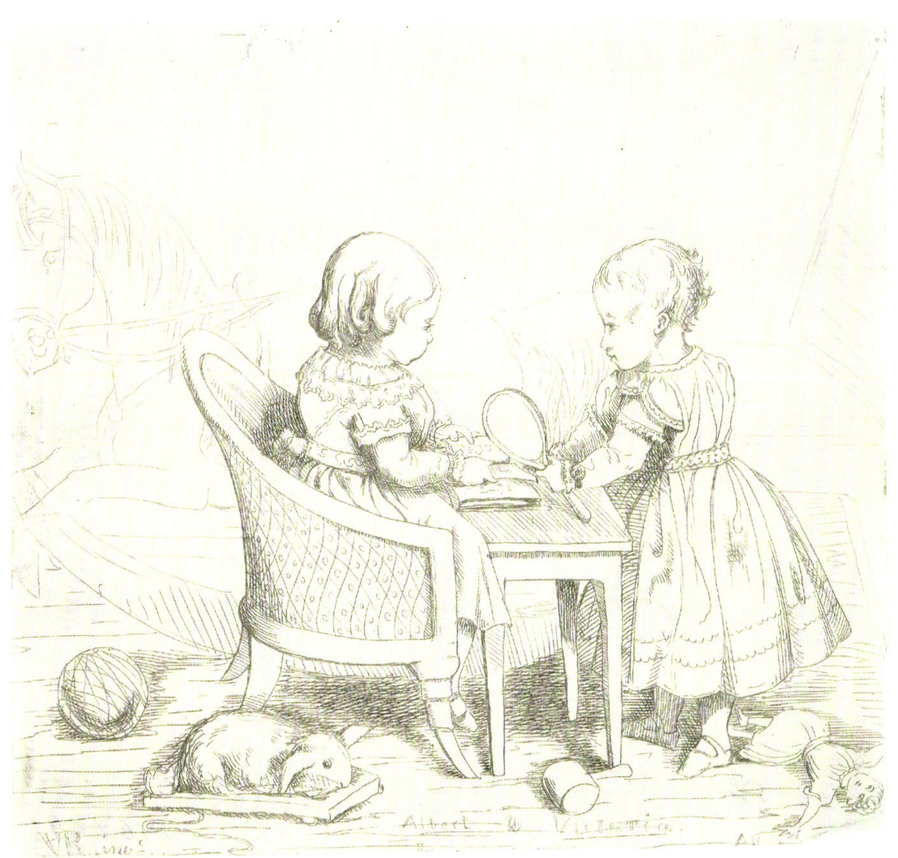

32
Prince Albert, Prince Consort, *Albert and Victoria*, dated 8 Jan 1843, etching on India paper, 14.8 x 16 cm, Royal Collection Trust

confessed to her uncle that confessed to her uncle that: '*All* the numerous children are as *nothing* to me when *he is away*; it seems as if the whole life of the house and home were gone, when he is away!'[46]

The role that images of their children played in Victoria and Albert's marriage reflects modern sensibilities, and demonstrates how much royal portraiture had evolved by the nineteenth century. Tracing a line from images by Holbein through Peake, Van Dyck, Dobson and Zoffany to Landseer and Winterhalter, it is evident that expectations of royal children had shifted considerably. Depictions of royal children have been shaped by the interests and passions of individual monarchs, the different talents of court artists and by the changing demands of society. However, we have only to remember Henry VIII's description of his son as a 'precious jewel', or Henrietta Maria's careful display of Van Dyck's portrait of her three children in her final home in France, to realize that perhaps not so much had changed between royal parents and their children over the centuries.

Notes

I am grateful to Anna Reynolds and Karen Hearn for their insightful comments on this chapter

1 'our most moost noble and moost precyous joyelle', Hayward 2007, p. 210.
2 London 2006, p. 100.
3 This inscription was composed by the humanist scholar Richard Morison. For the full inscription see London 1995–96, p. 41.
4 Loach 1999, p. 35.
5 A fragment of Holbein's preparatory cartoon shows the full-length figure of Henry VIII (National Portrait Gallery, NPG 4027) and a copy of the complete mural by Remigius van Leemput dated 1667 is in the Royal Collection, RCIN 405750. Further full-length copies of the King were produced soon after his death and are at Petworth House, West Sussex, and in the Walker Art Gallery, Liverpool. The later portraits show that Holbein changed the orientation of Henry's head after making the preparatory cartoon, from three-quarter turn to full frontal.
6 The drawings of Edward, Prince of Wales are at Windsor, RCIN 912200 and RCIN 912202. Both have suffered from rubbing and retouching by later hands. Foister 1983, pp. 49 and 55–56. Unusually the head in the Washington portrait of Edward is larger than in the portrait drawing, suggesting that Holbein may have enlarged it after transfer. London 1995–96, p. 41.
7 Christina of Denmark sat for Holbein for three hours for the full-length portrait that is now in the National Gallery, London, 1538, NG 2475. During this time Holbein made preparatory sketches, completing the painted portrait on his return to England. Foister 2004, pp. 40–65.
8 A work close to the Compton Verney painting is the so-called 'Lumley Portrait' of Edward VI, sold by the Weiss Gallery in 1998 to a private collection. This is thought to have been painted c. 1542–45 and is distinguished by a painted *cartellino*, added in 1590, signifying that the painting once belonged to John, 1st Lord Lumley (c. 1533–1609). A second portrait type features the prince holding a rose, and is found in several versions including the National Portrait Gallery, NPG 1132. Strong 1969, p. 92, and London 2014, pp. 70–71.
9 Foister 1983, pp. 3–12, and London 1995, pp. 22–23.
10 Arnold 1988, pp. 252–53. The section detailing Edward's clothes lists three sets of matching doublets and hose and a small selection of jewellery and weapons.
11 Sarcenet was a lightweight fabric used for 'pullings out' similar to those shown on Edward's sleeves. Edward wears the same garment in a group portrait by an unknown artist in *The Family of Henry VIII* painted c. 1545 in the Royal Collection, RCIN 405796. Warrants from 1539, 1544 and 1545 show Henry VIII ordering highly decorative garments for his son, reflecting his increasing age and maturity. Hayward 2007, pp. 210–13.
12 This painting may also relate to a lost original

drawing by Holbein, the existence of which is suggested by a profile drawing in the Royal Collection attributed to a follower of Holbein, RCIN 912202, and a number of paintings that employ the profile format,.

13 Accounts suggest that the portrait of Edward delighted visitors to Whitehall Palace at the end of the sixteenth century, who viewed the painting through a telescopic device. It is unlikely that the Holbein portrait was viewed using such a device. Foister 2004, p. 216.

14 Other half-length portraits of this type include a painting in the National Portrait Gallery, NPG 442; a portrait at Knole, National Trust; a portrait at Wilton House, WLN 69561; and a portrait in the Victoria and Albert Museum, inv. 493-1882.

15 Karen Hearn, 'Edward VI: A Boy King and his Portraits', lecture delivered at Compton Verney, 4 August 2005.

16 The flowers are illustrated on page 854 of John Gerard's *The Herball*, first published in 1597.

17 Fisher 2011, pp. 28, 124 and 139.

18 The original patron may have been Sir Michael Stanhope (c. 1508-1552). Brother-in-law of Edward Seymour, the Lord Protector, Stanhope was Chief Gentleman of the Privy Chamber by 1549 but fell from power at the end of the year and was eventually beheaded in 1552. The portrait is thought to have hung at Elvaston Castle, the estate acquired by Stanhope's son Thomas Stanhope, since the seventeenth century.

19 It is suggested that the unusual staging of this painting may derive from woodcut illustrations found in George Gascoigne's treatise *The Noble Art of Venerie, or Hunting* (1575). London 2012a, pp. 70-71. The format was first used to depict Prince Henry in an earlier double portrait now in New York: Robert Peake, *Henry Frederick (1594-1612), Prince of Wales, with Sir John Harington (1592-1614), in the Hunting Field*, dated 1603, Metropolitan Museum, New York.

20 For more on the relationship between Van Dyck and King Charles I see the essays in London 2009.

21 Van Dyck's Italian sketchbook, British Museum, fol. 108r. London/Antwerp 1999, p. 169.

22 Haarlem/Antwerp 2000, p. 19.

23 Piper 1968, p. 18.

24 Barnes 2004, pp. 477-78; Ferrero 1881, pp. 39-40.

25 The Savoy minister in London, Benoît Cize, reported to the Duke of Savoy that: *'le Roy estoit faché contre le peintre Vandec por ne leur avoir mis leur Tablié, comme on accoustume aux petits enfans, et qu'elle enscriproit à Madame sa soeur, pour le leur faire mettre'*. The Duchess of Savoy requested that the picture should not be altered. London/Antwerp 1999, p. 295.

26 London/Antwerp 1999, p. 295; Millar 1963, pp. 98-99.

27 London 2013, p. 123.

28 Hugget, Malcolm-Davies and Mikhaila 2013, pp. 26-27.

29 Millar, 1963, p. 99.

30 The only other picture hung in the King's Breakfast Chamber was Guilio Romano's *Mermaid Feeding Her Young*, perhaps a comical reference to the fact that every creature considers its own offspring to be beautiful. London 2018, p. 243. For a list of the copies after these compositions see Millar 1963, nos. 151 and 152; Barnes 2004.

31 The English painter Richard Gibson (1615-1690) sat for Van Dyck and described how: 'Vandyke would take a little piece of blue paper upon a board before him & look upon the Life & draw his figures & postures all in Suden lines, as angles with black Chalk, & heighten with white chalk'. London 2009, p. 153.

32 Sir Anthony van Dyck, Charles II as Prince of Wales, c. 1637, black chalk heightened with white on blue paper, 46 × 30.3 cm, RCIN 913018

33 It has been suggested that Van Dyck would have produced an oil sketch for the heads of the other children too. New York 2016, pp. 205-07.

34 Ibid., pp. 20-21.

35 Reckitt 1952, p. 54.

36 Royal Armouries 2003. Dobson painted the Prince of Wales in the same armour two years later, in a portrait now in the Royal Collection: William Dobson, *Charles II when Prince of Wales*, 1644, RCIN 404921. See London 2013, pp. 225-48.

37 London 2009, p. 101.

38 Queen Charlotte evidently knew Locke's publication; a copy of it appears beside her in Allan Ramsay's portrait of *Queen Charlotte with her Two Eldest Sons*, c. 1764. See also chapter 3, fig. 34.

39 Gordenker 2001, p. 77.

40 RCIN 400501, see London 2004, p. 31.

41 London 2009, pp. 164-65.

42 Victoria's pen-and-ink sketch, on gold-headed notepaper, is in the Royal Collection (RCIN 980057). It differs slightly from Winterhalter's painting and is an interesting record of the Queen's perception of the painting. Scott 2010, pp.144-46.

43 Butchart 2015, p. 52. Prince William wore a sailor suit as a child during the 1980s; in 2015 the Duchess of Cambridge photographed Prince George in nautical clothing.

44 London 2010, p. 431.

45 Warner 1979, p. 125.

46 Benson and Esher 1908, vol. 3, p. 240.

'That beloved object'
Child Portraiture, Memory and Mourning[1]

EMILY KNIGHT

William Hogarth's group portrait of *The Graham Children* offers a lively rendering of mid-eighteenth-century childhood (fig. 33). Royal Apothecary Daniel Graham's four children, Thomas, Henrietta, Anna Maria and Richard, play together in a domestic setting seemingly unaware of the viewer. Only the eldest child, Henrietta, looks out and invites us into the scene, demonstrating her maturity and impending transition into adulthood. Scholars have understood this portrait as a breakthrough moment in child portraiture – 'one of the greatest depictions of children from the period' – highlighting Hogarth's innovative experimentation with portrait conventions during a period in which the concept of childhood was the subject of much discussion.[2] Despite the seemingly unselfconscious poses of the Graham children, the portrait is rich in symbolism of transience and mortality.[3]

Richard, positioned on the far right-hand side of the canvas, turns the handle of a mechanical organ while looking up to a caged bird, which seems to sing along to its tune. Unbeknownst to the boy, a cat hovers behind his head with eyes wide open ready to pounce on the cage, perhaps the real cause of the bird's sound. This moment of suspense and impending danger has been read as a commentary on the transition from childhood to adulthood, further accentuated by the depiction of the eldest child, Henrietta, who holds a pair of cherries in her left hand, traditionally symbolic of virginity. Here she stands on the brink of adulthood, still part of the world of children but approaching the next phase of her life. The cherries, however, serve a dual function that contributes to the more sombre aspect of the painting. Considered the fruits of paradise, cherries were also used in portraits to symbolize heaven and, by implication, death. It is not, however, Henrietta who has been portrayed posthumously but her youngest brother Thomas, who eagerly reaches out to the fruit with an entranced expression. Furthermore, immediately above the toddler's head there is a clock topped by a figure holding a scythe, a common trope that suggests the passing of time and ultimately death.

Portraiture is inextricably bound to absence whether through physical separation or death. When a portrait is taken from life to mark a particular moment in a person's life, there is an expectation that it will outlast the sitter.[4] During the eighteenth century in Britain, this sense of everlasting commemoration was particularly pronounced in portraits of children. Parents, acutely aware of the precarious reality of childhood, sought images of their offspring that, at best, would commemorate their early years and, at worst, provide visual comfort after their premature death. At times, death would come too soon. As Hogarth's portrait of the Graham children demonstrates, parents who may not have commissioned a portrait of their child in life sought to capture their image in death, often including their deceased child within group portraits in order to maintain their place in the family. This practice was by no means unique to the period and there are earlier examples of group portraits in which a deceased child is included.[5] The manner in which artists and their patrons sought to do this in the eighteenth century, however, speaks to a particular cultural moment in which emotions were expressed more openly in art and literature.

The layered meaning of Hogarth's portrait hints at this desire to preserve the image of deceased children. In this chapter, close analysis of several eighteenth-century

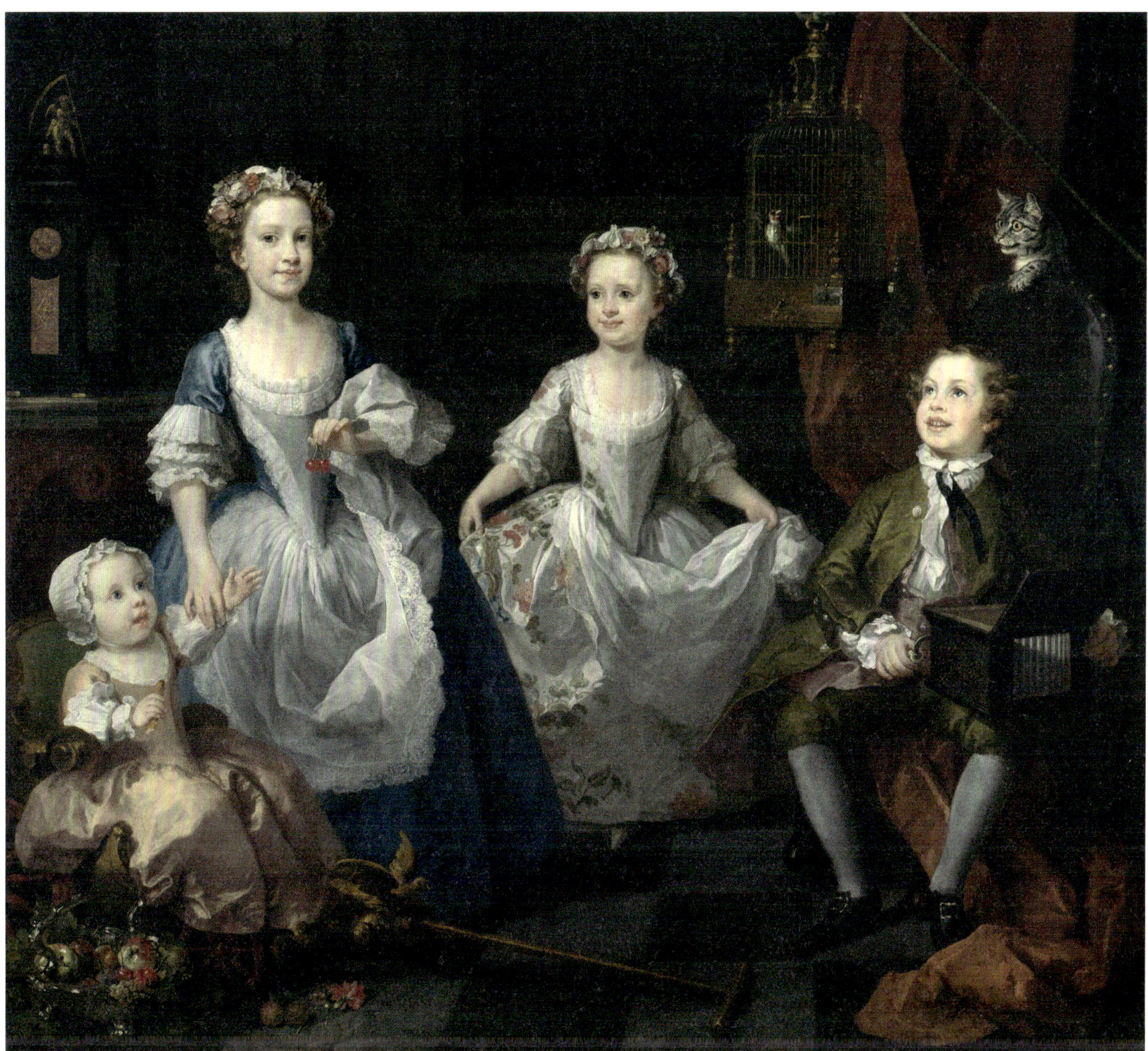

33
William Hogarth, *The Graham Children*,
1742, oil on canvas, 160.5 x 181 cm,
National Gallery, London

portraits included in *Painting Childhood* will reveal new conceptions of childhood and the more outward expression of emotion by parents that occurred during this 'Age of Sensibility'. These changes are anchored in two key themes. First is that of the philosophical and intellectual developments that shifted notions of childhood and their impact to child portraiture. The second is the manner in which artists and their patrons portrayed children after their death in such a way as to maintain their presence within the family and to assuage the grief of those left behind. Positioning these works alongside textual sources enriches our understanding of the motivation behind their creation and the effect that they had on grieving parents. This demonstrates the crucial role that portraiture played

34
Allan Ramsay, *Queen Charlotte with her two Eldest Sons*, 1764–69, oil on canvas, 247.8 x 165 cm, Royal Collection Trust

in mourning practices and the drive to make a child's absence present within the home.

The debates surrounding conceptions of childhood during this period in Britain were a key influence on the changing manner in which children were portrayed in portraiture.[6] Crucial to this shift were the intellectual and philosophical foundations provided by John Locke's *Some Thoughts Concerning Education* (1693), and Jean-Jacques Rousseau's *Émile* (1762). In Locke's text he argues that children are not inherently sinful and that the development of a child's intellect and morality should be carefully nurtured.[7] Describing the young child's mind as 'white Paper, or Wax, to be moulded and fashioned as one pleases', with an inherent capacity for reason, he contends that the early years of a child's education should prepare their mind for the intellectual development discussed in his earlier work, *An Essay Concerning Human Understanding* (1689).[8] Crucially, Locke purports that childhood is a state of development distinct from adulthood, and children should thus 'not be hindered from being children, or from playing, or doing as children, but from doing ill'.[9]

Locke's text became hugely popular, reprinted numerous times by the end of the eighteenth century and widely commented upon in contemporary journals and novels, even achieving the recognition of Queen Charlotte. Painted by Allan Ramsay (1713–1784) around 1764–69 with her two children Prince Frederick and Prince George (later George IV) (fig. 34), the Queen rests her elbow on the top of a spinet, directing the viewer's attention to a copy of Locke's text. This overt inclusion clearly indicates her beliefs concerning the nature of childhood and the role of education in the upbringing of 'virtuous, useful, and able men'. Close familial bonds are emphasized by the physical proximity of the family group: the Queen gently embraces Prince George on her lap with Prince Frederick at her side resting his arm on her knee. A reference to play, advocated by Locke, is provided by the older prince, who holds a bow in his left hand and a drum behind him.[10] As Locke argues in *On Education*, 'For, All their innocent Folly, Playing, and *Childish* actions, [children] are to be left perfectly free and *unrestrained*, as far as they can consist with the Respect due to those that are present; and that with the greatest Allowance.'[11]

This idea of independence and freedom is similarly discussed in Rousseau's highly influential book *Émile*, first published in English in 1763, which was also owned by Queen Charlotte. He argues that children are fully innocent creatures who are eventually corrupted by society and that it is the role of parents to protect their children from these dangers for as long as possible.[12] Furthermore, Rousseau emphasized the importance of allowing children to learn through experience and for this to occur in nature, as 'All things are good as their Creator made them, but every thing [sic] degenerates in the hands of man'.[13]

Hogarth's celebrated portrait of the Graham children draws on contemporary notions of childhood that were informed by Locke's writing and would continue to be discussed following the publication of Rousseau's *Émile*.[14] It was, however, the artist's attempt to capture the precarious nature of childhood that is crucial to this chapter, whether it be the loss of innocence as a child approached adulthood and the corrupting forces of society, or the very real threat of childhood mortality.

One of the key challenges that faced artists when depicting a deceased sitter was the ability to capture a likeness. In the Graham portrait Hogarth has depicted the dead infant Thomas as if he is alive, denying his death for the sake of the coherent narrative of the painting. In order to do this, it is probable that Hogarth worked from a sketch that he had made of the child immediately following his death (fig. 35). When this drawing came into the British Museum collection in 1895, it was understood to be an

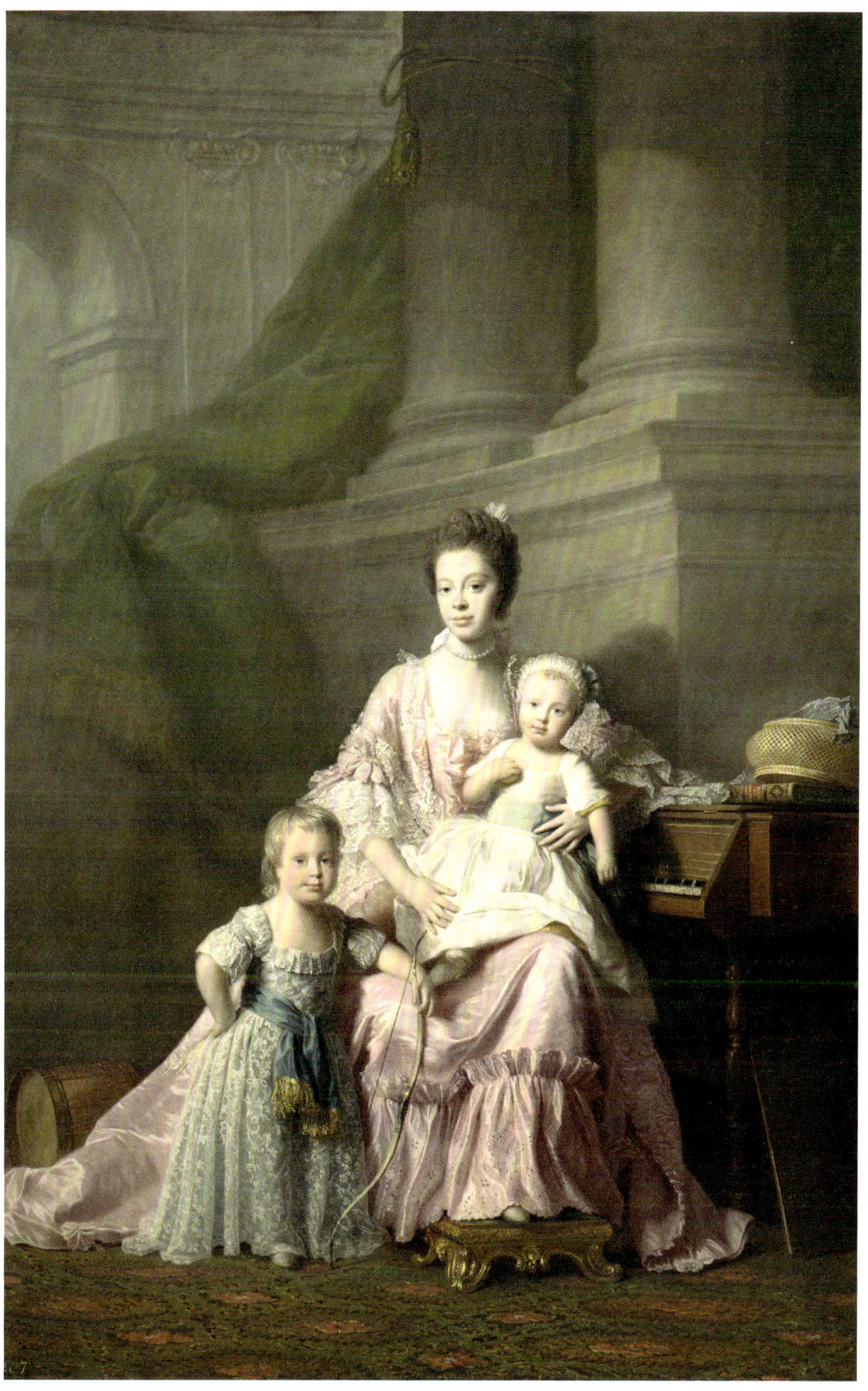

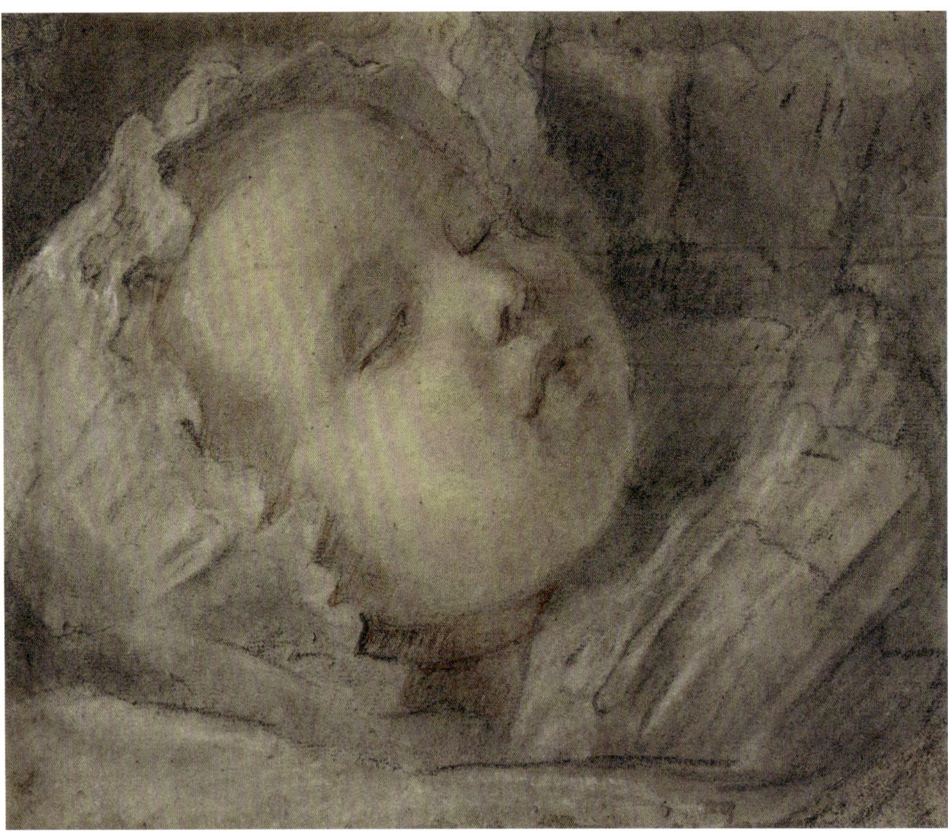

35
William Hogarth, *Study of a Sleeping Child*, 1740–42, drawing, 22.8 x 27 cm, British Museum

unidentified sleeping child. The image of the sleeping child had existed in European painting since the Renaissance, including Domenichino's two sheets of studies of a sleeping child (figs. 36 and 37). Works like these allowed the artist to capture the proportions of a child without the risk of them moving or wriggling away. The sleeping child gained renewed prominence in the eighteenth century and artists such as Reynolds similarly painted several comparable works, including *A Child Asleep* (fig. 38), albeit a little older in this instance. The baby drawn by Hogarth, however, was later identified as the young Thomas Graham.[15] It is easy to see how Hogarth's deathbed sketch could have been misconstrued as a child sleeping but its creation indicates the artistic and, perhaps, emotional value of a final image of a corpse. By making use of his sketch, the artist could adequately portray and lend a sense of authenticity to his depiction of baby Thomas alongside his living brothers and sisters. It is not known whether Hogarth's drawing was ever owned by the Graham family or if it simply served as an artistic tool, but there are a number of other examples of deathbed portraits of children that demonstrate the emotional value of such works to the grieving family.

Allan Ramsay, the prominent and fashionable Scottish artist, was hit by a string of losses that began with the death of his son Allan, who died aged just fourteen months in 1741 (fig. 39). Years later, the artist recounted to Lady Bute how, sitting in tears next to his son, he used his skills as a painter to overcome his grief, if only for a moment. Her daughter, Lady Louisa Stuart, recorded the conversation: 'while thoroughly occupied thus, [Ramsay] felt no more concern than if the subject had been an

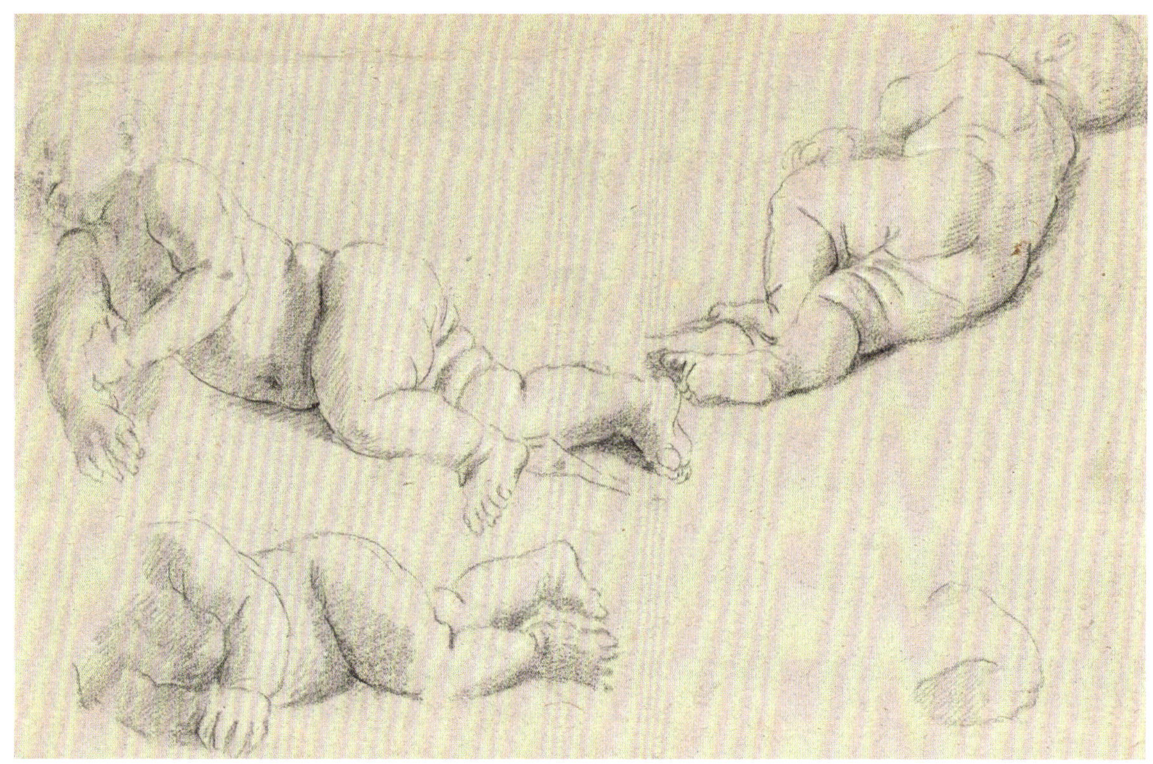

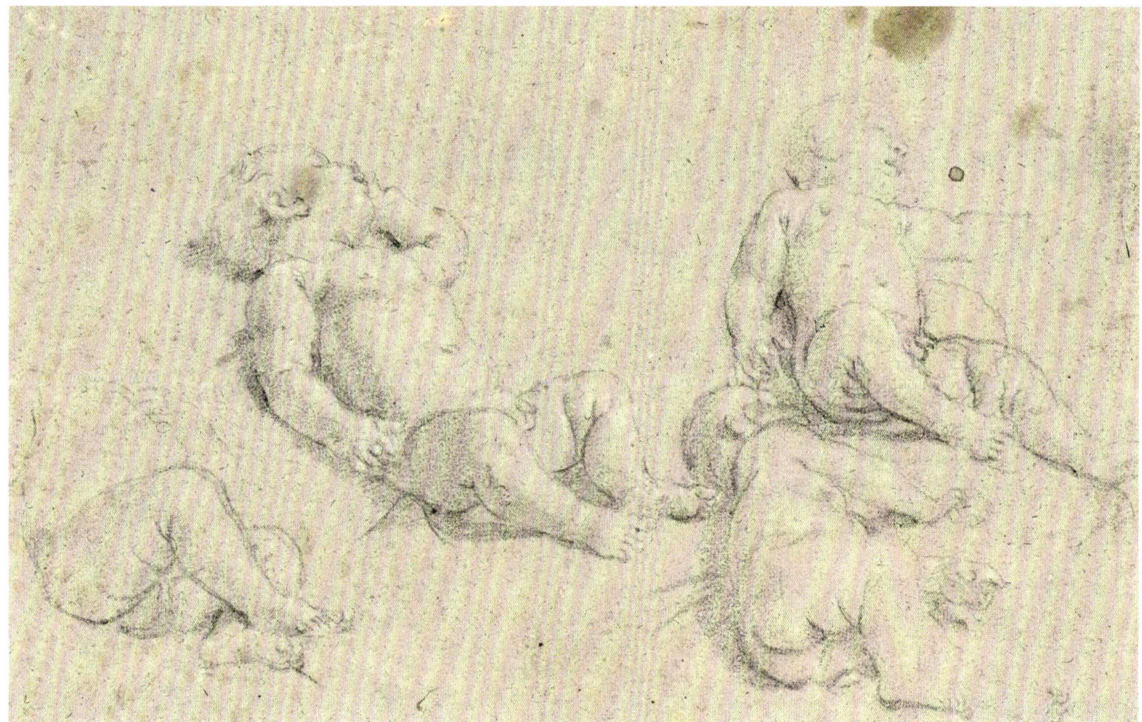

36
Domenico Zampieri, called Domenichino, *Three studies of a sleeping child*, undated, black chalk heightened with white on grey paper, 22.6 x 34.1 cm, Royal Collection Trust

37
Domenico Zampieri, called Domenichino, *Four studies of a sleeping child*, undated, black chalk heightened with white on light brownish grey paper, 20 x 31.6 cm, Royal Collection Trust

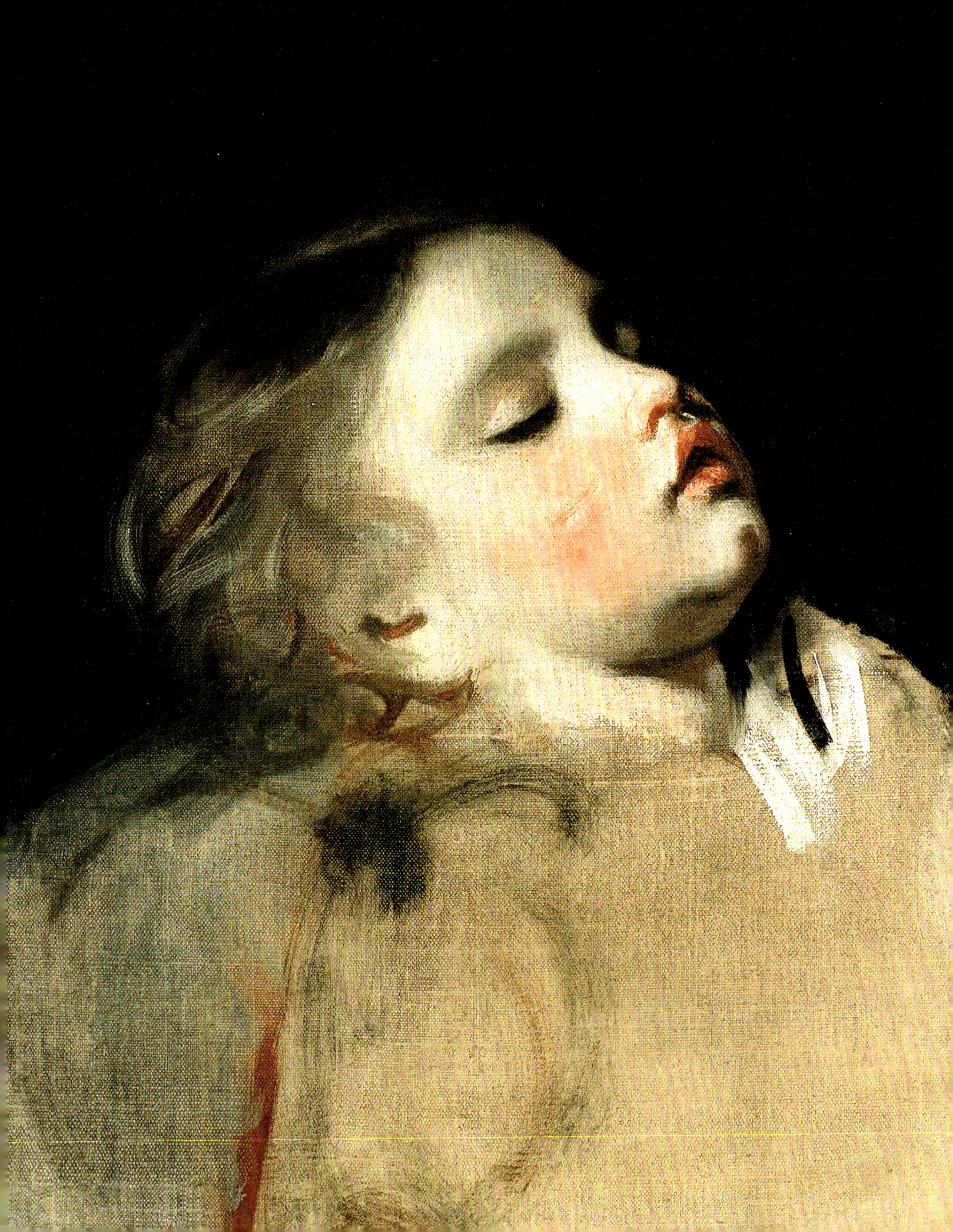

38
Sir Joshua Reynolds, *A Child Asleep*, c. 1782, oil on canvas, 41.6 x 36 cm, Christopher Tower Collection

indifferent one. All his grief was gone. When he laid down his pencil it returned.'[16]

By gently daubing paint on to the canvas for those few minutes Ramsay was able to forget about the death of his child and focus on his practice as an artist. As soon as he stopped, the fiction dissolved, and the grief came flooding back. The portrait, realized on unstretched canvas, was never shown publicly and remained unknown until it was discovered amongst Ramsay's effects following his own death.[17] This was not a work for public consumption, nor a sketch for a later portrait like Hogarth's deathbed portrait of Thomas Graham. In fact, it is hard to classify it as a portrait in the normative sense of the word but rather a record and summation of his grief. It is the material residue of feeling, something that did not require a viewer because the true significance of the work could only be fully understood by the artist himself. Indeed, much like the drawing of Thomas Graham, Ramsay's painting was, for a long time, catalogued as a depiction of a sleeping child, preserved for its value as a sensitive portrayal of a child by one of the era's greatest artists, rather than for its emotional value as a repository for the artist's grief.

While there are few examples of posthumous portraits by artists of their own children, the Ramsay oil sketch shows how the act of rendering a portrait could relieve the intense feelings of loss and sadness felt by parents. Similarly, the act of commissioning a portrait of a deceased child and the experience of viewing it or, indeed, the lack of such a work, could have a profound effect on grieving parents. For example, in the aftermath of the birth of his stillborn son and the death of his beloved wife Princess Charlotte, Prince Leopold of Saxe-Coburg was filled with regret that he did not have a picture of his child: 'My grief did not think of it, but if [only] I could have had a drawing of it!'[18] This clearly demonstrates the value ascribed to portraiture as a consoling artefact. Similarly, a near contemporary series of letters describes the practice of commissioning a posthumous portrait of a child and illustrates its ability both to comfort the viewer and simultaneously perpetuate feelings of grief. On 25 September 1815, Maria Capel, known as 'Muzzy', wrote from Brussels to her grandmother, Dowager Countess of Uxbridge, telling her of 'the death of our dear little Baby', the teenager's baby sister Priscilla.[19] Muzzy goes into great detail explaining Priscilla's illness and the various treatments her mother, Caroline Capel, had used in hope of curing her. To the family's dismay, 'the little angel expired with her face on Mama's breast'.[20] The baby was removed from her embrace, washed, dressed and laid out, and, for the next three days, Caroline cried and knelt by her baby's deathbed. As Muzzy notes, it was during this time that they 'had her picture taken'.[21]

Muzzy sent a further update to her grandmother on the day of the baby's interment in the Protestant burial ground just outside the city, in which she describes how, having laid Priscilla in her coffin the previous night, Caroline had been left alone with the corpse of her baby. Over the course of these few days, Caroline clearly felt compelled to sit with the body of her deceased baby and to commission an artist to record her appearance before the burial. Just a few days after the tragic event, her husband, who had been ill for some time, was advised by his physicians to leave Brussels for a change of scene in hope that it would improve his health. Caroline notes, 'I go with a heavy heart, but I have got the Picture of My Baby to gaze upon & so remind me of the foolish pride I took in her Beauty & the blind security I felt in her flourishing health & strength – Oh Mama, how dare we boast of any thing [sic]!'[22]

While this portrait is lost and one cannot, therefore, know the manner in which Caroline's baby was portrayed, it clearly demonstrates her desire to record the features of her deceased baby and in doing so, maintain her presence

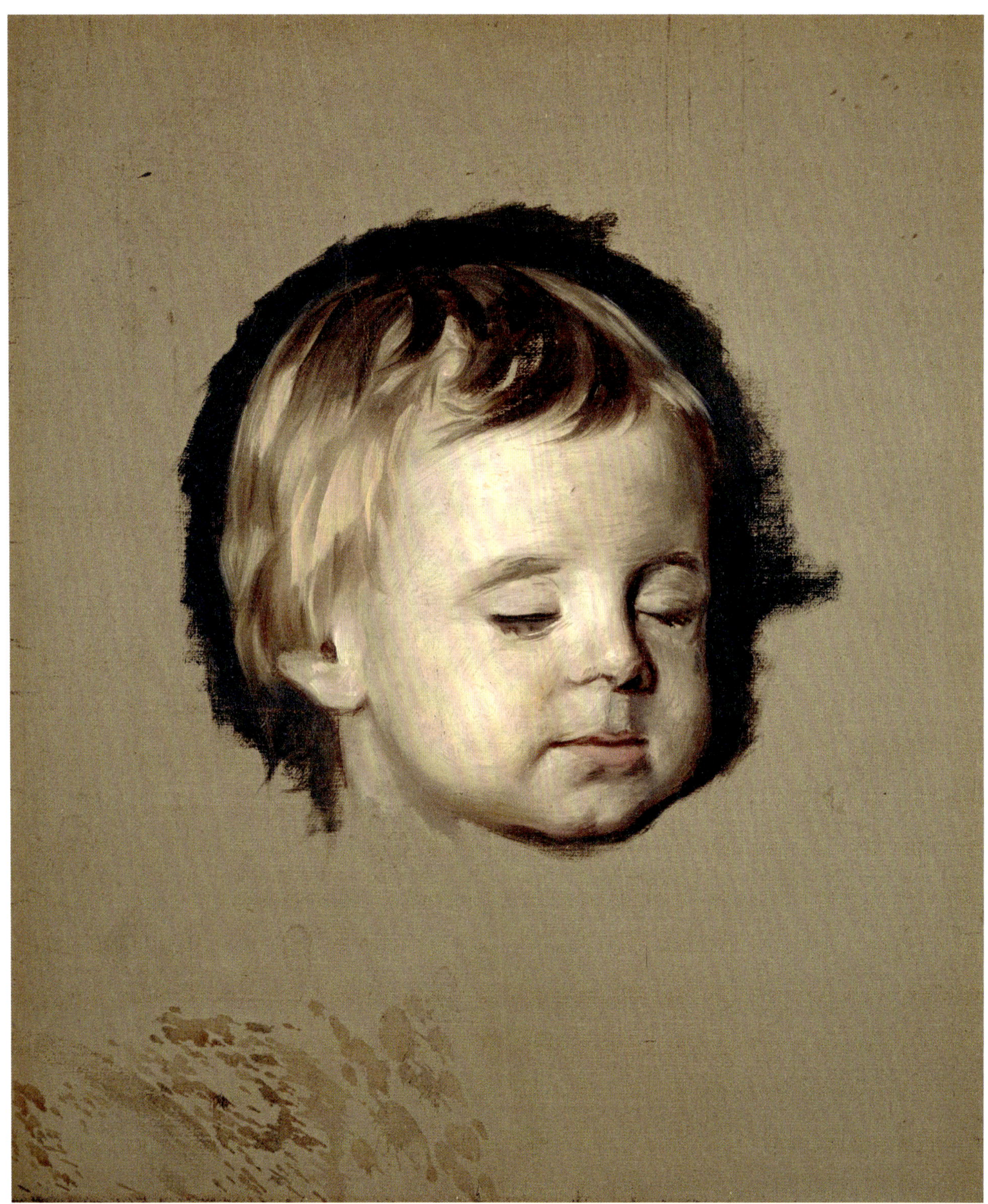

39
Allan Ramsay, *Infant Son of the Artist*,
1741, oil on canvas, 32 x 27.3 cm,
National Galleries of Scotland

through a material artefact. For Caroline, the portrait also acted as a punishing reminder of her perceived indulgence in the health of her baby without regard to the dangers of infancy. While the portrait may have comforted her in one way, it also acted as a cruel reminder of all that she had lost.

This idea of dwelling on the loss of a child is similarly found in the emotional outpouring of grief that followed the death of Penelope Boothby, famously portrayed by Reynolds just a couple of years before her death (fig. 40). His portrait came to epitomize popular eighteenth-century ideas about the innocence of children and was widely copied after it was first exhibited in public almost a century after its creation in 1871. The dark landscape that surrounds the child emphasizes the white of Penelope's dress and large mobcap and, in turn, her childish innocence and purity.[23] Indeed, the encroaching darkness seems almost apocryphal because, less than three years after Penelope sat to Reynolds, her parents, Sir Brooke Boothby and Susanne Bristoe, were faced with the most heartbreaking event of their lives when their five-year-old daughter passed away. Her death had a profound effect on the couple, who separated shortly afterwards. Devasted by their loss, they poured their emotion into her commemoration.

First, Henry Fuseli (1741–1825) was commissioned to paint Penelope Boothby on her ascent to heaven within the arms of an angel (fig. 41). Known for the dramatic compositions and supernatural subject matter of much of his painting, Fuseli was an obvious choice to carry out such a commission. Fuseli's work is a dramatic display of earthly departure with a muted palette and focus on the sharp contrast between light and dark. The five-year-old Penelope casts her eyes upwards to the darkness as a putto descends in extreme perspective with an otherworldly sprite-like face. The raised wings of the angel and dramatic posture of the young girl create a sense of swift upwards ascent, typical of the drama that typifies much of Fuseli's work, and, perhaps, emphasizing the speed with which she has been separated from her parents. At the bottom of the composition, just visible amid the darkness, Fuseli has included a butterfly, symbolic of the fleeting and fragile life of the deceased Penelope, along with an urn tipped on its side, another common trope that indicates death.

The Boothby parents also commissioned a monument for Ashbourne Church, Derbyshire, from Thomas Banks which had quite a different effect but clearly spoke to the parents' emotional trauma. It depicts the child as if sleeping along with seven inscriptions in English, Latin, Italian and French, quoting Catullus, the Bible and, significantly, Rousseau's *La Nouvelle Eloise,* the philosopher's meditation on authenticity as moral value. In fact, Boothby was well acquainted with the French philosopher, who had spent over a year living in Staffordshire not far from Boothby's home, which resulted in Boothby's translation and publication of Rousseau's autobiographical *Premier Dialogue* (1780).[24] Boothby would have been familiar with Rousseau's writing on children, which is visually evident through this innocent and vulnerable portrayal of his 'sleeping' daughter. Considering this work in relation to Fuseli's painting shows the extent to which Boothby celebrated the spotless purity of his child, born into this world innocent, in line with Rousseauean philosophy.

Thomas Banks exhibited the model of the monument at the Royal Academy in 1793, where it 'attracted a crowd of admiring spectators', including Queen Charlotte and her daughter, who 'stood over it for a considerable time in silence, and were affected even to tears'.[25] The fascinating account of a royal display of emotion shows how successful Banks was in creating an image of death that elicited deep feeling regardless of whether the viewer knew the child depicted. The 'sleeping' Penelope was an emotive cipher of mourning for everyone.

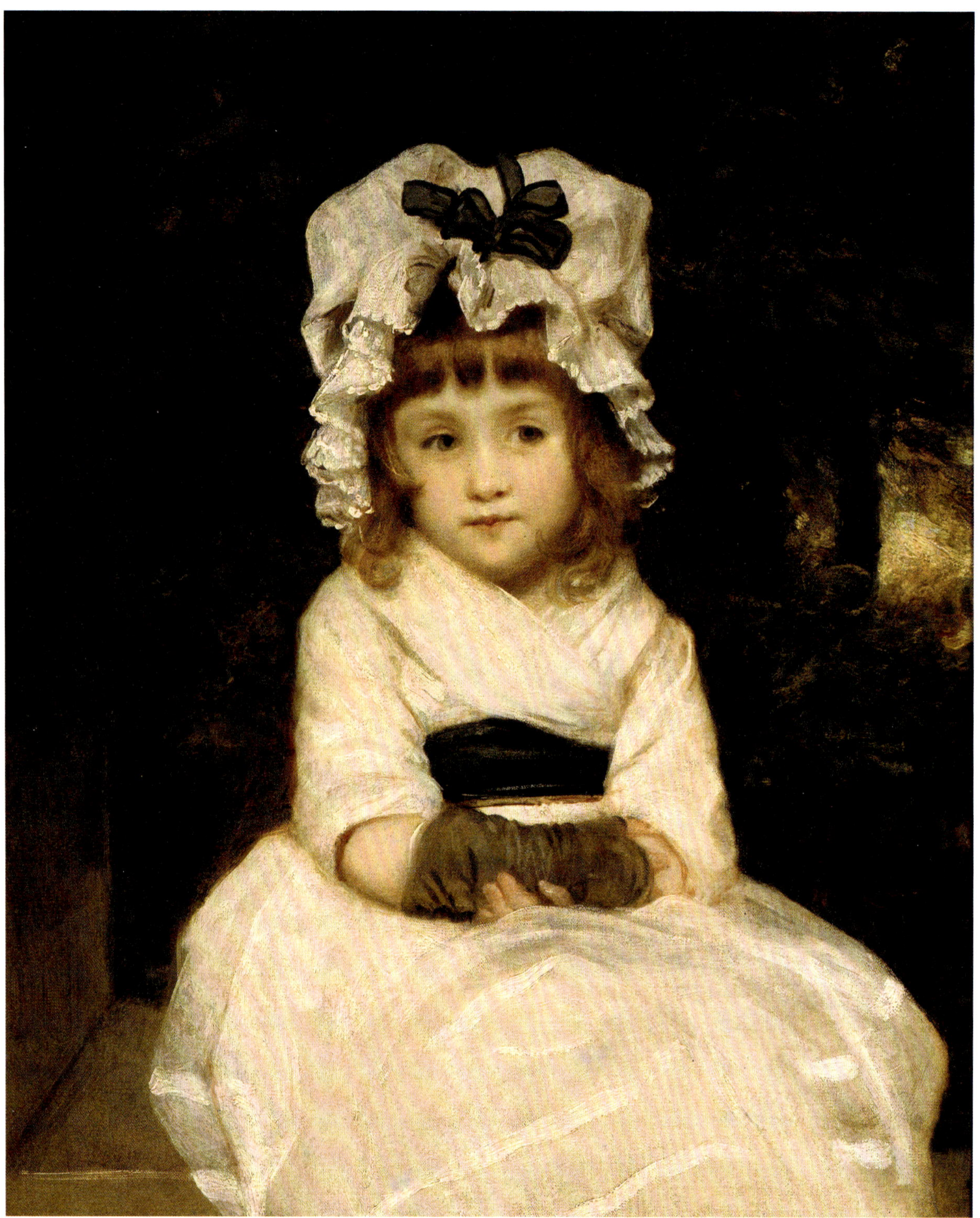

40
Sir Joshua Reynolds, *Portrait of Penelope Boothby*, 1788, oil on canvas, 75 x 62 cm, private collection on loan to Ashmolean Museum, University of Oxford

The Boothby parents attempted to deal with their grief by finding permanent ways of commemorating Penelope, so that the mark she made on their lives would never be forgotten. Brooke Boothby's expressions of grief were not just limited to painting and sculpture; he also turned to print through the publication of *Sorrows Sacred to the Memory of Penelope* (1796), a literary outpouring of emotion, comprising twenty-four sonnets and two elegies. The text is accompanied by reproductions of both Fuseli's *Apotheosis* and Banks's monument, along with Thomas Kirk's engraving of Reynolds's portrait of *Penelope Boothby*, scenes that relate to her home, and various symbols that allude to the fragility of life, including a butterfly flying out of a cocoon, a broken and dying tree, and an extinguished torch. Boothby begins his work with an address to the reader:

> The following little works were written to relieve a mind overburthened with grief, and are here collected as a frail monument, designed to withhold for a moment, from the grasp of oblivion, one loved 'not wisely, but too well'. They have small pretensions to poetical merit; but they are the expressions of real feelings .... Receive them with complacency, gentle reader, and mayest thou never experience the sorrows they describe![27]

Boothby's publication was hailed as a 'most elegant monument of paternal regret', combining as it did 'the allied arts of poetry, painting, and sculpture, with that of typography'.[28] What Fuseli did in paint and Banks in marble, Boothby's publication did in words. His collection of sonnets and elegies epitomize the sentimental expression of 'real feeling' – 'a mind overburthened with grief' that could only process the trauma of his daughter's passing through various memorializing acts.[29] 'Sonnet XII' applauds the work of Banks and his ability to defeat the lifeless, whiteness of marble. He writes:

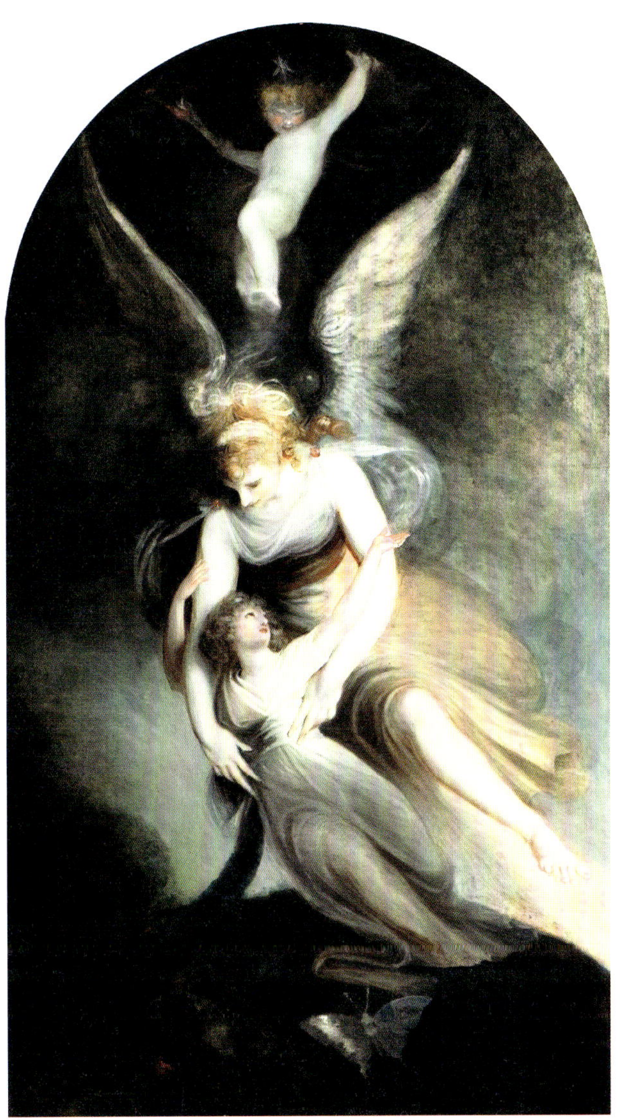

41
Henry Fuseli, *The Apotheosis of Penelope Boothby*, 1792, oil on canvas, 213.5 x 121.5 cm, Wolverhampton Art Gallery

Recorded there exists her every charm,
In vivid colours, safe from change or harm ....

The need to remember Penelope as she was is clearly evident in these lines. By commissioning the monument and the painting of her apotheosis, as well as writing these verses, Boothby could maintain a sense of paternal protection despite Penelope's passing. Boothby goes on, in 'Sonnet XVI', to celebrate Fuseli's ability 'to cheat these weary eyes,/ And raise [Boothby's] drooping spirit to the skies' by depicting Penelope's spiritual passing from this world to the next. The engraving produced by Michele Benedetti was used as the frontispiece of *Sorrows*, pointing to Boothby's own attempt to provide a literary apotheosis of his child.

The portraits discussed in this chapter highlight the crucial function of the posthumous image of children for grieving parents. Whether represented dead or alive, these works both maintained the presence of the child in the family unit and provided emotional solace and consolation. Furthermore, the process of creating such works and the impetus to do so, whether through the act of painting, writing or commissioning, could help to relieve parents of their sadness and help them come to terms with their loss. The inherent capacity for portraiture to outlast the sitter was put into even sharper focus in the creation of these commemorative works.

Emily Knight *is Assistant Curator of Paintings at the Victoria and Albert Museum. She recently submitted her doctorate on eighteenth-century posthumous portraiture in Britain at the University of Oxford.*

Notes

1 Letter from George III to Lord Dartmouth following the death of his son, Octavius, cited in Hibbert 1999, p. 99.
2 Berkeley/Memphis/Omaha 1995–96, p. 85.
3 Retford 2010, pp. 76–77.
4 Woodall 1997, pp. 8–9.
5 Eade forthcoming 2019.
6 For an in-depth discussion of the way in which child portraiture developed during the eighteenth century see Berkeley/Memphis/Omaha 1995–96 and Bath/Kendal 2005.
7 Ezell 1983, pp. 146–47.
8 Locke 1779, p. 319. This is a point discussed by Ezell 1983, p. 141. See also Hilton and Hirsch 2000, p. 3.
9 Locke 1779, p. 76.
10 The inclusion of these playthings may also have demonstrated Queen Charlotte's concern for 'the development of his masculine character'. See K. Retford, p.104.
11 Locke 1693, no. 63, p. 39.
12 C. Campbell Orr, 'Queen Charlotte, "Scientific Queen"', in Campbell Orr 2002, p. 266.
13 Rousseau 1763, p. 1.
14 Hogarth's 1732 portrait of the Cholmondeley family (private collection) similarly demonstrates his preoccupation with capturing the playfulness of children in portraiture.
15 Judy Egerton identified the child as Thomas Graham, the youngest child depicted in Hogarth's *The Graham Children* (1741), following on from Mary Webster's suggestion that Thomas was deceased at the time of its creation. See Webster 1989, pp. 171–77.
16 Letter from Lady Louisa Stuart to Miss Louisa Clinton, 13 October 1831, in Home 1903, p. 115.
17 Bath/Kendal 2005, p. 34.
18 Layard 1906, p. 111.
19 *The Capel letters being the correspondence of Lady Caroline Capel and her daughters with the Dowager Countess of Uxbridge from Brussels and Switzerland 1814–1817*, ed. the Marquess of Anglesey with an introduction by A. Bryant, London, 1955, p.140.
20 Ibid.
21 Ibid, p.141.
22 Ibid, p.144.
23 It is worth noting that, in this work, Reynolds used bitumen in his paint to create the darker tones, a non-drying substance that eventually darkens severely and causes cracks in the paints.
24 In his 1781 portrait by Joseph Wright of Derby (Tate), Brooke Boothby is shown holding a volume with *Rousseau* on the spine, in reference to this project.
25 Cited in Cunningham 1863, p. 4.
26 Penny 1977, p. 115.
27 Boothby 1796.
28 *The Monthly Review, or Literary Journal*, vol. 20, London, 1796, p. 316.
29 Parisot 2013, pp. 1–18. See T. Parnell's 'Night-Piece on Death' (1721), R. Blair's *The Grave* (1743), E. Young's *Night Thoughts* (1742–45).

Innocence and Experience
Childhood and the Fancy Picture

MARTIN POSTLE

In the early 1930s the three-year-old Shirley Temple launched her career in a series of spoof films collectively titled 'Baby Burlesks', in which she and other pre-school children were made to re-enact adult roles in popular films. In one film, *War Babies*, Temple played the role of a French prostitute, in which she uttered her first on-screen words, 'Mais oui, mon cher'.[1] Not surprisingly, in later years Temple described the films as 'a cynical exploitation of our childish innocence'.[2] In 1935 Temple was cast in the more wholesome role of an orphan adopted by a millionaire, who, albeit, had romantic designs upon her elder sister. The film, *Curly Top*, which was an instant box-office success, exploited Temple's precocious talent as a singer, dancer and actress.

In a key scene in the film, Temple's wealthy patron falls into a reverie as he imagines the paintings on the wall of his mansion coming to life in the persona of the little orphan. As he casts his eye across his collection, he watches as Temple animates successively *The Age of Innocence* by Joshua Reynolds, *The Blue Boy* by Thomas Gainsborough (fig. 42), and John Everett Millais's *My First Sermon*, where she smiles and blows him a kiss.[3] In reality the paintings were housed in public museums – *The Age of Innocence* in the National Gallery, London, *My First Sermon* in the Guildhall Gallery, London, and *The Blue Boy* in the Huntington, San Marino, California (acquired for over $700,000 in 1921 – at the time the highest price ever paid for an oil painting).[4] By now all three paintings had achieved international status as iconic depictions of childhood, revered as works of art and exploited for their merchandizing potential, reproduced on chocolate boxes, biscuits tins and other ephemera. They were also quintessential examples of an established genre which became known in the eighteenth century as the 'fancy picture'. Shirley Temple, in acting out a fantasy of childhood through the medium of high art, before the eyes of her on-screen patron and countless movie-goers, was now herself transformed into a fancy picture *vivant* – an emblem of childhood moulded by tradition, sentiment, and popular audience appeal, all oiled by the wheels of commerce.

This chapter explores aspects of the evolution of the fancy picture as it pertains to the image of childhood in British art, from the early decades of the eighteenth century to the high Victorian period, as well as its legacy upon modern manipulations of the image of childhood, as exemplified by the career of child-star Shirley Temple. It examines how the genre found its roots in Dutch seventeenth-century art and culture, and developed, through its close association with commerce and the print trade, to its adoption by Joshua Reynolds as a form of popularized history painting and its later revival in the mid to late nineteenth century, notably by John Everett Millais. It will also consider how the genre of the fancy picture was received by the public at exhibition, in terms of its validation of the condition of childhood, as well as its patronage by collectors.

The fancy picture, although it evades precise definition and parameters, typically takes the form of a vignette, the characters involved being representative of a typology rather than specific individuals. Subject matter includes, variously, wizened old beggars, market traders and winsome young women, and above all children, who range from young scholars and musicians to urban beggar children, ragged peasantry and scantily clad infant deities.

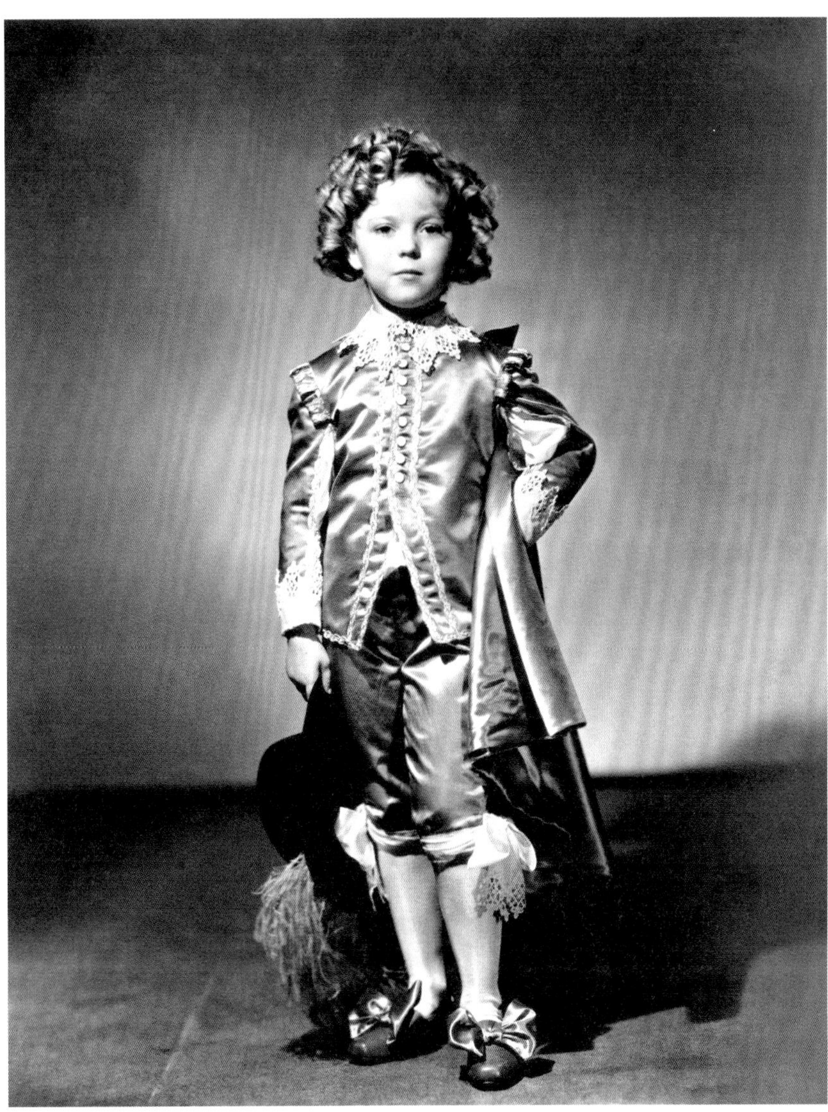

42
Photograph of Shirley Temple as *The Blue Boy* by Thomas Gainsborough, 1934, Getty Images

During the eighteenth century the evolution of the image of the child was allied to the promotion by Enlightenment philosophers of childhood purity and innocence, in contrast to traditional Christian doctrine, which centred on the redemption of a soul blighted by original sin. Yet, while the fancy picture had a popular modern appeal, the roots of the genre lay in the Old Master traditions of high art, stretching back to the Renaissance. Perhaps more than any other artist, the progenitor of the fancy picture was Michelangelo Merisi da Caravaggio (1571–1610), who looked to the city streets for his models as he infused observed reality into sacred subject matter, transforming unkempt urchins into palpable flesh-and-blood saints and deities. In eighteenth-century Britain, it was not Caravaggio, however, who proved influential in the fusion of the real and ideal, but the seventeenth-century Spanish master Bartolomé Esteban Murillo.

Murillo's success in his native Spain was conditioned by the large-scale altarpieces he produced for churches in Seville. However, he gained popularity further afield through his secular images of childhood, as well as his devotional images of child saints, such as the *Infant St John the Baptist* and the *Christ Child as the Good Shepherd*, a version of which Thomas Gainsborough copied from

43
Godfried Schalken, *A Boy blowing on a Firebrand to Light a Candle*, c. 1692–98, oil on canvas, 75 x 63.5 cm, National Galleries of Scotland

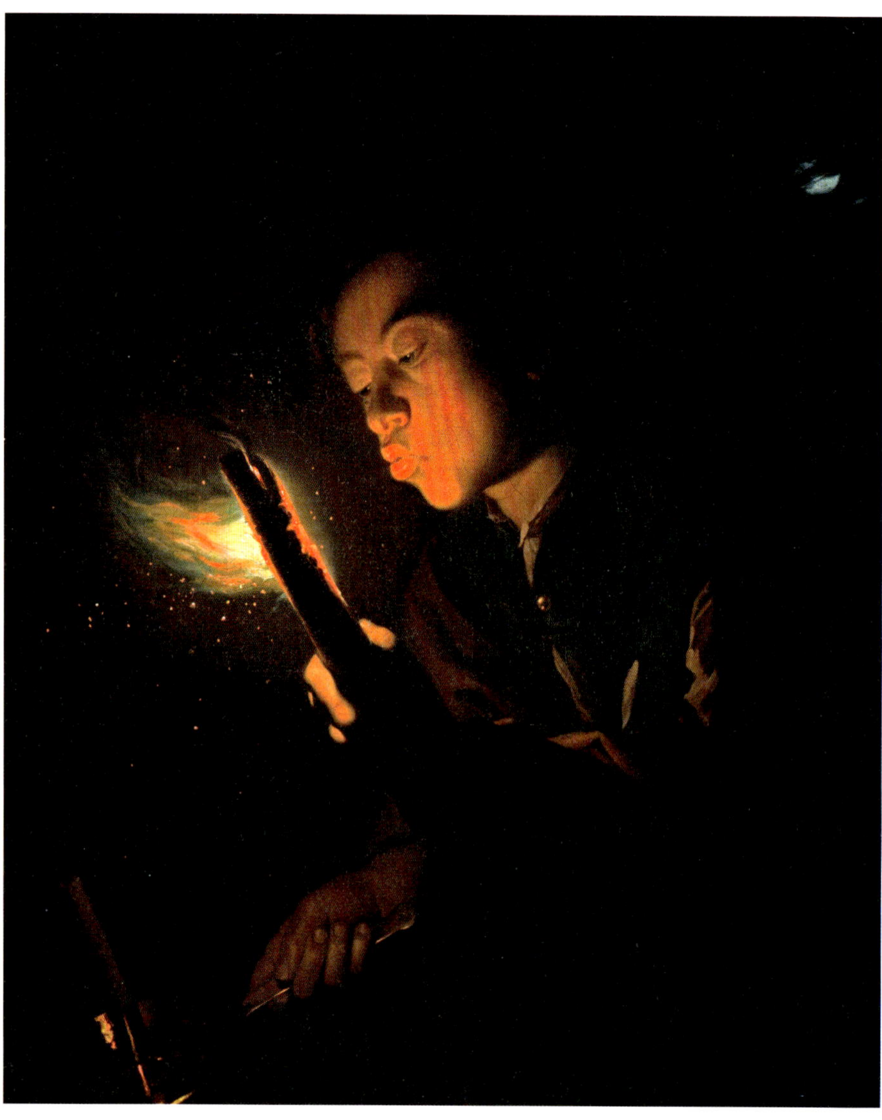

memory, when he saw it briefly on the London art market in the 1770s.[5] Among the secular paintings by Murillo of children that attracted the attention of art patrons and connoisseurs in London were two pictures, *Invitation to a Game of Argolla* and *Three Boys* (see fig. 6), which were in the collection of Lord Godolphin at Stable Yard, St James's Palace, and subsequently acquired by the art dealer Noel Desenfans.[6] Gainsborough evidently studied the former picture closely since he used the figure of the reclining boy as a compositional source for his own painting of a shepherd boy which he exhibited at the Royal Academy in 1781.[7] He also relied more immediately upon his own living model, a boy described in one newspaper of the time as 'the Beggar Boy of St James's Street'.[8] In addition to his fictive persona, the boy in question had a name and an identity: he was John Thomas Hill – known as Jack – baptized in the church of St Mary Magdalene, Richmond-upon-Thames on 6 December 1781, and educated subsequently, through the auspices of the Gainsborough family, at Christ's Hospital.[9] As in so many fancy pictures, the enduring fascination of Gainsborough's image relies upon the interstices between fantasy and fact, and the ambiguities generated by the shifting identities of the subjects in question.

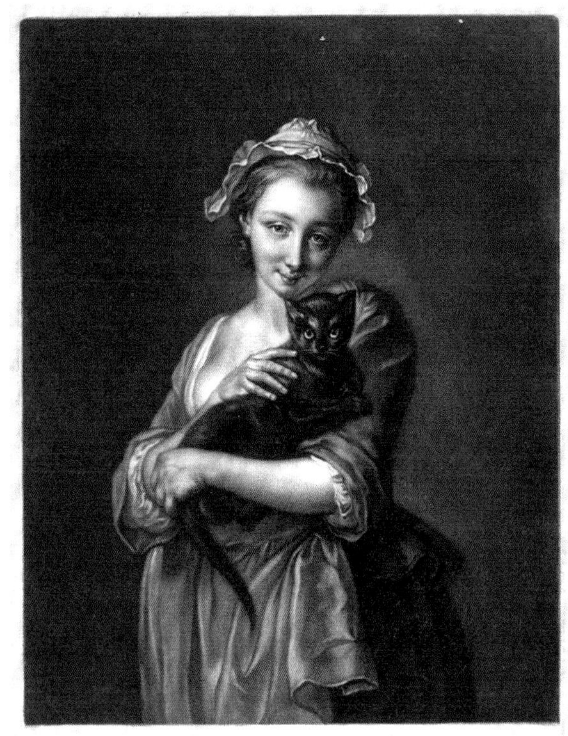

44
James MacArdell after Philip Mercier, *Girl with a Cat*, mezztotint engraving, 32.9 x 22.5 cm, British Museum

While Murillo was a conspicuous influence upon the evolution of the fancy picture in Britain, and upon Gainsborough in particular, as a genre it was rooted more firmly in the art and culture of the seventeenth-century Dutch Republic, and the strong commercial and constitutional ties that bound Britain increasingly to the Low Countries. By this time genre painting, including vignettes from everyday life, constituted a popular art form. And here the depiction of the child played a crucial role. As it has been argued, it was in the context of Dutch secular culture that the image of the ordinary child at play flourished, 'the replacement of the putto by the little perisher' being 'a moment of high significance not just in the history of art but in that of Western culture's view of its children'.[10] Emerging from this culture, where the playful nature of childhood was esteemed, the image of the child took on 'satirical' and 'tutorial' functions, provoking both enjoyment and lessons for adult life. Typical of such images is *A Boy and a Girl with a Cat and an Eel* of c. 1635 by the talented Haarlem-born painter Judith Leyster (fig. 3). Leyster's career flourished for only a few years prior to her marriage to a fellow-artist, Jan Molenaer (1610–1668), her obscurity until the late nineteenth century being the result of the misattribution of her works variously to her husband and Frans Hals. In the present painting, the finger-wagging girl, tugging on the cat's tail, and the clownish boy clutching the squirming cat and wriggling eel are clearly conveying a message to the viewer – one which has been interpreted as a warning about the consequences of misbehaviour, as well as a visual explication of the Dutch saying 'He who plays with cats gets scratched'.[11]

The impact of Continental images of childhood upon British audiences was achieved though the import of paintings and prints. It was also facilitated by the movement of artists themselves. They included, notably, Godfried Schalcken (1643–1706), who travelled from the Hague to London in 1692. Among Schalcken's most impressive paintings was a trademark series of character studies by candlelight, influenced in turn by prominent Utrecht artists, notably Hendrick ter Brugghen (1588–1629) and Gerard van Honthorst (1592–1656). They included *A Boy Blowing on a Firebrand* (fig. 43), which was executed probably for Robert Spencer, 2nd Earl of Sunderland and engraved subsequently by the Irish printmaker, Richard Purcell (fl. 1746–66). As with many character studies of this kind, it was infused with a double meaning, as the burning ember acts as a phallic emblem enflamed by lust.[12] While Schalcken remained in England for only a few years, the full potential of character studies of this kind was exploited by the French émigré artist, Phillipe Mercier (?1689–1760), who turned to making fancy pictures following the rapid decline in his fortunes as a society and court portrait painter. In 1737, the British engraver George Vertue described Mercier's pictures as 'pieces of some figures of conversation as big as the life: conceited plaisant Fancies and habits:

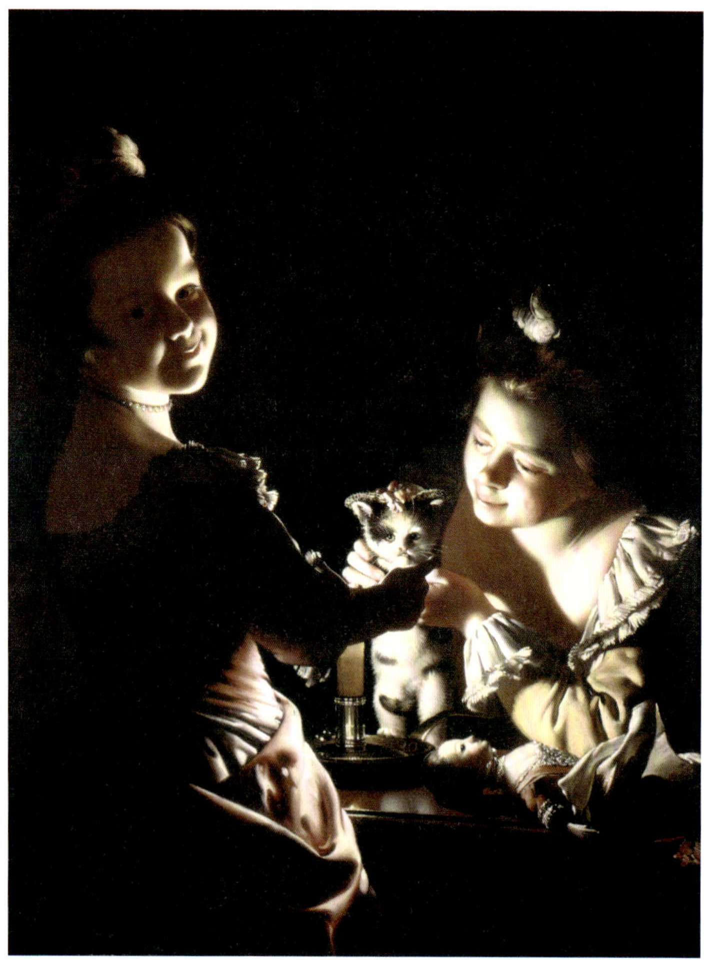

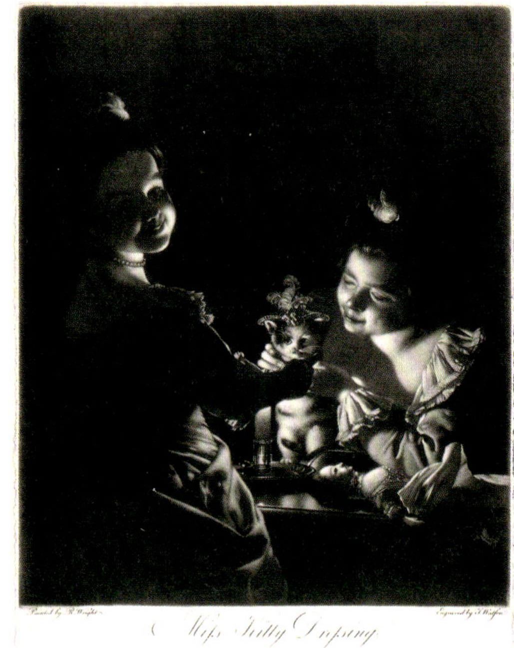

45
Joseph Wright of Derby, *Two Girls Dressing a Kitten by Candlelight*, c. 1768–70, oil on canvas, 89 x 68 cm, Kenwood House, London, The Iveagh Bequest

46
Thomas Watson after Joseph Wright, *Miss Kitty Dressing*, 1781, mezzotint, 40.9 x 32.8 cm, Wellcome Collection

mixed modes really well done – and much approved of'.[13] Among his most popular subjects were children at work and at play, as well as adolescent girls and young women performing household duties, or selling comestibles on city streets. Mercier's female images often contained barely suppressed sexual overtones, as for example in the *Girl with a Cat* (National Gallery of Scotland, Edinburgh), of around 1755, where the attractive, smiling girl clasps the black furry feline to her bosom. Like many of Mercier's images, with sharp contrasts between dark and light, the painting was calculated to serve as the basis for an engraving (fig. 44) available through print sellers, viewed in metropolitan shop windows as well as private residences.[14]

Phillipe Mercier was an artist of relatively modest abilities who turned to the fancy picture through expediency as other artistic ventures failed. None the less, his example proved that there was a ready market for such images, and others eagerly took up the challenge. Among the most gifted and innovative of the rising generation of artists who turned to the fancy picture was Joseph Wright, who, following a stint in London in the early 1750s, returned to his native Derby, where he worked for the majority of his career. While he pursued a successful career in portraiture, Wright's particular talent lay in producing innovative genre paintings, such as *A Philosopher Lecturing on the Orrery*, where the dramatic use of candlelight demonstrated his mastery of chiaroscuro, as well as his ability to elevate contemporary genre painting to the level of high art. He also employed candlelight in a series of smaller fancy pictures, the majority of which

47
John Singleton Copley, *Boy with a Flying Squirrel (Henry Pelham)*, 1765, oil on canvas, 77 x 63.8 cm, Museum of Fine Arts Boston

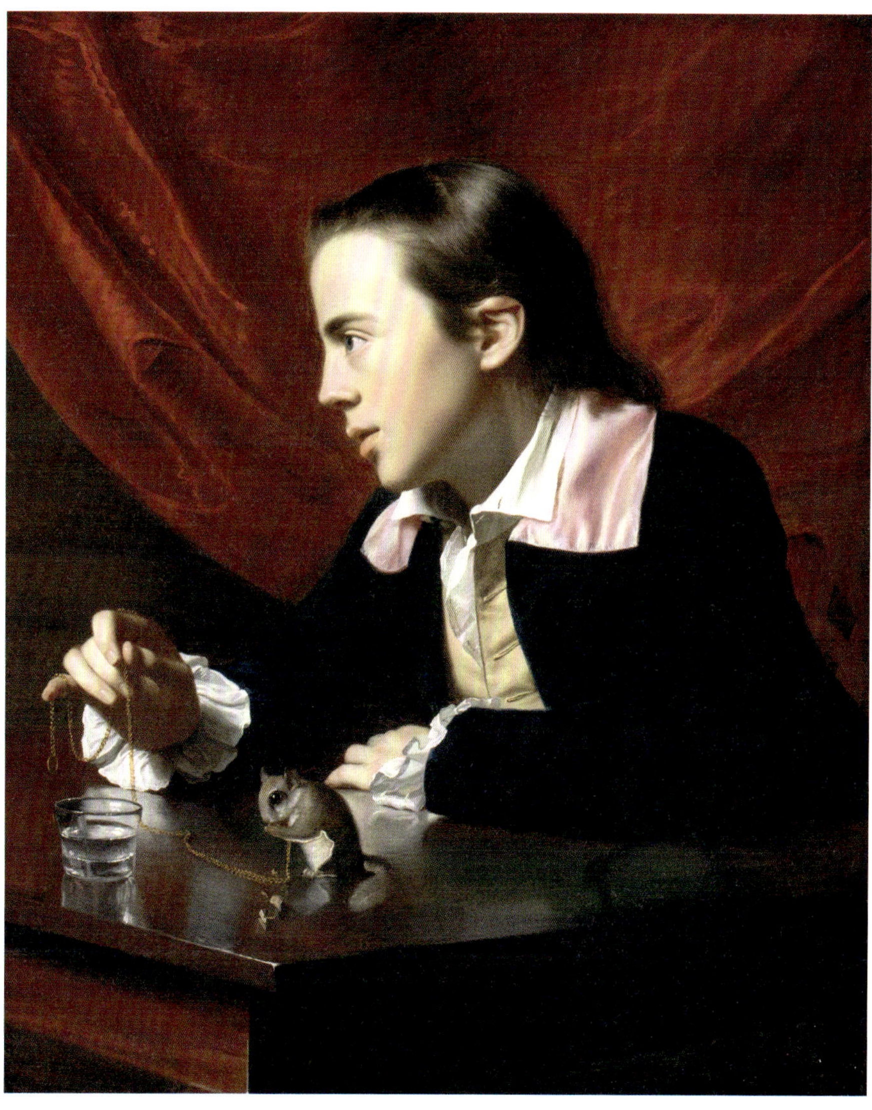

featured children and adolescents at play. Among the most striking is *Two Girls Dressing a Kitten by Candlelight* (fig. 45), which reached a mass market via a mezzotint engraving by Thomas Watson (1743–1781) entitled *Miss Kitty Dressing* (fig. 46).[15] Like its Dutch precedents the picture proffers an image that suggests the cruelty of which children are capable, as the demonic young girls toy with their unfortunate pet, its erect tail, and the prone figure of the female doll, with its skirt lifted, suggesting uncomfortable sexual undercurrents, which foreshadow the girls' potential for manipulation of the opposite sex in adulthood.[16]

By the 1760s the audience for art was expanded greatly through the inauguration of the public exhibition. Here, the fancy picture prospered, since it provided a ready means of demonstrating an artist's facility beyond the confines of specific portraiture, and without resorting to the complexities of multi-figure history painting. One artist, with otherwise limited access to the London art scene, was the largely self-taught American John Singleton Copley (1738–1815), then based in Boston, who shipped *A Boy with a Flying Squirrel* (fig. 47) across the Atlantic to be shown at the 1766 exhibition at the Society of Artists. While the boy, viewed in profile, was modelled

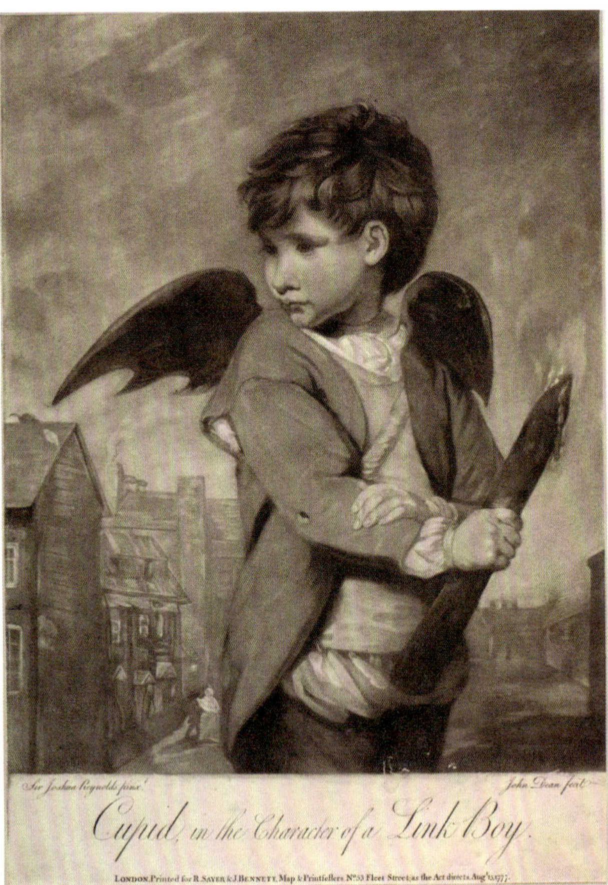

48
John Dean after Joshua Reynolds, *Cupid as a Link Boy*, mezzotint engraving, Victoria & Albert Museum

49
Joshua Reynolds, *Miss Crewe*, c. 1775, oil on canvas, 137 x 112 cm, private collection on loan to the Tate

upon Copley's half-brother, the composition was to all intents and purposes a fancy picture, the exotic New World pet seated upon the highly polished surface of the table alongside the half-filled glass of water, designed to demonstrate the artist's virtuosity. The picture attracted approval among the artistic community in London, not least Joshua Reynolds, who for a while displayed the picture in his own home. When he was first shown the picture, Reynolds, who knew only that it was painted by a young man from the provinces, supposed it to be by Joseph Wright – which was high praise indeed.[17]

Although he had only flirted with the genre previously, Joshua Reynolds himself turned to the fancy picture as a vehicle for artistic expression, self-promotion and financial gain in the early 1770s, shortly after he assumed the presidency of the Royal Academy. A frantically busy artist, Reynolds made fancy pictures principally during the summer months, when his portrait practice was slack.[18] Although he occasionally used his nieces as models, most of the children he employed were street urchins and beggars. At times he focused upon the head of the model only, as in the unfinished *A Child Asleep* (fig. 38) from the early 1780s. As Reynolds's studio assistant James Northcote recalled, 'when the Beggar Infant, who was sitting to him for some other picture, during the sitting fell asleep, Reynolds was so pleased with the innocence of the object, that he would not disturb its repose to go on with the picture on which he was then engaged, but took up a fresh canvas, and quickly painted the child's head as it lay before it moved'.[19] At other times, Reynolds would wilfully ignore the innocence of the child in order to use it as a vehicle for more knowing compositions, as in his pendant fancy pictures, *Cupid as a Link Boy* (fig. 48) and *Mercury as a Cutpurse*, where the subjects allude to the arousal and deflation of sexual passion; Cupid's flaming torch, bat-like wings, and lewd arm gesture acting as references to lust in a manner reminiscent of earlier images of children wielding and blowing upon firebrands. The pictures entered the collection of Reynolds's aristocratic patron, Frederick Sackville, 3rd Duke of Dorset, and neither was exhibited in public during the artist's lifetime.[20] They were, however, made available to the public in the form of mezzotint engravings by one of Reynolds's favoured printmakers, John Dean (1754–1798). An early impression of *Cupid as a Link Boy*, made prior to the addition of the inscription, belonged to the artist, Thomas Lawrence, whom we shall come to shortly.[21]

In addition to producing fancy pictures, Reynolds increasingly introduced an element of fantasy into his commissioned child portraits, who at times adopted

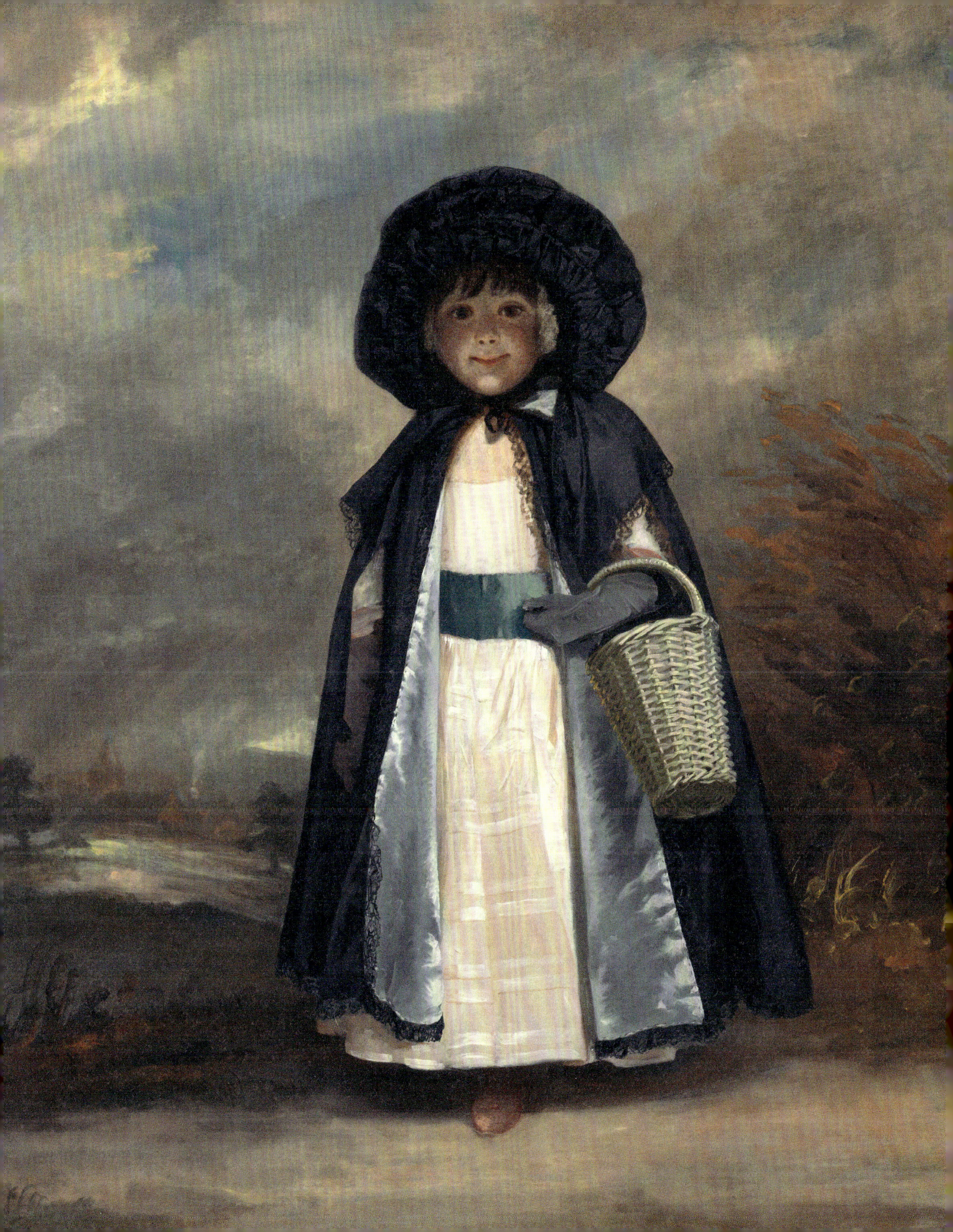

50
Thomas Gainsborough, *A Peasant Girl Gathering Faggots in a Wood*, 1782, oil on canvas, 169 x 123 cm, Manchester Art Gallery

the dress and masquerade costumes of adults, or even historical and allegorical characters. An instance was the portrait of John Crewe, son of the Whig politician, John, 1st Baron Crewe, who Reynolds depicted as Henry VIII, then a popular fancy-dress character at metropolitan masquerades.[22] When the picture was exhibited at the Royal Academy in 1776, the conceit was appreciated by the aesthete Horace Walpole, who enjoyed the 'humour and satire in Sir Joshua's reducing Holbein's swaggering and colossal haughtiness of Henry 8th. to the boyish jollity of Master Crewe'.[23] In later life, Crewe went on to assume his seat in the House of Lords, as well as following a successful career in the British army and diplomatic service. At the time Reynolds also painted the portrait of John Crewe's elder sister, Frances (fig. 49), in a fashionable black silk cape lined with satin, her face cast into shade by the over-large bonnet. Upon her arm she carries a wicker basket reminiscent of that carried by Reynolds's *Strawberry Girl*, a fancy picture he had exhibited at the Royal Academy a few years earlier.[24] Frances Crewe appears to have died before the picture was completed , as suggested by the sketchy handling of her gloved arm. Her early death serves as a reminder of the high child mortality rates, to which even the wealthy were not immune. As for Frances herself, the only record of her brief life and identity is to be found in Reynolds's portrait.[25]

In portraiture, Reynolds's principal rival by the 1770s was Thomas Gainsborough. Like Reynolds, he resorted increasingly to the fancy picture as a genre through which to explore childhood. Initially, he used his two girls as models, in works such as *The Painter's Daughters Chasing a Butterfly* (National Gallery, London) and *Margaret Gainsborough as a Gleaner* (Ashmolean Museum, Oxford), although, as we have seen, he also employed poor children from his neighbourhood in London and in Richmond-upon-Thames, where he had a country residence. With regard to the fancy picture, Gainsborough's interest lay in the rural poor, explored in works such as *A Girl with Pigs*, which he exhibited at the Royal Academy in 1782, where it was purchased by Reynolds.[26] He also produced several full-length 'fancy' portraits on the scale of life, notably *A Cottage Girl with a Dog and Pitcher* (National Gallery of Ireland, Dublin) and a *Peasant Girl Gathering Faggots in a Wood* (fig. 50), both also created during the 1780s, and which harked back to Old Master traditions in which secular subject matter was inflected with a quasi-spiritual dimension. Gainsborough's fancy pictures of this nature were conceived not only as sympathetic depictions of the rural poor but as a stimulus to perform the Christian duty of charity. Such sentiments were broadcast in a slightly later painting exhibited at the Royal Academy by William Beechey (1753–1839) in 1793 as 'Portraits of children relieving a beggar boy' (fig. 51). The fashionably attired children in question were the offspring of Sir Francis Ford, whose money derived from the ownership of slave plantations in Barbados. As Sir Francis noted to his young son at the time, in a letter written from Barbados, 'you have terrible times in England'; a reference presumably to the mass starvation due to bread shortages and the spectre of revolution spreading from France across the Channel.[27] The painting itself, which combined portraiture with subject matter more usually contained within the fancy picture, attracted social as well as artistic commentary, one critic stating that the beggar boy 'may suggest a Reform of our *Poor Laws*, and excite a temporary throb of pity in breasts, steeled, perhaps, against reality of distress'.[28] Even so, as the body language of Ford's children suggests, charity may begin at home, but its object is best kept at arm's length.

As we move into the nineteenth century, the presence of the fancy picture in British art persisted in painting and print culture, although increasingly the visualization of individuals from the lower echelons of society, and

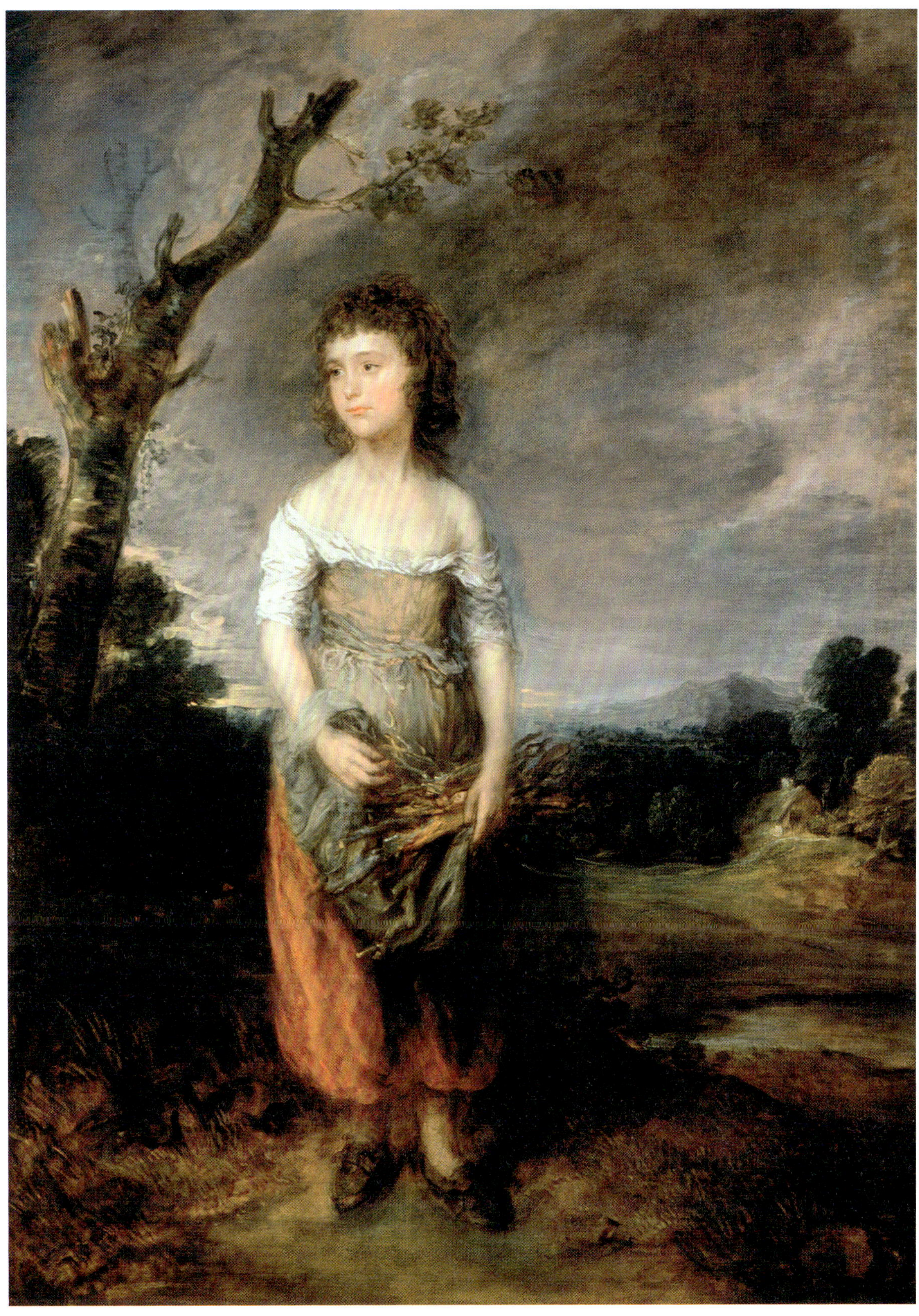

51
William Beechey, *Sir Francis Ford's Children giving a Coin to a Beggar Boy*, exhibited 1793, oil on canvas, 180.5 x 150 cm, Tate

their children, became subsumed into more ambitious narratives with social agendas linked to reform, and to concerns with the modern economy and the present-day world, where divisions between town and country, past and present, were more apparent.[29] Leading artists, including Thomas Lawrence (1769–1830), continued to paint fancy pictures, Lawrence's own Diploma Work, *A Gipsy Girl*, presented to the Royal Academy in 1794, on his election as an Academician, depicting a scantily clad adolescent female clutching a chicken to her barely concealed bosom. Lawrence's child portraiture, too, often relied heavily upon the conventions of the fancy picture, and was received as such, most notably in his depiction of the youthful Charles William Lambton (fig. 52), clad in a scarlet suit of velvet, whilst reclining dreamily upon a moonlit mossy bank as comfy as any living-room sofa. Charles Lambton died from tuberculosis aged thirteen, six years after the portrait was completed. His memory was eclipsed inevitably by the painting, which attained iconic status as the 'Red Boy', gracing assorted tin plates, toffee boxes, as well as a 1967 Royal Mail postage stamp. Even during Lambton's lifetime his personal association with the portrait was diminished, as critics in Paris, where the picture was exhibited, viewed it as an idealized image of the young Lord Byron –

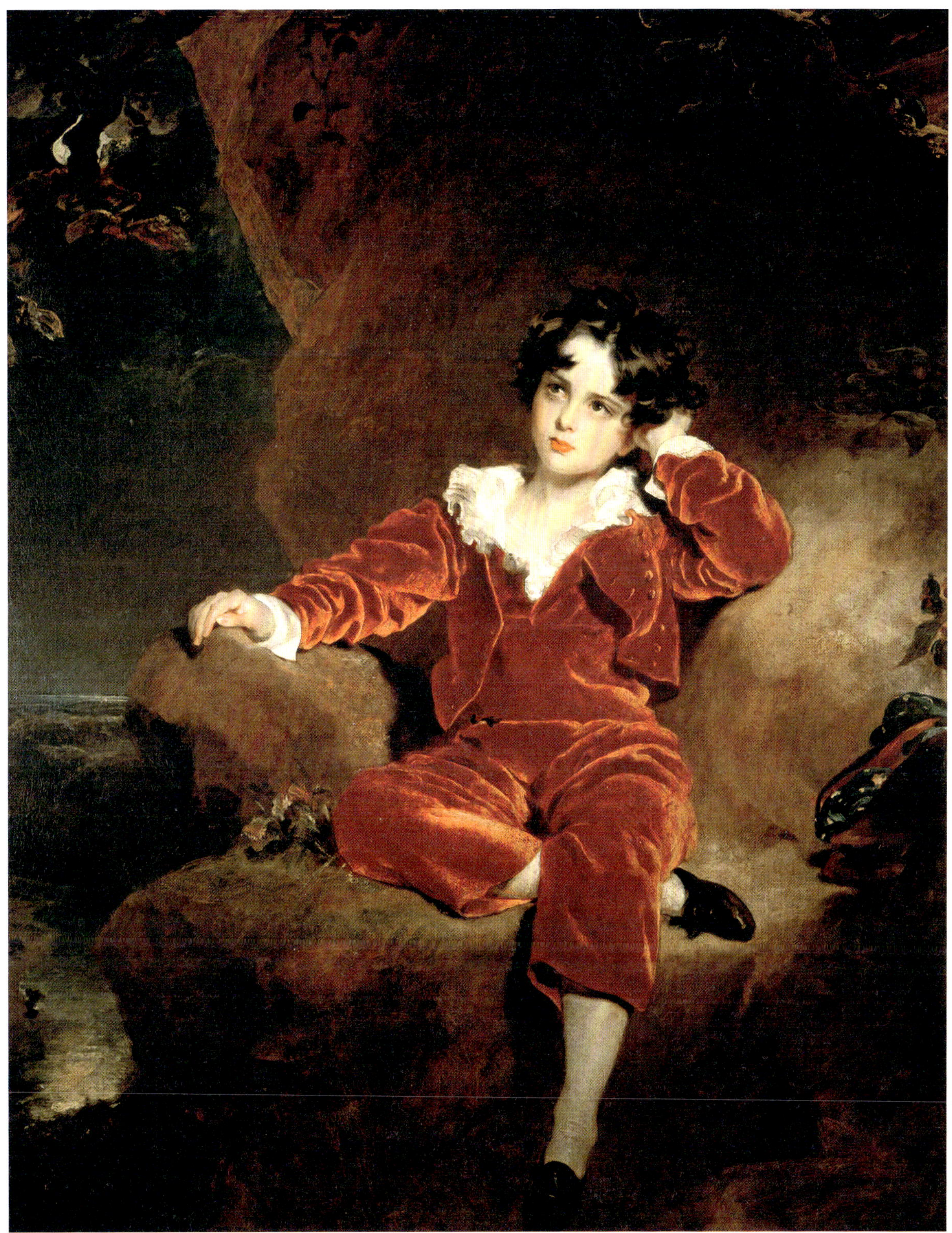

52
Thomas Lawrence, *The Red Boy (Master Lambton)*, 1825, oil on canvas, 140 x 110 cm, Private collection

53
Sir John Everett Millais, *A Souvenir of Velasquez*, 1868, oil on canvas, 102.7 x 82.4 cm, The Royal Academy of Arts

a quintessential poetic emblem for a Romantic Age.[30]

Despite critical success and lionization by fashionable society, following his death in 1830 Lawrence's reputation fell away swiftly. And with the advent of Pre-Raphaelitism in the late 1840s, and its adherents' disparagement of Reynolds, who they nicknamed 'Sir Sloshua', it seemed that the traditions of the fancy picture as it was upheld by the leading lights of the Georgian and Regency artistic community were exhausted. However, in an unlikely turn of events, John Everett Millais, one of the very artists who had done most to steer British art on a new course, began in the 1860s to embrace the Reynoldsian spirit of the fancy picture and its adherence to the art of the Old Masters. Millais's interest in the genre coincided with fatherhood, his children serving as models. Millais's daughter Effie posed for the pendant fancy pictures *My First Sermon* and *My Second Sermon* (Guildhall Art Gallery), painted in 1863–64, the former painting, as noted earlier, being later animated for cinema-goers by Shirley Temple. As well as the enjoyment Millais derived from creating such compositions, he was keenly aware of their commercial potential. It has also been pointed out that the timing of Millais's interest in the fancy picture coincided with a desire to promote himself as a successor to Reynolds and Gainsborough, a focal point of a national school of art and the Old Master traditions upon which it was constructed.[31]

In 1868 Millais was elected as a Royal Academician, presenting as his Diploma Work, *A Souvenir of Velasquez* (fig. 53). While the little girl was dressed in Spanish costume, clutching an orange branch, the principal inspiration for this very painterly composition was Reynolds as much as Velázquez – a deliberate ploy to underscore his affiliation to the traditions of the Royal Academy. And while the painting ostensibly promoted a 'natural' image of childhood, it was, like so many fancy pictures, brimming with artifice. The example of Reynolds continued to inform Millais's fancy pictures over the ensuing decades, notably in *Cherry Ripe* of 1879, which relied heavily upon *Penelope Boothby* (fig. 40) of nearly a century earlier. While the picture gained Millais an international reputation, its overt appeal to sentiment also damaged his standing as a 'serious' artist.[32] The suggestion that Millais had sold out through such paintings was confirmed in 1886 with *Bubbles*, for which the artist's young grandson posed. The upward gaze of the boy recalls earlier sacred images of children looking towards the Godhead, although here the child's eyes are directed towards a more transitory object. The exploitation of the image by the painting's subsequent owner to promote Pears' Soap confirmed its marketing potential beyond any intrinsic commercial value or the sale of reproductive prints made from it.

For some, the branding of *Bubbles* proved to be the final nail in the coffin for Millais's artistic integrity, the advertisement serving to 'prevent his ever standing on the dignified height of distinction with such masters in Art as Romney, Sir Peter Lely, Gainsborough and Reynolds'.[33] In the end, it was not Millais but his child model, William James, who had to endure the fallout engendered by the Pears' Soap debacle. For while James went on to gain a knighthood and earned distinction as an admiral in the Royal Navy, he remained forever 'Sir Bubbles'. As for Shirley Temple, the emblem of childhood innocence for modern movie-goers, the unsettling aspect of her performances, rooted in sentiment inspired by the fancy picture, were noted at the time by the novelist Graham Greene: 'Adult emotions of love and grief glissade across the mask of childhood, a childhood that is only skin-deep. It is clever, but it cannot last. Her admirers – middle-aged men and clergymen – respond to her dubious coquetry, to the sight of her well-shaped and desirable little body, packed with enormous vitality, only because

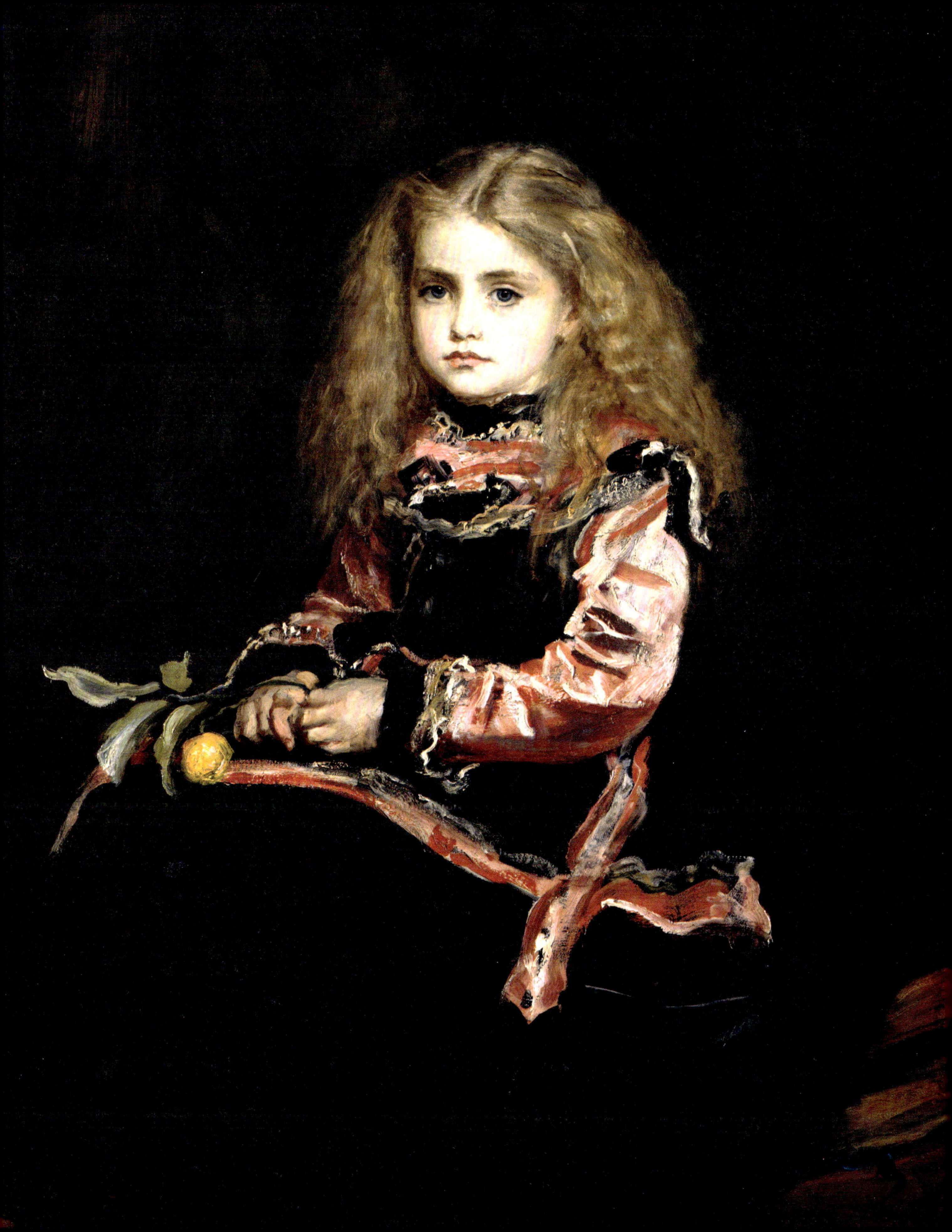

the safety curtain of story and dialogue drops between their intelligence and their desire'.[34] Greene was sued successfully by Temple's film company and fled to Mexico, fearing a jail sentence. Yet, while Greene's comments incited moral outrage at the time, they continue to highlight the point that such visualizations of childhood, which trade upon fantasies of innocence, are borne out of calculated adult experience.

Martin Postle *is Deputy Director for Grants & Publications at the Paul Mellon Centre for Studies in British Art. He has published widely on aspects of eighteenth-century British art and has curated a series of major exhibitions on a variety of subjects, including Joshua Reynolds, Johan Zoffany, Richard Wilson, Stanley Spencer, the artist's model, the fancy picture, and the art of the garden.*

Notes

1 Windeler, 1978, p. 111.

2 Temple Black, 1988, p. 16.

3 A fourth picture, *The Helping Hand (Un Coup de Main)* by the French artist, Émile Renouf, then in the Corcoran Gallery, Washington DEC, also featured in the sequence.

4 Reynolds's *Age of Innocence* was transferred from the National Gallery to the Tate Gallery in 1951.

5 Nottingham / London, 1998, pp. 59-60, no. 7.

6 Bray 2013, p. 16.

7 Gainsborough's original painting was destroyed in a fire at Exton Park, Leicestershire, in 1810. It was engraved in mezzotint by Richard Earlom in 1781. See Nottingham / London, 1998, p. 59, no. 6.

8 Whitley, 1915, p. 174.

9 Martin Postle, 'Location, Location, Location'. Reynolds, Gainsborough and the View from Richmond Hill', in *Windows on that World. Essays on British Art Presented to Brian Allen,* London: The Paul Mellon Centre for Studies in British Art, 2012, p. 103, and p. 112, n. 88.

10 Schama, 1991, p. 484.

11 https://www.nationalgallery.org.uk/paintings/judith-leyster-a-boy-and-a-girl-with-a-cat-and-an-eel, accessed 20 December 2018.

12 San Francisco / Baltimore / London 1997, pp. 239-240, no. 36.

13 'The Note-Books of George Vertue relating to Artists and Collections in England', Vertue III, *The Walpole Society*, vol. XXII, 1934, p. 82.

14 Mercier's painting was engraved by James McArdell in 1756 with the inscription 'Love me – Love my Cat'. Yale Center for British Art, B1970.3.571. An inferior engraving produced by the fictive engraver, Charles Corbutt, was entitled 'Miss and her Kitten', British Museum, 2010, 7081.1962.

15 Wright's painting was made around 1768-70, and was purchased at auction in 1771 by Henry Temple, 2nd Viscount Palmerston. The painting was engraved by Thomas Watson and published on 20th February 1781.

16 Bryant, 1996, pp. 18-19; Bryant, 2012, pp. 408-11.

17 Kamensky, 2016, p. 115.

18 Postle, 1995, chapter two, 'The Infant Academy', pp. 58-120.

19 Northcote, 1815, p. LXV-LXVI. Northcote was referring in particular to Reynolds's fancy picture, *Children in the Wood*, which he exhibited at the Royal Academy in 1770. See Mannings and Postle, 2000, vol. 1, p. 518, no. 2044.

20 Mannings and Postle, 2000, vol. 1, pp. 523-24, no. 2060, pp. 544 45, no. 2104.

21 The engraving is now in the collection of the Metropolitan Museum, New York, Accession Number 41.105.29.

22 Mannings and Postle, 2000, vol. 1, p. 153, no. 449.

23 Walpole, 1782, vol. 4, p. ix.

24 Mannings and Postle, 2000, p. 564, nos. 2165 and 2166. It is uncertain which of the two versions Reynolds exhibited at the Royal Academy in 1773.

25 Mannings and Postle, 2000, p. 153, no. 446. The dates of Frances Crewe's birth and death are unrecorded. She was born around 1767 and died around 1775, but is not mentioned in the family's genealogy.

26 Nottingham / London 1998, pp. 90-91, no. 85.

27 For Francis Ford's record of slave ownership and the correspondence with his son see 'Legacies of Slave Ownership. Sir Francis Ford 1st Bart', University College London, https://www.ucl.ac.uk/lbs/person/view/2146638825 accessed 21 December 2018.

28 See Nottingham / London 1998, p. 93.

29 For an account of this sea change in the earlier decades of the nineteenth century see Solkin, 2008, passim.

30 See Levey, 2005, p. 256.

31 Alison Smith, 'Fancy Pictures', in exh. cat., London / Amsterdam / Fukuoka / Tokyo 2007-2008, p. 172.

32 Ibid., pp. 182-83, no. 106.

33 The quotation is from *The Sorrows of Satan*, the best-selling Faustian novel of 1895 by Marie Corelli. See Ibid., p. 184.

34 Edwards, 1988.

A Portrait of the Artist's Children
Autobiography and Painting Children Now

JILL SEATON

> The people I like most are interested in portraiture, the symbolic and recognizable unique essence of a person. I, on the other hand, am interested in the portraiture of a relationship, how a relationship can be twisted, the effect people have on another.
> —Louise Bourgeois, 1992[1]

> Most of all I want people to be excited by the possibilities of paint: what has not been painted before, how individual paintings relate to a world of paintings throughout history, and the particularities of what paint can do that no other medium can – even in terms as simple as a fortuitous drip or an oily lump of colour.
> —Matthew Krishanu, 2018[2]

In 1994, Louise Bourgeois (1911–2010) produced a folio of fourteen dry-point etchings collectively titled *Autobiographical Series*.[3] Many of the prints were based on drawings from an earlier printmaking period in the 1940s: the process of revisiting and reinventing themes is intrinsically linked to Bourgeois's autobiographical approach to her work, and in this instance the ability to revisit a specific moment or memory was helped by the volume of material the artist compulsively collected, including photographs, letters, clothing and diaries recording daily thoughts, observations and emotions.[4] Bourgeois would return to these 'documents' throughout her career, which often produced a delay between the work's creation and public reception. *Birth* (1994, fig. 54) is based on an earlier drawing, and depicts the painful separation of mother and baby during childbirth. Of the drawing, Bourgeois said, 'it's a self-portrait, but I'm in a really difficult position. It's not flattering and it's not simple.'[5]

The birth is that of her third son Alain in 1941 (Bourgeois's second experience of childbirth, given that her eldest son was adopted). Bourgeois was to revisit Alain's birth again in 2003, when it formed the subject of *The Reticent Child*, an installation made for the Freud Museum in Vienna, where a sequential portrayal of birth plays out through six small figurative sculptures on tiny plinths. In the text accompanying the installation, she describes Alain as 'a child who simply refused to be born ... he is the reticent child'.[6] In *Birth*, Bourgeois is also addressing the difficulty of a mother 'letting go' of her child. She has frozen the moment where the baby is half-born, past the point of no return. The mother's hands on her womb are simultaneously holding on to her rounded belly and pushing the baby out – an act inhibited by her hair, which wraps around him like a cocoon, holding him close. The equal size of their heads is both a figurative description of the mother's acute pain as well as recognition of the baby as an individual entity – attached yet separate, the paradoxical nature of the parent-child relationship. The figures are balanced because the baby's head is enlarged to match the size of the mother's, so that there is a playing card-like symmetry to the composition. This is reinforced by the mirrored angles of the bent arms and legs and the lines across the necks of mother and child: Bourgeois is perhaps returning to the 'safety' and comfort of her early love of geometry to rationalize the anxiety of childbirth and parenthood.[7] The mother's facial expression conveys concentration and intensity, but not agony, while the child's expression is serene, with eyes gently closed. Bourgeois, an

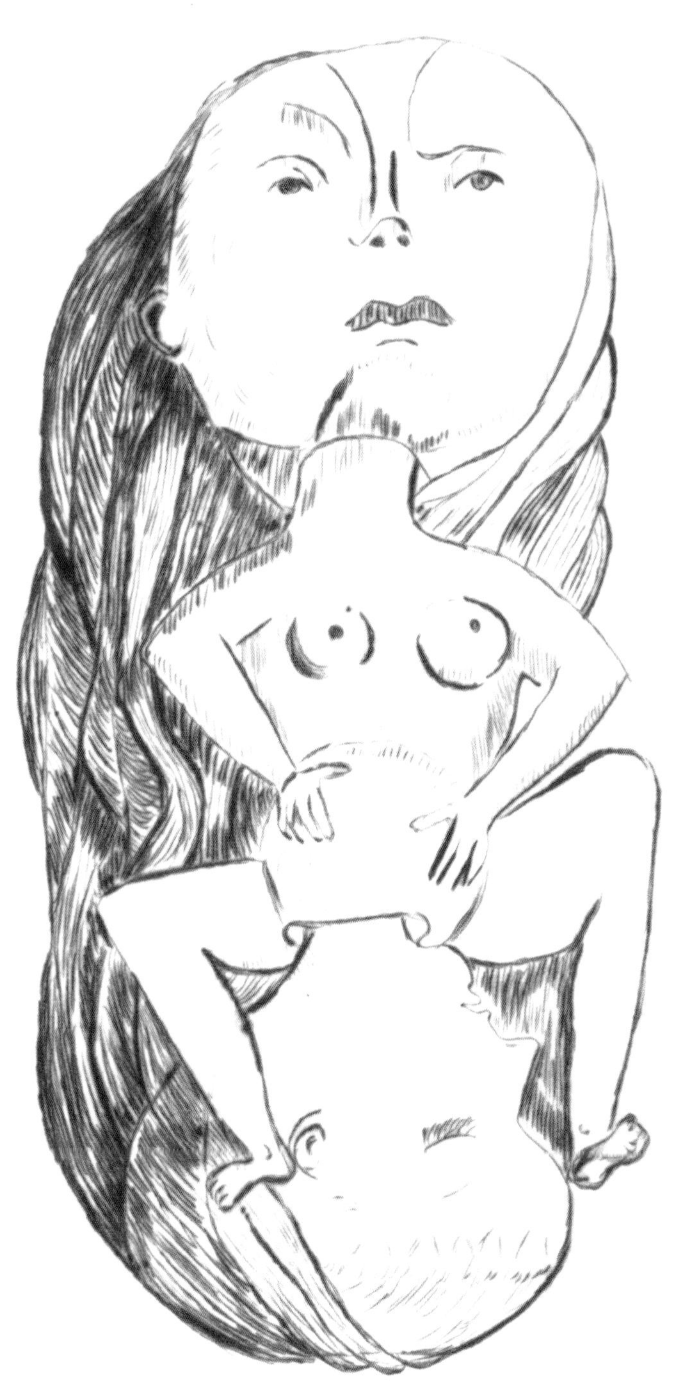

54
Louise Bourgeois, *Birth*, 1994, drypoint on paper, based on a drawing made in 1941, 23.6 x 18.2 cm, Tate

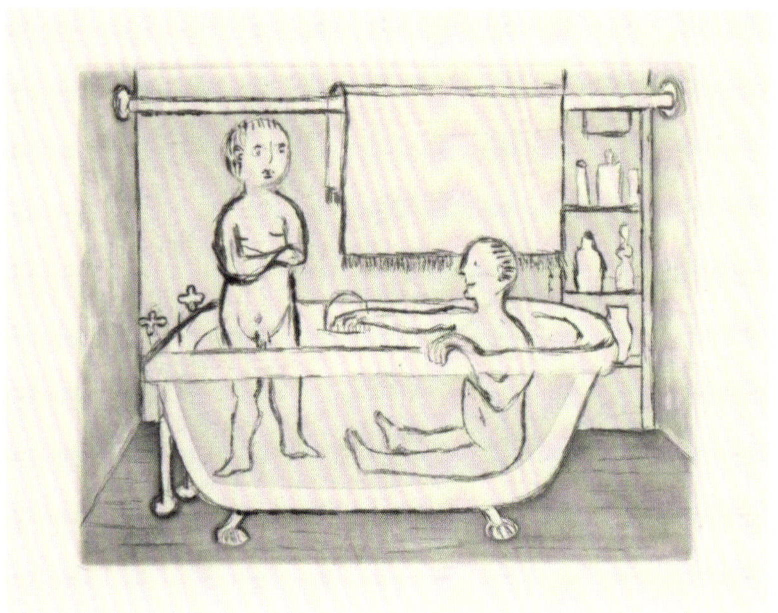

55
Louise Bourgeois, *Children in Tub*, 1994, drypoint and aquatint on paper, based on a drawing made in 1941, 10.6 x 13.7 cm, Tate

56
Winifred Nicholson, *The Artist's Children, Kate and Jake, at the Isle of Wight* (detail), 1931–32, oil on canvas, 67 x 75 cm, Bristol Museums, Galleries and Archives

artist with a capacity to convey anguish, instead chooses to present us with a mother internalizing the pain of childbirth, so that the baby remains undisturbed, innocent, untroubled. There is tenderness in this gesture and, as Bourgeois claimed, 'I only learned tenderness with the arrival of my own children'.[8] Tenderness can be seen again in the domestic simplicity conveyed by another etching in the series, *Children in Tub*, 1994 (fig. 55).[9] One boy stands with arms crossed, while his brother sits and points directly to his lower torso. The expressions caught by their mother in the moment suggest an animated discussion, perhaps one of many focused on body parts. The setting for this image is the New York apartment Bourgeois lived in with her family in the 1940s, when her children were small. She recalls:

> This is the bathroom at 18th Street. Everything is exactly the same ... the cabinet ... the tub with the feet ... it is very accurate. I'm asked all the time ... but I never say ... it was a lot of work to get through the day .... It was really something to have three children and also try to work. It was a lot of physical work. I could never carry a child, even when they were very little ... I had to have ways to hoist them. So here they help each other. They are happy ... it is very tender.[10]

Winifred Nicholson (1893–1981) was a contemporary of Louise Bourgeois and also chose her own children as artistic subjects, in works such as *The Artist's Children, Kate and Jake, at the Isle of Wight* (fig. 56).[11] Nicholson's impressionistic style characteristically combined elements of landscape and still-life painting in a portrait of four-year-old Jake and two-year-old Kate at the table in the seaside conservatory. In the foreground a snack set out for the children doubles as a still-life composition of round plates of fruit sitting atop the vertical and horizontal lines of the tablecloth, a space where figuration meets abstraction. For Nicholson colour usually expressed harmony and joy, but this painting was produced during a period of upheaval and adjustment for the family.[12] In July 1931, Nicholson gave birth to her third child, Andrew, in Cumberland. By autumn, her husband Ben Nicholson had met fellow artist Barbara Hepworth on holiday and moved to London to live with her. Winifred took her three young children to Fishbourne, Isle of Wight, in the immediate aftermath of the separation. In the painting there is a poignant contrast between the bright colours and cheerful party hats and the sombre expressions of the children, who have been described by Jake's son Jovan Nicholson as looking 'bewildered and lost'.[13] Nicholson's unwavering

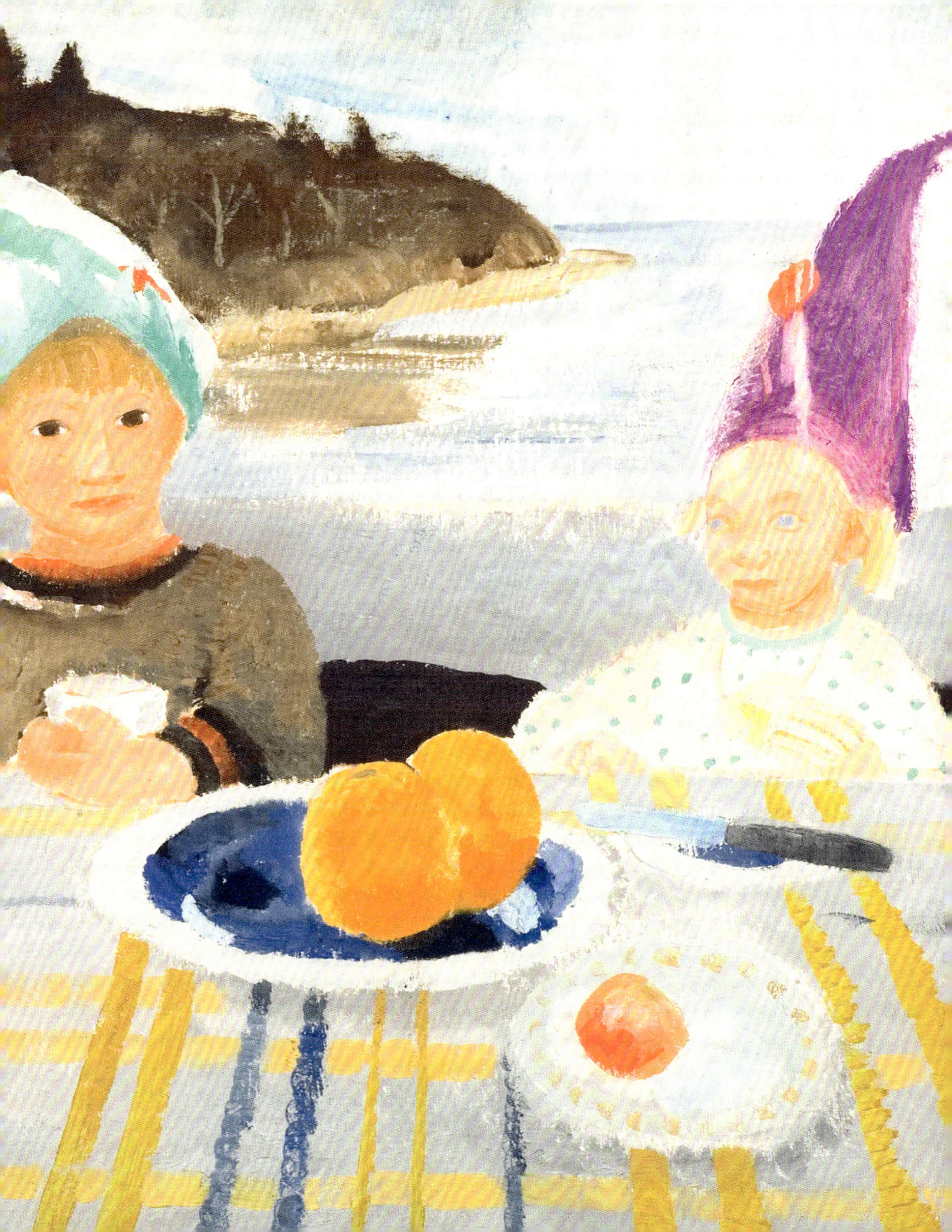

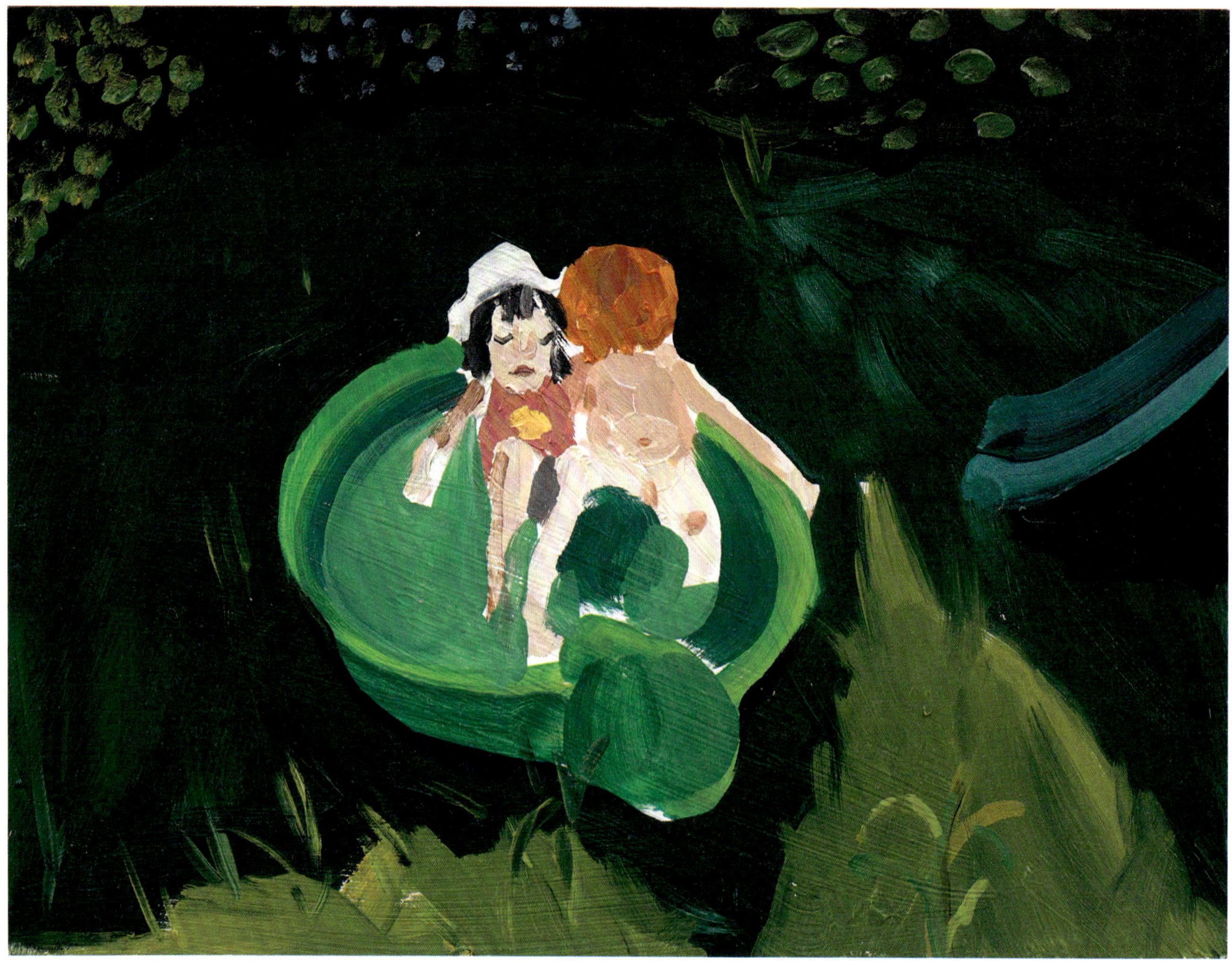

exploration of the depths of colour and light underpin the composition with stability and a sense of place.

The portraits produced by contemporary painter Chantal Joffe are similarly colourful and strewn with the familiar objects of family life, such as the green 'turtle pool' occupied by the toddlers in *Paddling Pool I* (fig. 57). Joffe has revealed that she is besotted by beauty, but not the kind found in fashion magazines. Instead, 'it's the actual instant, the shifty, wriggling person inside their hapless, gorgeous suit of flesh'.[14] Joffe's daughter, Esme, is an enduring subject for the artist, who has charted her daughter's development from newborn to teenager. Joffe is adamant that she will only paint Esme as she currently is, never revisiting an earlier stage.[15] *Esme, First Portrait* (fig. 58) captures Joffe's earliest impressions of her daughter, with her face still swollen and reddened from birth. Having stated that she hasn't experienced something until she has painted it, Joffe took almost a month to paint this first encounter, joking, 'I wasn't really in a fit state to paint her the day she was born.'[16]

A theme of unapologetic motherhood runs through Joffe's portraits of Esme – her dual role as mother and artist cohabiting the domestic spaces that unfold like a walk through her home. We see where Esme played, her toys and pastimes, play dates and birthday parties, and the silly jumpers she liked to wear. The recently completed portrait of *Esme on the Sofa* (fig. 59) confirms Joffe's unwavering resolution to capture the immediacy

57
Chantal Joffe, *Paddling Pool I*, 2008,
oil on board, 30 x 40 cm

of her relationship with her daughter, with details such as the yellow lanyard around the girl's neck (missing its identification badge) and her synthetic school uniform. Due to Joffe's prolific chronicling Esme is instantly recognizable, despite her generic uniform. She lolls back against the sofa after a long day at school, part adolescent, and part Venus. Interestingly, as Esme started to get older, Joffe deliberately ceased painting her without clothes.[17] This shift is symbolized in *Esme in a Blue Skirt*. Esme stands topless in a blue skirt, eyes averted, one arm protectively covering her front. According to Joffe, it was a new skirt and featured *appliqué* animals, so Esme wanted to show it off, but it is the last time she is shown (almost) nude.

In this respect, Joffe's work stands in contrast to that of Lucian Freud, a noted influence on her work.[18] Whereas Freud acknowledged fathering fourteen children by six different women, three of them by three different women in the same year, he never lived with any of his children, and only knew some of them as adults. He painted many of his acknowledged children, but not all of them had his phone number, and he decided when he would see them.[19] The portrait encounter thus began, as for any other sitter, with an invitation to enter their father's space. Freud resisted sentiment in his work, but the 'sexually loaded, penetrating gaze [that] was part of his weaponry' meant that he still conveyed, in paint, something uniquely intimate.[20] This can be seen in two rather different portraits of his daughters Annie and Annabel, whom he fathered with his first wife, Kitty Garman, the daughter of sculptor Sir Jacob Epstein and his mistress Kathleen Garman. In *Annabel* (fig. 60), Freud's characteristic broad brushstrokes, high viewpoints, tilted furniture and smaller than life-size scale are representative of the painting style he adopted from the 1950s onwards.[21] Though refined and elegantly posed, Annabel sits awkwardly in the worn chair, her gaze averted. The spatial elements of the

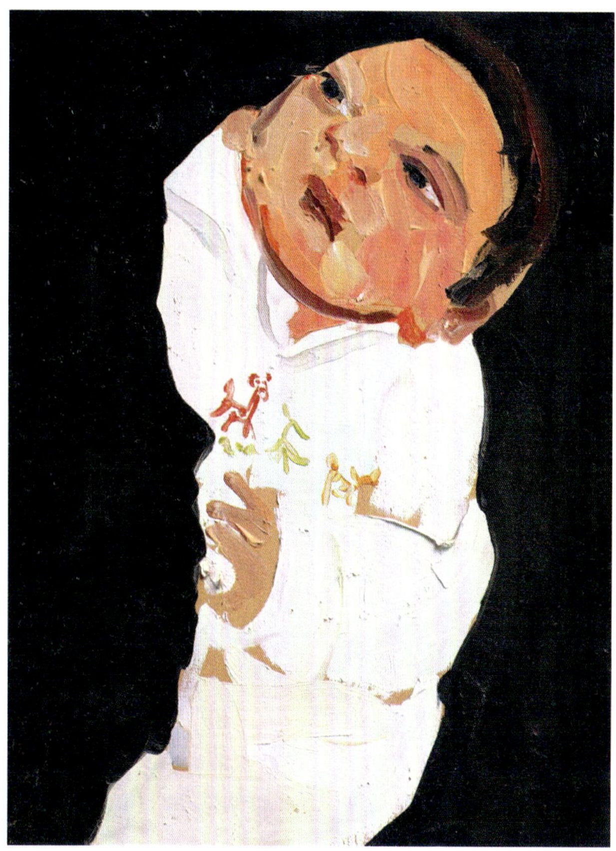

58
Chantal Joffe, *Esme (First Portrait)*, 2004,
oil on board, 29.2 x 21.8 cm

composition convey a distance between the artist and his fifteen-year-old daughter, and the viewer studies her from above. Annabel's expression is thoughtfully ambiguous, the averted gaze of her large, expressive eyes implying a level of submission and the hint of a smile appearing at her mouth. Freud was known to keep sitters in a pose for hours on end, and Annabel's arm comes across her body as if required to support her other arm on the side of the chair. She wears a modest green and brown striped dress, her only adornment a delicate watch on her wrist.

Annabel is a portrait of a young lady, the embodiment of the idea of the well-mannered daughter Freud envisioned when he admonished Annie, Annabel's elder sister, for smoking outside. Annie recalled, 'He told me that prostitutes smoked in the street and wanted me to know that if I did it again I could be regarded as a prostitute'. When asked if she knew why he was being so

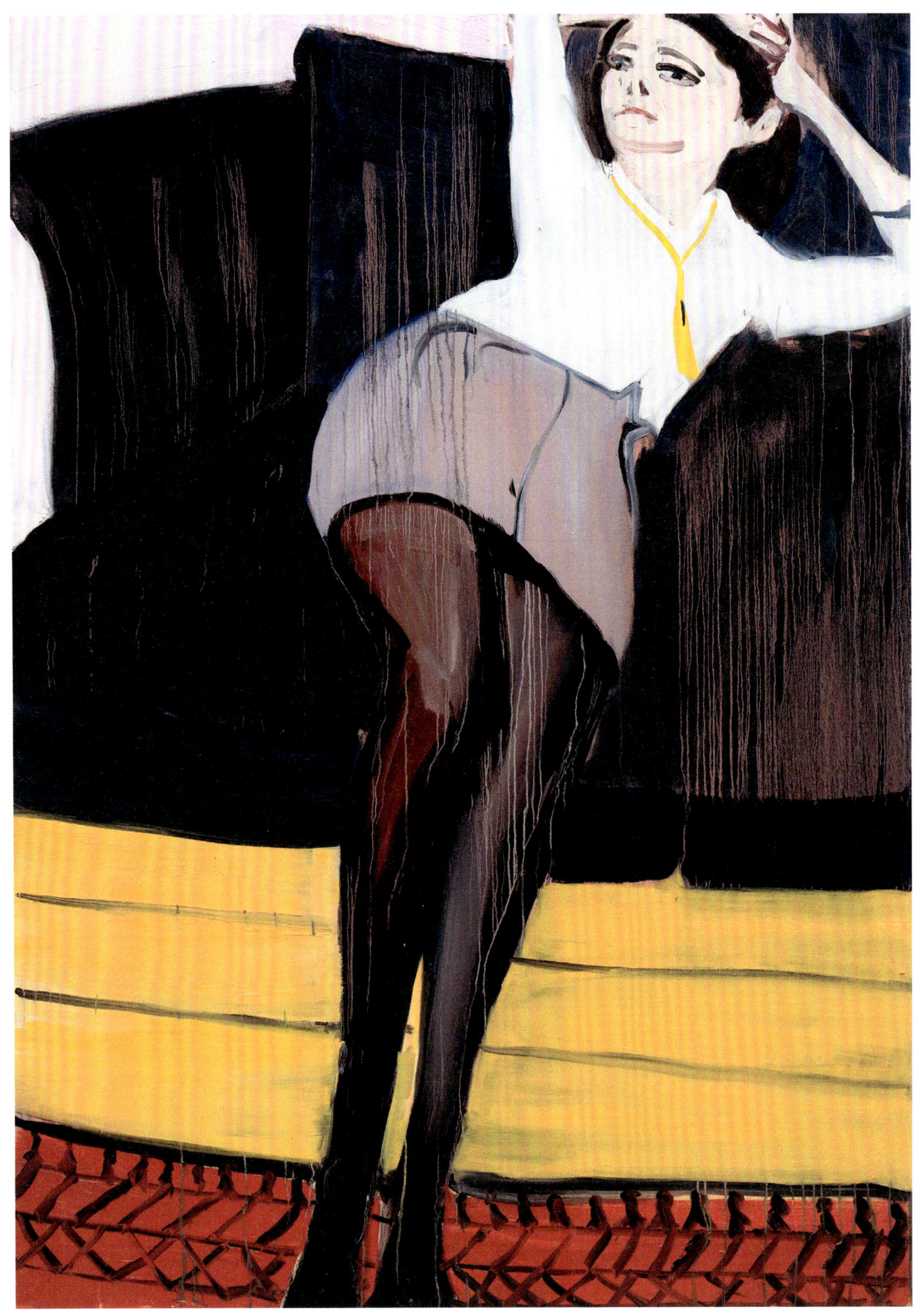

59
Chantal Joffe, *Esme on the Sofa*, 2018,
oil on canvas, 213.5 x 152.5 cm

60
Lucian Freud, *Annabel*, 1967, oil on canvas, 35 x 27 cm, New Art Gallery, Walsall

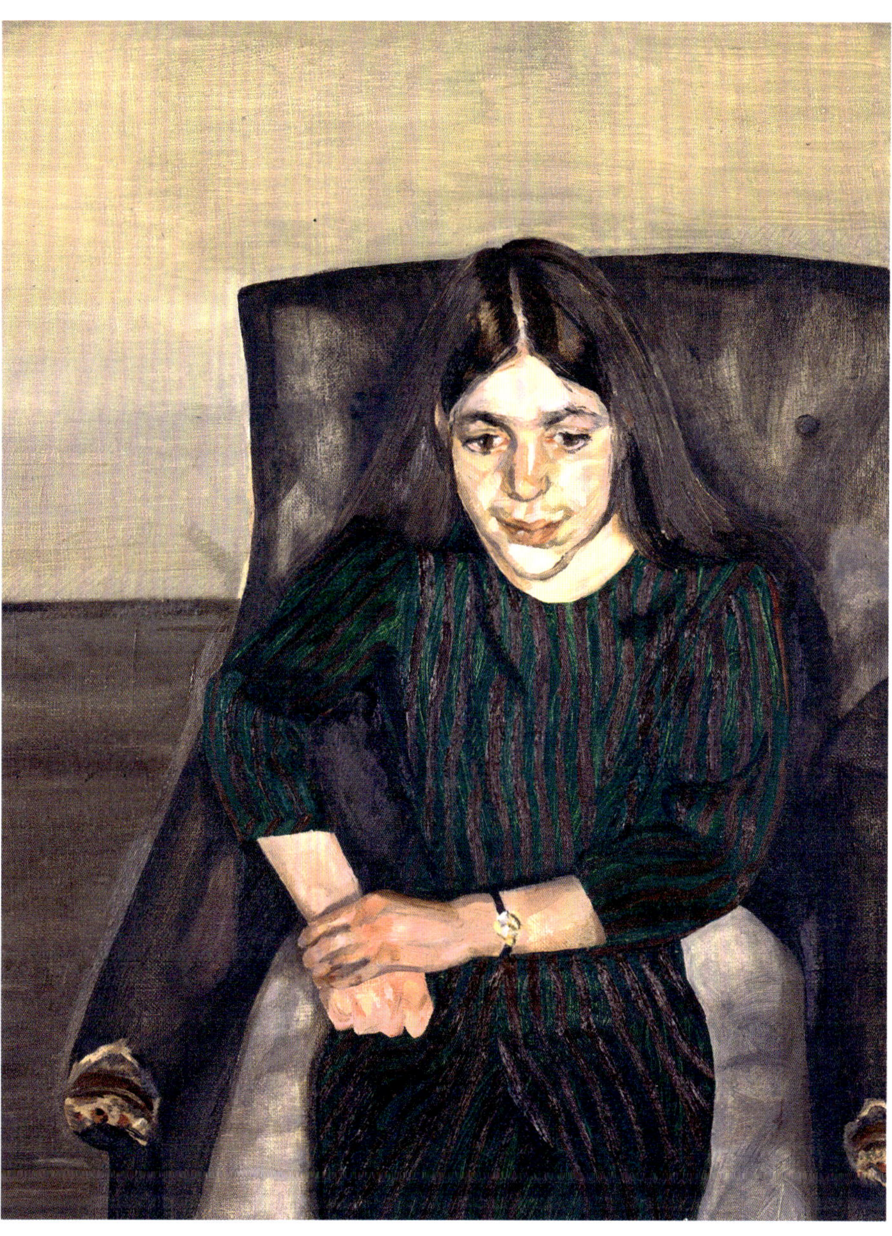

adamant, she replied, 'Because you are my father', and he replied, 'That's completely irrelevant. It's because I care about you.'[22] Whilst Annie found his objectivity to their biological link difficult, it might help to understand Freud's relationship with his children in simpler terms. While not given to sentimentality, Freud had to be interested in someone if he was to paint him or her, stating: 'My work is purely autobiographical. It is about myself and my surroundings. It is an attempt at a record. I work from the people that interest me and that I care about, in rooms that I live in and know. I use the people to invent my pictures with, and I can work more freely when they are there.'[23] Freud's objectivity is grounded in a deliberate resistance to sentimentality, a lesson he took from the painters of the past, once commenting that Rembrandt's pictures of his son Titus were ruined by sentimentality.[24] The notion of overcompensating for any embedded sentimentality might help contextualize Freud's nude portrayals of his pubescent

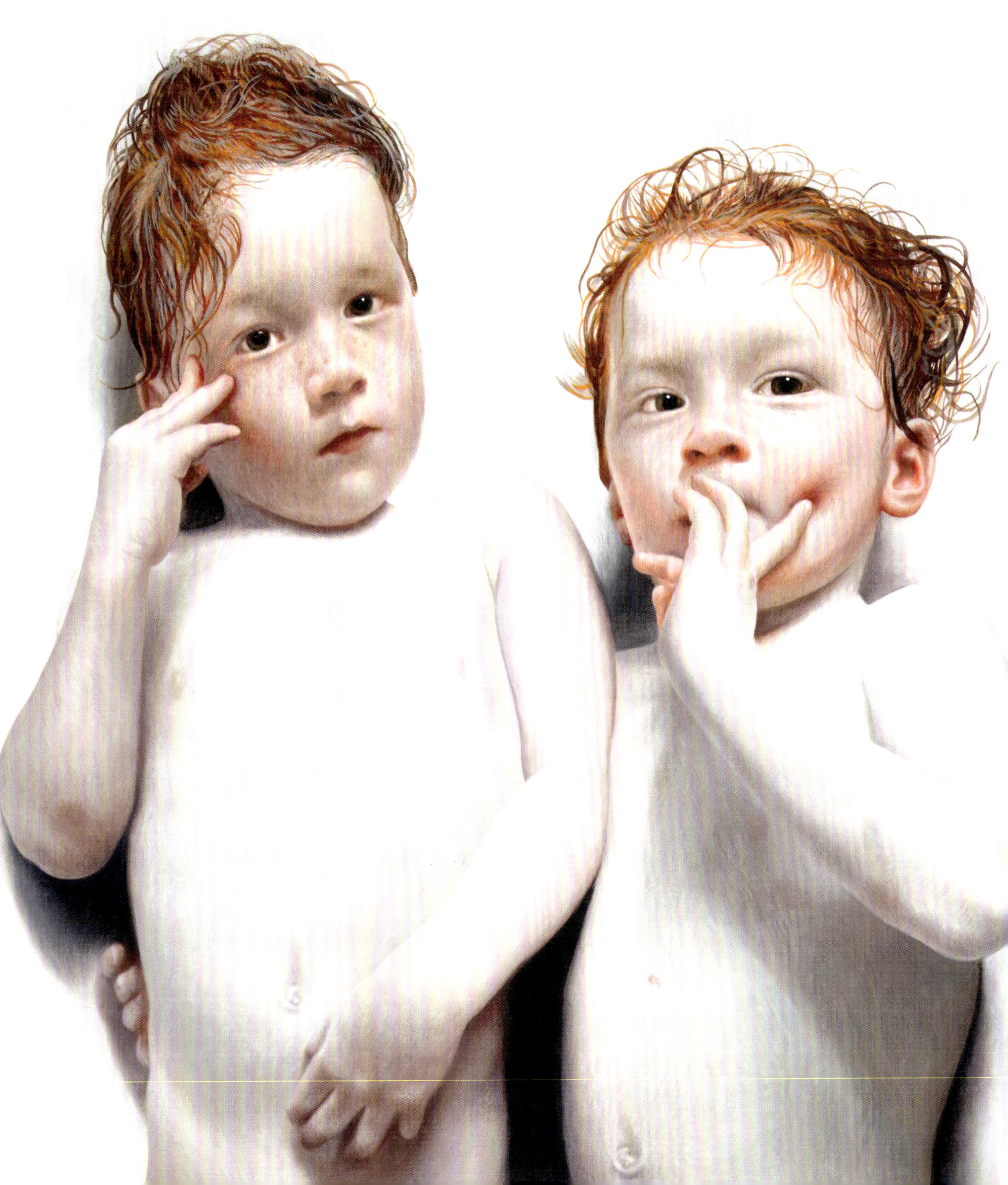

61
Mark Fairnington, *Lee and Jason*, 2011, oil on panel, 49 x 44 cm, Artist's Collection

62
Mark Fairnington, *Jason's Eye*, 2011, oil on panel, 7 x 7 cm, Artist's Collection

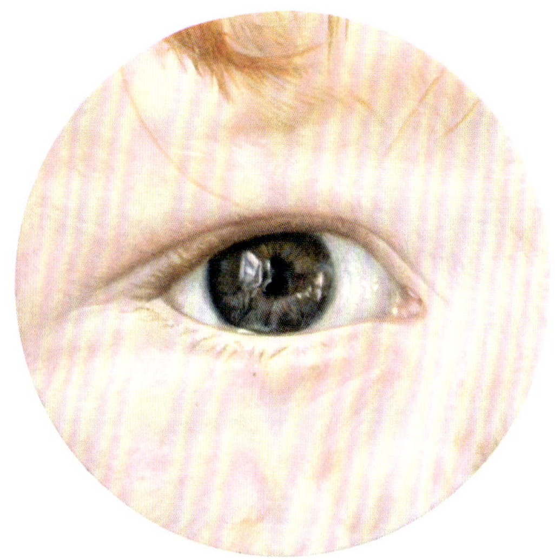

children. In *Naked Child Laughing* (1963), Freud depicts his fourteen-year-old daughter Annie nude sitting on a sofa. Freud reportedly asked his daughter to remove her 'clothes and teenage inhibitions' for the portrait, but the painting involves more modesty than some of his later works.[25] Annie's folded legs are turned to the left to hide her pubis and her breasts are partially obscured by her long hair. With her laughing smile and shy, hunched posture, boundaries between childhood innocence and artistic objectivity, and appropriate and inappropriate behaviour between a father and his teenage daughter, collide. In her own words, Annie stated, 'He knew that nudity changed everything, bringing new levels of revelation and exposure'.[26]

While not his first painting of people, *Lee and Jason* (fig. 61) is the first painting that Mark Fairnington considers to be a portrait.[27] Fairnington applies a scientific process of collection, documentation and observation to the production of the portraits of his two children, which developed from painting insect specimens, where multiple photographs were used to generate images that had detailed and complex surfaces. Fairnington has discussed how as boys, redheads and identical twins, Lee and Jason already inhabit specific taxonomies. In painting them, Fairnington sought to record both their likeness and their similarities, but also to 'take pleasure in their differences, the hand gestures, the bruising on the legs from football ...'[28] In *Lee and Jason* the boys are posed naked against a stark white background and their snowy pale skin, combined with the cropping of the image at their waists, presents them as taxonomic specimens. The setting of the portrait is ambiguously sterile – the children could be on an operating table, but for the casual deployment of Jason's arm, which unites the pair and suggests that they have just got out of the bath. Their damp curly hair is aflame with colour, reds and oranges suffusing the boys' faces with a warm glow. Devoid of devices and props, the viewer is left to focus on the children, and encouraged to continue looking, a process which is simultaneously intriguing and unsettling. Fairnington describes how:

'They are with each other, self-contained and assertive, in spite of their nakedness. The suggestion of narrative does not destroy the painting and the power relationship between the viewer and the subject oscillates.'[29]

The boys are intimately familiar to Fairnington, but he has described how in the moment of painting them his intimacy is by necessity with the touch of the brush on the painted surface, not with the subject of the painting. The highly detailed, life-size seven-centimetre tondos of *Lee's Eye* (2011) and *Jason's Eye* (fig. 62) reproduce a cropped, single eye of each twin (a left and a right respectively). These works recall the tradition of portrait miniatures, in particular the subgenre of 'lover's eye' miniatures which gained popularity after 1785, when the Prince of Wales, later George IV, proposed marriage to Maria Fitzherbert by letter, enclosing a miniature portrait of his eye instead of a ring.[30] Inspired by these historic examples, Fairnington wanted to explore how such disembodied fragments might come to represent the possession of a whole person.[31] In other portraits Fairnington records the boys at full length, enabling him to document their favourite outfits, including baggy shorts, football kits and wetsuits.

Two boys are also the subject of Matthew Krishanu's paintings, but the boys here are Krishanu and his brother

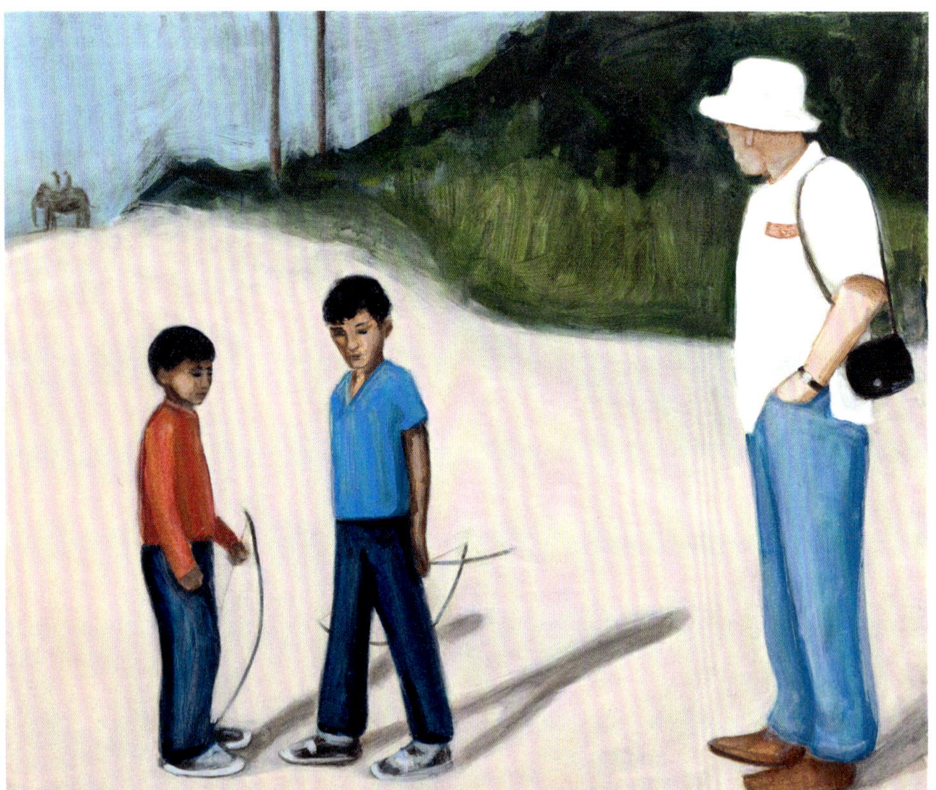

63
Matthew Krishanu, *Safari*, 2013, oil and acrylic on linen, 50 x 60 cm, Collection Amrita Jhaveri

64
Matthew Krishanu, *Skeleton*, 2014, oil on canvas, 150 x 200 cm, Arts Council Collection, Southbank Centre, London

as children. The inspiration for *Two Boys* (2012) was a photograph from his family album of the pair playing on an abandoned water tank in India. Once he started painting, Krishanu put the photograph away, using his memory to sketch in broadly the colours, subject and features of the two boys.[32] Although he later returned to the photograph to refine details, Krishanu's process involved deliberately taking the 'reality' of a photograph and dissolving it, and then remaking it in a parallel world – his 'painting world'.[33] He explains: 'I've always liked the idea that our past selves continue to exist as if in a foreign land. With that in mind, the paintings are like windows on to the past, animated in paint.'[34] Born in Bradford in 1980, Krishanu lived in Bangladesh from the age of one to twelve, with annual visits to his mother's family in India, before moving back to England. These experiences mean that for Krishanu the period of childhood is strongly demarcated in both another place and another time.

The relationship between painting and digital images can be explored in the process behind the creation of *Safari* (fig. 63). The painting is based on a photograph which shows the artist's family standing in front of two elephants – a mother with two riders on her back, and a small calf. Krishanu removed four of the figures and the baby elephant from the central group, leaving himself (in red), his brother (in blue) and his grandfather, who has a camera slung over his shoulder. Krishanu returned to this piece over a period of three years, at one point removing himself from the picture, then deciding to put himself back in for balance. The changes made to the painting affect our interpretation: removed from the family group, the lighter skin of Krishanu's grandfather and his camera suggest that he is a tourist, and his relationship to the two boys becomes ambiguous. Krishanu aligns working from digital images with working from memory and imagination, and finds that painterly solutions frequently surpass those of the digital. An example of this is found in *Skeleton* (fig. 64), a composition that Krishanu struggled with in its earlier stages. Two boys stand behind a large, indistinct carcass. One wears a white shirt, the other blue. The initial blue

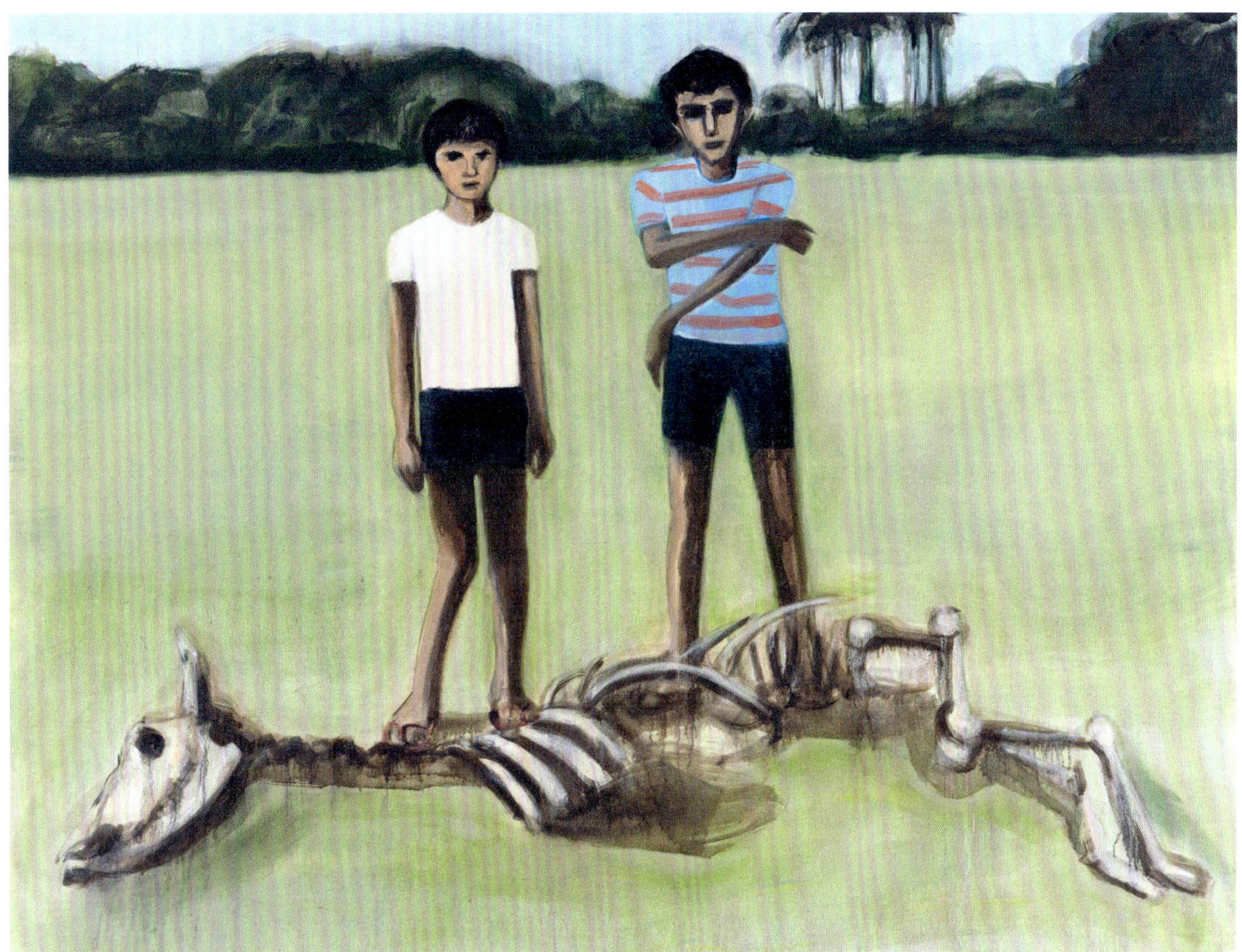

shirt was plain, and this, as it transpired, was the problem. Krishanu found his solution in the red horizontal stripes he added to the blue shirt, with the artist stating 'a new layer of paint can bring a new layer of life'.[35]

Access to digital technology does not diminish the desire to paint, it enhances it, opening up new opportunities and methods within this traditional medium. Chantal Joffe, Matthew Krishanu and Mark Fairnington all use photography in their work, but they dismantle the digital image and reassemble it for their own purposes. While the approaches encountered in this chapter might be different, all of the artists share a fundamental interest in observing people. Within this the child occupies a special place – whether as a route back to the distant lands of the past in the work of Krishanu and Bourgeois, or as a present and constantly evolving subject in the work of Fairnington and Joffe. In the case of Freud, sentiment was actively resisted when portraying his own children; however, for other artists the intimate moments of family life were valuable creative stimuli. The works surveyed here demonstrate a shared process of questioning and pulling apart a highly personal subject or emotion, to be reassembled in a finished work.

Jill Seaton *is an independent art historian and curator. She holds a PhD in History of Art from the University of Edinburgh and her research interests include the history of display in public and private spaces. Recent projects include working with NGOs (Non-governmental organizations) to promote contemporary art as a facilitator of critical dialogue on environmental, social, economic and cultural issues faced by societies.*

Notes

1 Louise Bourgeois, source unknown, 1992. Cited in Crone and Schaesberg 2008, p. 49.

2 Priseman 2018.

3 Acquired by Tate 1994. The portfolio was published in an edition of thirty-five plus ten artist's proofs by Peter Blum Edition, New York, and printed by Harlan & Weaver Intaglio, New York.

4 Bourgeois claimed 'I need my memories; they are my documents' in Küster 2011, p.43.

5 The original drawing is dated 1941, *Untitled*, Museum of Fine Arts, Bern. See Bernadac and Obrist 1998, p. 294.

6 *Il était réticent. Mais j'ai l'ai relève* [He was reticent. But I found him out]. Morris 2007, p. 38.

7 When her mother died in 1932, Bourgeois suffered deeply from the loss. That same year, she started studying mathematics at the Sorbonne in Paris, seeking refuge in the constancy of geometric principles, a safe haven from her turbulent family life. Bourgeois spoke widely of her early passion for Euclidean geometry, a system that represented stability and order. See Coxon 2010, p.12.

8 Declaration made by Louise Bourgeois in 1995, in Gorovoy and Asbaghi, op. cit. (note 5), p. 18.

9 The original source is the drawing, *Untitled*, 1945, charcoal and ink on paper, Easton Foundation, New York. The alternate titles 'Tub' and 'Hazing' were given by the artist, as cited in New York 1994, p. 234. Conversely, in other versions of this image, the bathtub is opaque, and the viewer cannot see through into the water. Only through comparison (of her revisited subject) do we discover a suspension of sentimentality by the invitation to question themes of (prepubescent) sexuality and voyeurism.

10 New York 1994, p. 234.

11 Another version makes the conservatory setting clearer, showing the windows of the conservatory behind the children, with a ship on the horizon in the watery background. See *The Artist's Children, Kate and Jake at the Isle of Wight*, 1931, Scottish National Gallery of Modern Art.

12 The dominance of colour in Nicholson's work dates back to a trip to India in 1919 that inspired a lifelong interest in the portrayal of light, shade and space using colour. Nicholson stated: 'I like harmony to be expressed in colour. For colour is one of the surest means of expressing joy – the joy that resides in a happy home.' Nicholson, 'Unknown Colour', reprinted in Glasgow 1979, pp. 29–32.

13 Jovan Nicholson spoke at the *Ways With Words* festival in Dartington on 9 July 2014. The talk coincided with an exhibition he curated, *'Art and Life: Ben Nicholson, Winifred Nicholson, Christopher Wood, Alfred Wallis, William Staite Murray, 1920 – 1931'*, London, Dulwich Picture Gallery, 2014.

14 Laing 2018, p. 162.

15 This pertains to all of Joffe's sitters, not just Esme. Conversation with Chantal Joffe, studio visit, London, 22 November 2018.

16 Ian Youngs, 'Chantal Joffe: Painting Pregnancy and Parenthood', *BBC News*, 7 June 2018.

17 Joffe said that she 'can't paint children naked now that they've become self-conscious' in an interview with Sarah Howgate in London 2015, p. 2.

18 On her artistic influences, Joffe said, 'I was always trying to inhabit other people, particularly other artists; Diane Arbus for instance. And that happened with Freud ... I love them so much I want to be them.' Interview with Sarah Howgate in London 2015, p. 10.

19 The exception are his four children by Katherine McAdam. Greig 2013, p. 187.

20 Lampert 2011.

21 From this point Freud stood up to paint, swapped fine sable brushes for clipped hog's hair brushes that allowed for larger, coarser brushstrokes with more pigment. See Moroney 2007, p. 84. On this stylistic shift, Malcolm Ruel stated, 'It was as though he no longer wished to imitate flesh but rather to convey some of its texture, immediateness, solidity.' See Ruel 1995, p. 20.

22 Greig 2013, p. 183.

23 Lucian Freud quoted in London 1974, p. 13, and London 2012b, p. 14.

24 As William Feaver reported, for Freud it is no good for the painter to be too tender towards his subjects, because that way lies the sentimentality that ruined, for example, Rembrandt's pictures of Titus. '"Rembrandt loved Titus so much he couldn't quite do him straight," Freud once said. "I'm very conscious of Titus disease."' London 2002.

25 Greig 2013, pp. 175–76. Freud painted six daughters and one son nude, dating from a small-scale portrait of Annie, *Naked Child Laughing*, 1963, 28 × 34 cm, to a large-scale painting of his son Freddy, born in 1971, *Freddy Standing*, 2001, 248.9 × 172.7 cm.

26 Greig 2013, p. 176.

27 Mark Fairnington, email to Amy Orrock, 25 November 2018.

28 Ibid.

29 Ibid.

30 Instead of a ring, the proposal included a miniature portrait of the Prince's right eye, painted by his friend the celebrated miniaturist Richard Cosway (1742–1821). Grootenboer 2006, p. 496.

31 In 1998 Fairnington saw a miniature portrait of the eye of Baroness Louise Lehzen by Sir William Charles Ross (1794–1860). Lehzen (1784–1870) was the governess, and later advisor and companion, to Queen Victoria.

32 Priseman 2018.

33 Matthew Krishanu, 'Why Paint in the Digital Age', lecture, *The Immediacy of Paint: The Role of Painting in the Digital Age*, University Campus Suffolk, 18 September 2015.

34 The concept of this parallel world relates to the L.P. Hartley line, 'The past is a foreign country; they do things differently there', and Krishanu's series of paintings are titled 'Another Country.' See Priseman 2018.

35 Ibid.

WORKS EXHIBITED

PAINTING CHILDHOOD

Federico Barocci (c. 1533–1612)
The head and shoulders of a swaddled baby, lying down, c. 1595
Pastels on blue paper, 16 x 22.1 cm
Lent by Her Majesty The Queen [fig. 7]

Domenico Zampieri, called Domenichino (1581–1641)
Three studies of a sleeping child, undated
Black chalk heightened with white on grey paper, 22.6 x 34.1 cm
Lent by Her Majesty The Queen [fig. 36]

Domenico Zampieri, called Domenichino (1581–1641)
Four studies of a sleeping child, undated
Black chalk heightened with white on light brownish grey paper, 20 x 31.6 cm
Lent by Her Majesty The Queen [fig. 37]

Francesco Salviati (1510–1563)
Study of a child, c. 1530
Red chalk on off-white paper, 27 x 27.2 cm
The Ashmolean Museum, University of Oxford. Purchased, 1950

School of Raphael (c. 1499–1546)
Two life studies of a nude child, c. 1520–46
Brush drawing in brown ink over metalpoint with some yellow ink on off-white paper, 16 x 20.3 cm
The Ashmolean Museum, University of Oxford. Presented by a Body of Subscribers, 18462

Domenico Zampieri, called Domenichino (1581–1641)
Study of a child trying on a cap, c. 1600
Black chalk, heightened with a little white, on grey paper, 29.3 x 18.2 cm
The Ashmolean Museum, University of Oxford. Bequeathed by Francis Douce, 1834

The Royal Portrait

Hans Holbein the Younger (1497/8–1543)
Edward, Prince of Wales, later Edward VI, c. 1540–43
Black and coloured chalks, and pen and ink on pale pink prepared paper, 27.3 x 22.7 cm
Lent by Her Majesty The Queen [fig. 14]

Follower of Hans Holbein the Younger (1497/8–1543)
Edward, Prince of Wales, later Edward VI, c. 1542
Oil on panel, 53 x 41.5 cm
Compton Verney Art Gallery & Park [fig. 11]

Attributed to William Scrots (active 1537–1553)
Edward VI, c. 1550
Oil on panel, 58 x 68 cm
Compton Verney Art Gallery & Park [fig. 15]

Robert Peake the Elder (c. 1551–1619)
Henry, Prince of Wales (1594–1612) with Robert Devereux, 3rd Earl of Essex (1591–1646) in the Hunting Field, c. 1605
Oil on canvas, 190.5 x 165.1 cm
Lent by Her Majesty The Queen [fig. 16]

Sir Anthony van Dyck (1599–1641)
The Five Eldest Children of Charles I, 1637
Oil on canvas, 163.2 x 198.8 cm
Lent by Her Majesty The Queen [fig. 21]

Sir Anthony van Dyck (1599–1641)
Princess Elizabeth (1635–1650) and Princess Anne, (1637–1640). Daughters of Charles I, 1637
Oil on canvas, 29.8 x 41.8 cm
National Galleries of Scotland. Purchased with the aid of the Heritage Lottery Fund, the Scottish Office and the Art Fund 1996 [fig. 23]

William Dobson (1611–1646)
Charles, Prince of Wales, later Charles II, with a page, c. 1642
Oil on canvas, 153.6 x 129.8 cm
National Galleries of Scotland. Purchased 1935 [fig. 24]

Dutch
Armour of King Charles I as a Boy, c. 1616
Steel, 144.8cm
Royal Armouries Museum, II 90 [fig. 25]

Johan Joseph Zoffany (1733–1810)
George, Prince of Wales, later George IV, with Prince Frederick, later Frederick, Duke of York, c. 1770
Oil on canvas 131 x 202 cm
Lent by Her Majesty The Queen [fig. 27]

Sir Edwin Landseer (1802–1873)
Victoria, Princess Royal, with Eos, 1841
Oil on canvas, 71.8 x 91.8 cm
Lent by Her Majesty The Queen [fig. 29]

Franz Xaver Winterhalter (1805–1873)
Albert Edward, Prince of Wales, later Edward VII, 1846
Oil on canvas, 127.1 x 88 cm
Lent by Her Majesty The Queen [fig.12]

Queen Victoria (1819–1901)
Victoria asleep aged 3 weeks, 1840
Pencil with touches of watercolour, 22.3 x 27.5 cm
Lent by Her Majesty The Queen [fig. 31]

Queen Victoria (1819–1901)
Victoria, 1841
Etching on India laid paper, 25.4 x 22.6 cm
Lent by Her Majesty The Queen

Queen Victoria (1819–1901)
Victoria, 1841
Etching on India laid paper, 15.2 x 11.4 cm
Lent by Her Majesty The Queen

Prince Albert (1819–1861), Consort of Queen Victoria (1819–1861)
Albert and Victoria, 1843
Etching on India paper, 14.8 x 16 cm
Lent by Her Majesty The Queen [fig. 32]

Queen Victoria (1819–1901)
Victoria, 1843
Etching, 27.6 x 32.6 cm
Lent by Her Majesty The Queen

Queen Victoria (1819–1901)
The Prince of Wales with a Parrot, 1843
Watercolour and bodycolour over pencil, 15 x 15.2 cm
Lent by Her Majesty The Queen

Queen Victoria (1819–1901)
Five studies of the Royal Children, 1845
Etching on India laid paper, 15.1 x 22.8 cm
Lent by Her Majesty The Queen

Queen Victoria (1819–1901)
Alfred, 1846
Lithograph, 27.8 x 37.7 cm
Lent by Her Majesty The Queen

Queen Victoria (1819–1901)
Helena, Alfred and Alice, 1847
Pen and ink, 16.8 x 18.3 cm
Lent by Her Majesty The Queen

Queen Victoria (1819–1901)
Victoria, 1851
Etching, 38.1 x 54.2 cm
Lent by Her Majesty The Queen

William Charles Bell (1831–1904)
Thirteen miniatures mounted on a gold box: Queen Victoria; Victoria, Princess Royal (x2); King Edward VII when Prince of Wales; Princess Alice; Prince Alfred; Princess Helena (x2); Princess Louise (x2); Prince Arthur; Princess Beatrice; and William II, Emperor of Germany, when Prince William of Prussia, , 1850–61
Gold and enamel, 8.5 x 12.7 cm
Lent by Her Majesty The Queen

William Essex (1784–1869)
Bracelet with miniatures of the Royal children by William Essex, c. 1845–50
Gold and blue champlevé enamel, pearls, enamel, hair, 18 x 3 x 0.8 cm
Lent by Her Majesty The Queen [fig. 30]

Playing and Growing

British (English) School
Arabella Stuart, later Duchess of Somerset (1575–1615), aged 23 months, 1577
Oil on panel transferred to canvas, 55.9 x 41.5 cm
National Trust: Hardwick Hall, Derbyshire

Attributed to the Dutch School
Portrait of Cornelia Burch, Aged 2 months, 1581
Oil on canvas, 54 x 77.5 cm
Ferens Art Gallery: Hull Museums

Marcus Gheeraerts the Younger (1561/2–1636)
A Boy Aged Two, 1608
Oil on panel, 114.3 x 85.7 cm
Compton Verney Art Gallery & Park [fig. 1]

Judith Leyster (1609–1660)
A Boy and a Girl with a Cat and an Eel, c. 1635
Oil on panel, 59.4 x 48.8 cm
The National Gallery, London. Bequeathed by C.F. Leach [fig. 3]

Jan Steen (1626–1679)
A School for Boys and Girls, c. 1670
Oil on canvas, 81.7 x 108.6 cm
National Galleries of Scotland. Purchased by Private Treaty with the aid of the National Heritage Memorial Fund 1984 [fig. 2]

William Hogarth (1697–1764)
The Graham Children, 1742
Oil on canvas, 160.5 x 181 cm
The National Gallery, London. Presented by Lord Duveen through the Art Fund, 1934 [fig. 33]

William Hogarth (1697–1764)
Study of a Sleeping Child, 1740–42
Black and red chalk, with stump, heightened with white on grey paper, 22.8 x 27 cm
British Museum [fig. 35]

Jean-Baptiste Greuze (1725–1805)
Boy with a Lesson-Book, c. 1757
Oil on canvas, 62.5 x 49 cm
National Galleries of Scotland. Bequest of Lady Murray of Henderland 1861

Jean-Baptiste Greuze (1725–1805)
Silence!, 1759
Oil on canvas, 62.2 x 50.5 cm
Lent by Her Majesty The Queen

Johan Joseph Zoffany (1733–1810)
Three Daughters of John, 3rd Earl of Bute, c. 1763–64
Oil on canvas, 101.2 x 126.5 cm
Tate: Accepted by HM Government in lieu of tax with additional payment (General Funds) made with assistance from the National Lottery through the Heritage Lottery Fund, the Art Fund and Tate Members 2002 [fig. 9]

William Mulready (1786–1863)
The Fight Interrupted, 1816
Oil on a gesso ground on panel, 71.8 x 93.2 cm
Victoria and Albert Museum. Given by John Sheepshanks, 1857

Fantasy and Reality

Bartolomé Esteban Murillo (1617–1682)
Three Boys, c. 1670
Oil on canvas, 168.3 x 109.8 cm
Dulwich Picture Gallery, London [fig. 6]

Jeffrey, Allen & Co (manufacturer)
Wallpaper after Murillo's *Invitation to a Game of Argolla*, c. 1843
Chiaroscuro prints from wood blocks, 81 x 53.4 cm
Victoria and Albert Museum

Thomas Gainsborough (1727–1788)
A Peasant Girl Gathering Faggots in a Wood, 1782
Oil on canvas, 169 x 123 cm
Manchester Art Gallery [fig. 50]

Sir Joshua Reynolds (1723–1792)
Miss Crewe, c. 1775
Oil on canvas, 137 x 112 cm
On long term loan from a private collection to Tate [fig. 49]

Sir Joshua Reynolds (1723–1792)
A Child Asleep, c. 1782
Oil on canvas 41.6 x 36 cm
The Christopher Tower Collection [fig. 38]

Sir Joshua Reynolds (1723–1792)
Portrait of Penelope Boothby, 1788
Oil on canvas, 75 x 62 cm
Lent from a private collection, courtesy of The Ashmolean Museum, University of Oxford [fig. 40]

Sir Thomas Lawrence (1769–1830)
Portrait of the Hon. George Fane (1819–1848), later Lord Burghersh, when a boy, c. 1822
Oil on canvas, 34.5 x 34.5 cm
Private collection

Sir John Everett Millais (1829–1896)
A Souvenir of Velazquez, 1868
Oil on canvas, 102.7 x 82.4 cm
The Royal Academy of Arts [fig. 53]

Sir John Everett Millais (1829–1896)
Bubbles, 1886
Oil on canvas, 113 x 82 cm
Unilever PLC. On loan to National Museums Liverpool, Lady Lever Art Gallery [fig. 4]

Jules Bastien-Lepage (1848–1884)
Pas Mèche (Nothing Doing), 1882
Oil on canvas, 132.1 x 89.5 cm
National Galleries of Scotland, Purchased 1913

Family Life

Mary Beale (1633–1699)
Head study of a boy, probably Charles Beale, the artist's younger son, c. 1664
Oil on paper laid down on canvas, 34 x 29 cm
Private collection

Allan Ramsay (1713–1784)
Infant Son of the Artist, 1741
Oil on canvas, 32 x 27.3 cm
National Galleries of Scotland. Presented by Lady Murray of Henderland as a memorial to her husband, Lord Murray of Henderland 1860 [fig. 39]

John Constable (1776–1837)
Maria Constable with Two of her Children, c. 1820
Oil paint on mahogany, 16.6 x 22.1 cm
Tate: Purchased 1984

Auguste Rodin (1840–1917)
The Young Mother, 1885
Marble, 61 x 48.3 cm
National Galleries of Scotland. Sir Alexander Maitland Bequest 1965

Pierre Bonnard (1867–1947)
The Evening Meal, c. 1903
Oil on canvas, 37.4 x 45.6 cm
The Henry Barber Trust, the Barber Institute of Fine Art

Winifred Nicholson (1893–1981)
The Artist's Children, Kate and Jake, at the Isle of Wight, 1931–32
Oil on canvas, 67 x 75 cm
Bristol Culture: Bristol Museums & Art Gallery [fig. 56]

Sir Stanley Spencer (1891–1959)
A Family Portrait (Hilda, Unity and Dolls), c. 1937
Oil on canvas, 76.2 x 50.8 cm
Leeds Museums and Galleries

Camille Pissarro (1830–1903)
Jeanne holding a fan, 1863
Oil on canvas, 56 x 46.5 cm
The Ashmolean Museum, University of Oxford. Presented by the Pissarro Family, 1952 [frontispiece]

Sir Jacob Epstein (1880–1959)
The Sisters (Anna and Annabel Freud), 1950–53
Bronze, 25 x 36 cm
The New Art Gallery Walsall, Garman Ryan Collection

John Ward (1917–2007)
The Newspaper Boys, 1960
Oil paint on canvas, 137.2 x 91.5 cm
Tate: Purchased with assistance from the Charlotte Bonham Carter Trust 1998

Lucian Freud (1922–2011)
Annabel, 1967
Oil on canvas, 35 x 27 cm
The New Art Gallery Walsall, Garman Ryan Collection [fig. 60]

Louise Bourgeois (1911–2010)
Children in Tub, 1994
Drypoint and aquatint on paper, based on a drawing made in 1941, 10.6 x 13.7 cm
Tate: Purchased 1994 [fig. 55]

Louise Bourgeois (1911–2010)
Birth, 1994
Drypoint on paper, based on a drawing made in 1941, 23.6 x 18.2 cm
Tate: Purchased 1994 [fig. 54]

CHILDHOOD NOW

Chantal Joffe, b. 1969

Chantal Joffe, b. 1969
Esme (First Portrait), 2004
Oil on board, 29.2 x 21.8 cm
Courtesy the artist and Victoria Miro, London/Venice
[fig. 58]

Chantal Joffe
Self-Portrait with Esme, 2008
Oil on board, 305 x 153 cm
National Portrait Gallery

Chantal Joffe
Paddling Pool I, 2008
Oil on board, 30 x 40 cm
Courtesy the artist and Victoria Miro, London/Venice
[fig. 57]

Chantal Joffe
Esme and Vita, 2008
Oil on canvas, 31 x 31 cm
Courtesy the artist and Victoria Miro, London/Venice

Chantal Joffe
Self-portrait combing Esme's hair, 2009
Oil on board, 40.7 x 51 cm
Courtesy the artist and Victoria Miro, London/Venice

Chantal Joffe
Vita, Alba and Esme, 2009
Oil on canvas, 36 x 46 cm
Victoria Miro

Chantal Joffe
Esme's 7th Birthday, 2011
Oil on canvas, 38 x 46 cm
Courtesy the artist and Victoria Miro, London/Venice
[fig. 10]

Chantal Joffe
Self-Portrait with Esme Watching TV, 2012
Oil on board, 244 x 183 cm
Courtesy the artist and Victoria Miro, London/Venice

Chantal Joffe
Poppy, Esme, Oleanna, Gracie and Kate, 2014
Oil on canvas, 40 x 80 cm
Courtesy the artist and Victoria Miro, London/Venice

Chantal Joffe
Esme in a Blue Skirt, 2014
Oil on canvas, 183 x 122 cm
Courtesy the artist and Victoria Miro, London/Venice

Chantal Joffe
Self-Portrait with Vita and Esme on the swings, 2015
Oil on canvas, 36 x 46 cm
Courtesy the artist and Victoria Miro, London/Venice

Chantal Joffe
Esme in a Green T-shirt, 2017
Oil on board, 35.6 x 28 cm
Courtesy the artist and Victoria Miro, London/Venice

Chantal Joffe
Self-portrait with Esme at bedtime, 2018
Oil on board, 38.5 x 46.2 cm
Courtesy the artist and Victoria Miro, London/Venice
[back cover]

Chantal Joffe
Esme on the Sofa, 2018
Oil on canvas, 213.5 x 152.5 cm
Courtesy the artist and Victoria Miro, London/Venice
[fig. 59]

Mark Fairnington, b. 1957

Mark Fairnington
Lee (Green), 2013
Oil on panel 69.5 x 65.5 cm
Artist's Collection

Mark Fairnington
Jason, 2013
Oil on panel, 80 x 35 cm
Artist's Collection

Mark Fairnington
Lee's Eye, 2011
Oil on panel, 7 x 7 cm
Artist's Collection

Mark Fairnington
Jason's Eye, 2011
Oil on panel, 7 x 7 cm
Artist's Collection [fig.62]

Mark Fairnington
The Blue Boys, 2015
Oil on canvas, 104 x 60 cm

Mark Fairnington
Jason (Grey), 2014
Oil on panel 28.5 x 40 cm
Artist's Collection

Mark Fairnington
Lee and Jason, 2012
Oil on panel, 57 x 31 cm
Artist's Collection

Mark Fairnington
Lee and Jason, 2011
Oil on panel, 49 x 44 cm
Artist's Collection [fig. 61]

Mark Fairnington
Lee, 2013
Oil on panel 80 x 35 cm
Artist's Collection

Mark Fairnington
Lee and Jason, 2012
Oil on panel, 57 x 31 cm
Artist's Collection

Mark Fairnington, b. 1957
The Swimming Hole, 2018
Oil on panel, 17 x 15 cm
Artist's Collection

Matthew Krishanu, b. 1980

Matthew Krishanu
Two Boys, 2012
Oil on board, 21 x 30 cm
Private Collection

Matthew Krishanu
Boys on a Rock, 2018
Oil on canvas, 55 x 70 cm
Private Collection

Matthew Krishanu
Swimming Pool, 2018
Oil on canvas, 60 x 75 cm
Artist's Collection

Matthew Krishanu
Kashmir, 2014
Oil on canvas, 125 x 175 cm
Artist's Collection

Matthew Krishanu
Bows and Arrows, 2018
Oil on canvas, 200 x 140 cm
Artist's Collection

Matthew Krishanu
Boy in Water, 2013
Oil on board, 21 x 30 cm
Private Collection

Matthew Krishanu
Boy on a Bed, 2005
Acrylic on canvas, 40 x 30 cm
Artist's Collection

Matthew Krishanu, b. 1980
Safari, 2013
Oil and acrylic on linen, 50 x 60 cm
Collection Amrita Jhaveri [fig. 63]

Matthew Krishanu, b. 1980
Skeleton, 2014
Oil on canvas, 150 x 200 cm
Arts Council Collection [fig. 64]

Matthew Krishanu
Limbs, 2014
Oil on canvas, 180 x 140 cm
Private Collection [frontispiece]

BIBLIOGRAPHY

ARNOLD 1988
Janet Arnold, *Queen Elizabeth's Wardrobe Unlock'd*, Leeds, 1988

BARNES 2004
Susan J. Barnes et al., *Van Dyck: A Complete Catalogue of the Paintings*, New Haven/London, 2004

BATH/KENDAL 2005
Amina Wright, *Pictures of Innocence, Portraits of Children from Hogarth to Lawrence*, exh. cat. Bath (The Holburne Museum)/Kendal (Abbot Hall Art Gallery), 2005

BENSON & ESHER 2009
Arthur Christopher Benson and Viscount Reginald Baliol Brett Esher, The Letters of Queen Victoria: A Selection from Her Majesty's Correspondence between the Years 1837 and 1861, vol. 3, 1854-1861., Project Gutenberg ebook, 2009

BERKELEY/MEMPHIS/OMAHA 1995–96
J. C. Steward, *The New Child: British Art and the Origins of Modern Childhood, 1730–1830*, exh. cat. Berkeley (University of California Art Museum)/ Memphis (Dixon Galleries)/Omaha (Joslyn Art Museum), Baltimore, 1995-96

BERNADAC AND OBRIST 1998
Marie-Louise Bernadac and Hans-Ulrich Obrist (eds.), *Louise Bourgeois: Destruction of the Father/ Reconstruction of the Father: Writings and Interviews 1923–1997*, Cambridge Mass./London, 1998

BOOTHBY 1796
Brooke Boothby, *Sorrows Sacred to the Memory of Penelope*, London, 1796

BRAY 2013
Xavier Bray, *Murillo at Dulwich Picture Gallery*, London 2013

BRYANT 1996
Julius Bryant, 'The dark side of *The Kitten*: A Wright of Derby for Kenwood', *Apollo*, December 1996, vol. 144, no.418, pp. 18–19

BRYANT 2012
Julius Bryant, *Kenwood: Paintings in the Iveagh Bequest*, New Haven/London, 2012

BUTCHART, 2015
Amber Jane Butchart, *Nautical Chic*, London, 2015

CAMPBELL 1990
Lorne Campbell, *Renaissance Portraits: European Portrait Painting in the fourteenth, fifteenth and sixteenth centuries*, New Haven/London, 1990

CAMPBELL ORR 2002
Clarissa Campbell Orr (ed.), *Queenship in Britain 1660–1837: Royal Patronage, Court Culture and Dynastic Politics*, Manchester, 2002

COXON 2010
Ann Coxon, *Louise Bourgeois*, London, 2010

CRONE AND SCHAESBERG 2008
Rainer Crone and Petrus Graf Schaesberg, *The Secret of the Cells*, Munich/London, 2008

CROWN 1984
Patricia Crown, 'Portraits and fancy pictures by Gainsborough and Reynolds: Contrasting Images of Childhood', *British Journal for Eighteenth-Century Studies*, vol. 7, 1984, pp. 159-167

CUNNINGHAM 1863
P. Cunningham, 'New Materials for the Life of Thomas Banks, R.A.', *The Builder*, vol. 21, 3 January 1863

DEKKER AND GROENENDIJK 1991
Jeroen J. H. Dekker and Leendert F. Groenendijk, 'The Republic of God or the Republic of Children? Childhood and Child-Rearing after the Reformation: An Appraisal of Simon Schama's Thesis about the Uniqueness of the Dutch Case', *Oxford Review of Education*, vol. 17, no. 3, 1991, pp. 317-335

DURANTINI 1983
Mary Frances Durantini, *The Child in Seventeenth-Century Dutch Painting*, Epping: Bowker, 1983

EADE 2019 (FORTHCOMING)
J. Eade, 'The Early Modern Child: Portraiture', in *The Early Modern Child*, ed. A. French, London, forthcoming 2019

EDWARDS 1988
Anne Edwards, *Shirley Temple. American Princess*, New York, 1988

EZELL 1983
M. J. M. Ezell. 'John Locke's Images of Childhood: Early Eighteenth Century Response to Some Thoughts Concerning Education', *Eighteenth-Century Studies*, vol. 17, no. 2, 1983, pp. 146–47

FISHER 2011
Celia Fisher, *Flowers of the Renaissance*, London, 2011

FOISTER 1983
Susan Foister, *Drawings by Holbein from the Royal Library, Windsor Castle*, New York, 1983

FOISTER 2004
Susan Foister, *Holbein and England*, New Haven/ London, 2004

FRANKFURT/LONDON 2007
Mirjam Neumeister, *The Changing Face of Childhood: British Children's Portraits and their Influence in Europe*, exh. cat. Frankfurt (Städel Museum)/London (Dulwich Picture Gallery), 2007

FRIJHOFF AND SPIES 2004
Willem Frijoff and Marijke Spies, *Dutch Culture in a European Perspective*, Assen/Basingstoke, 2004

GERARD 1633
John Gerard, *The herball, or, Generall historie of plantes/gathered by John Gerarde of London, master in chirurgerie; very much enlarged and amended by Thomas Johnson, citizen and apothecarye*, London, 1633

GLASGOW 1979
Christopher Carrell and Cordelia Oliver (eds.), *Winifred Nicholson: Paintings 1900–1978*, exh. cat. Glasgow (Third Eye Centre), 1979

GOMBRICH 2007
E. H. Gombrich, *The Story of Art*, 16th edn. London, 2007

GORDENKER, 2001
Emilie E. S. Gordenker, *Anthony van Dyck (1599–1641) and the Representation of Dress in Seventeenth-Century Portraiture*, Turnhout, 2001

GOROVOY AND ASBAGHI 1997
Jerry Gorovoy and Pandora Tabatabai Asbaghi, *Louise Bourgeois: Blue Days and Pink Days*, Milan, 1997

GREIG 2013
Geordie Greig, *Breakfast with Lucian: The Astounding Life and Outrageous Times of Britain's Great Modern Painter*, New York, 2013

GROOTENBOER 2018
Grootenboer, Hanneke, 'Treasuring the Gaze: Eye Miniature Portraits and the Intimacy of Vision,' *The Art Bulletin*, vol. 88, no. 3, 2006, pp. 496-507

HAARLEM/ANTWERP 2000
Jan Baptist Bedaux and Rudi Ekkart, *Pride and Joy: Children's Portraits in the Netherlands 1500–1700*, exh. cat. Haarlem (Frans Halsmuseum)/Antwerp (Koninklijk Museum voor Schone Kunsten), New York, 2000

HAYWARD, 2007
Maria Hayward (ed.), *Dress at the Court of King Henry VIII*, Leeds, 2007

HOFRICHTER 1989
Frima Fox Hofrichter, *Judith Leyster: A woman painter in Holland's Golden Age*, Doornspijk, 1989

HOMANS, 1998
Margaret Homans, *Royal Representations: Queen Victoria and Visual Culture 1837–1876*, Chicago, 1998

HOME 1903
J. A. Home (ed.) *Letters of Lady Louisa Stuart to Miss Louisa Clinton*, 2nd edn, Edinburgh, 1903

HIBBERT 1999
Christopher Hibbert, *George III: A Personal History*, London, 1999

HILTON AND HIRSCH 2000
Mary Hilton and Pam Hirsch, *Practical Visionaries: Women, Education and Social Progress, 1790–1930*, Harlow, 2000

HUGGETT, MALCOLM-DAVIES AND MIKHAILA 2013
Jan Huggett, Jane Malcolm-Davis and Ninya Mikhaila, *The Tudor Child: Clothing and Culture 1485 to 1625*, London, 2013

KAMENSKY 2016
Jane Kamensky, *A Revolution in Color. The World of John Singleton Copley*, New York/London, 2016

KÜSTER 2011
Ulf Küster, *Louise Bourgeois*, Ostfildern, 2011

LAMPERT 2011
Catherine Lampert, 'Lucian Freud Obituary', *The Guardian*, 22 July 2011

LANGMUIR 2006
Erika Langmuir, *Imagining Childhood*, New Haven/London, 2006

LAYARD 1906
G.S. Layard (ed.), *Sir Thomas Lawrence's Letter-Bag*, London, 1906

LEVEY 2005
Michael Levey, *Sir Thomas Lawrence*, New Haven/London, 2005

LOACH 1999
Jennifer Loach, *Edward VI*, New Haven, 1999

LOCKE 1693
John Locke, *Some Thoughts Concerning Education* (1693) and *Of the Conduct of the Understanding* (1706), ed. Ruth W. Grant and Nathan Tarcov, Indianapolis/Cambridge, 1996

LOCKE 1779
John Locke, *Some Thoughts Concerning Education & of the Conduct of the Understanding* (1779), ed. Ruth Grant and Nathan Tarcov, Indianapolis, 1996

LONDON 1974
John Russell, *Lucian Freud*, exh. cat. London (The Arts Council of Great Britain), 1974

LONDON 1983
Malcolm Rogers, *William Dobson, 1611–46*, exh. cat. London (National Portrait Gallery), 1983

LONDON 1995
Susan Foister, 'The Production and Reproduction of Holbein's Portraits', in Karen Hearn (ed.), *Dynasties: Painting in Tudor and Jacobean England 1530–1630*, exh. cat. London (Tate), 1995, pp. 21–26

LONDON 1995–96
Karen Hearn (ed.), *Dynasties: Painting in Tudor and Jacobean England 1530–1630*, exh. cat. London (Tate), 1995–96

LONDON 2002
William Feaver, *Lucian Freud*, exh. cat. London (Tate), 2002

LONDON 2003
Titian, exh. cat. London (National Gallery), 2003

LONDON 2004
Jane Roberts, *George III and Queen Charlotte: Patronage, Collecting and Court Taste*, exh. cat. London (Queen's Gallery), 2004

LONDON 2006
Susan Foister, *Holbein in England*, exh. cat. London (Tate Britain), 2006

LONDON 2007
Frances Morris (ed.), *Louise Bourgeois*, exh. cat. London (Tate Modern), 2007

LONDON 2009A
Karen Hearn (ed.), *Van Dyck & Britain*, exh. cat. London (Tate), 2009

LONDON 2009B
Desmond Shawe-Taylor, *The Conversation Piece: Scenes of Fashionable Life*, exh. cat. London (Queen's Gallery), 2009

LONDON 2010
Jonathan Marsden, *Victoria & Albert: Art & Love*, exh. cat. London (Queen's Gallery), 2010.

LONDON 2012A
Catharine MacLeod, *The Lost Prince: The Life & Death of Henry Stuart*, exh. cat. London (National Portrait Gallery), 2012

LONDON 2012B
Sarah Howgate, *Lucian Freud: Portraits*, exh. cat. London (National Portrait Gallery), 2012

LONDON 2013
Anna Reynolds, *In Fine Style: The Art of Tudor and Stuart Fashion*, exh. cat. London (Queen's Gallery), 2013

LONDON 2013–14
Tarnya Cooper, *Elizabeth I & Her People*, exh. cat. London (National Portrait Gallery), 2013–14

LONDON 2014
Charlotte Bolland and Tarnya Cooper, *The Real Tudors: Kings and Queens Rediscovered*, exh. cat. London (National Portrait Gallery), 2014

LONDON 2015
Sarah Howgate, 'Chantal Joffe in conversation with Sarah Howgate' in *Friendship Portraits: Chantal Joffe and Ishbel Myerscough*, exh. cat. London (National Portrait Gallery), 2015

LONDON 2018A
David H. Solkin, *Gainsborough's Family Album*, exh. cat. London (National Portrait Gallery), 2018

LONDON 2018B
Desmond Shawe-Taylor and Per Rumberg (eds.), *Charles I: King and Collector*, exh. cat. London (Royal Academy of Arts), 2018

LONDON/AMSTERDAM/FUKUOKA/TOKYO 2007–08
Jason Rosenfeld and Alison Smith, *Millais*, exh. cat. London (Tate)/Amsterdam (Van Gogh Museum)/Fukuoka (Kitakyushu Municipal Museum of Art)/Tokyo (Bunkamura Museum of Art), 2007–08

LONDON/ANTWERP 1999
Christopher Brown and Hans Vlieghe, *Van Dyck 1599–1641*, exh. cat. London (Royal Academy)/Antwerp (Royal Museum), 1999

LONDON/FRANKFURT 2007
Mirjam Neumeister (ed.), *The Changing Face of Childhood: British Children's Portraits and their Influence in Europe*, exh. cat. London (Dulwich Picture Gallery)/Frankfurt (Städel Museum), 2007

LONDON/MUNICH 2001
Xanthe Brooke and Peter Cherry, *Murillo: Scenes of Childhood*, exh. cat. London (Dulwich Picture Gallery)/Munich (Alte Pinakothek), 2001

LONDON/PARIS 1988
Richard Ormond and Carol Blackett-Ord, *Franz Xaver Winterhalter and the Courts of Europe (1830–70)*, exh. cat. London (National Portrait Gallery)/Paris (Musée du Petit Palais), 1988

MACLAREN AND BROWN 1991
Neil MacLaren and Christopher Brown, *The Dutch School, 1600–1900* (National Gallery London), London/New Haven, 1991

MANNINGS AND POSTLE 2000
David Mannings and Martin Postle, *Sir Joshua Reynolds: A Complete Catalogue of His Paintings*, London/New Haven, 2000

MILLAR 1992
Oliver Millar, *The Victorian Pictures in the Collection of Her Majesty the Queen*, Cambridge, 1992

MILLAR 1963
Oliver Millar, *The Tudor, Stuart and Early Georgian Pictures in the Collection of Her Majesty the Queen*, London, 1963

MORONEY 2007
Mic Moroney, 'Lucian Freud: Prophet of Discomfort,' *Irish Arts Review*, vol. 24, no. 2, Summer, 2007, pp. 80–85

NEW YORK 1994
Deborah Wye and Carol Smith, *The Prints of Louise Bourgeois*, exh. cat. New York (Museum of Modern Art), 1994

NEW YORK 2016
Stijn Alsteen and Adam Eaker, *Van Dyck: The Anatomy of Portraiture*, exh. cat. New York (The Frick Collection), 2016

NICHOLSON 1987
Andrew Nicholson (ed.), *Unknown Colour; Paintings, Letters, Writings by Winifred Nicholson*, London, 1987

NORTHCOTE 1815
James Northcote, *Supplement to the Memoirs of the Life, Writings, Discourses, and Professional Works of Sir Joshua Reynolds, Knt.*, London, 1815

NOTTINGHAM/LONDON 1998
Martin Postle, *Angels & Urchins, The Fancy Picture in 18th-Century British Art*, exh. cat. Nottingham (Djanogly Art Gallery, University of Nottingham)/London (Kenwood House, Hampstead), 1998

ORME 2001
Nicholas Orme, *Medieval Children*, New Haven/London, 2001

PARISOT 2013
Eric Parisot, *Graveyard Poetry: Religion, Aesthetics and the Mid-Eighteenth-Century Poetic Condition*, Farnham, 2013

PAULSON 1997
Ronald Paulson (ed.), *William Hogarth, The Analysis of Beauty (1753)*, New Haven, 1997

PENNY 1977
Nicholas Penny, *Church Monuments in Romantic England*, London, 1977

PIPER 1968
David Piper, *Van Dyck*, London, 1968

POINTON 1993
Marcia Pointon, *Hanging the Head, Portraiture and Social Formation in Eighteenth-Century England*, New Haven/London, 1993

POLLOCK 1987
Linda Pollock, *A Lasting Relationship: Parents and Children over Three Centuries*, Hanover/London, 1987

POSTLE 1995
Martin Postle, *Sir Joshua Reynolds: The Subject Pictures*, Cambridge, 1995

PRISEMAN 2018
Robert Priseman, 'Matthew Krishanu: From Bradford to Bangladesh and onward,' *Art UK*, 10 April 2018

RECKITT 1952
Basil N. Reckitt, *Charles the First and Hull, 1639–1645*, London, 1952

RETFORD 2010
Kate Retford, 'A death in the Family: Posthumous Portraiture in Eighteenth-Century England, *Art History*, vol. 33, no. 1, February 2010, pp. 76–77

ROUSSEAU 1763
Jean-Jacques Rousseau, *Emilius; or, A New System of Education. Translated from the French of Mr. J. J. Rousseau, Citizen of Geneva, by The Translator of Eloisa*, London, 1763

ROYAL ARMOURIES 2003
Royal Armouries, *An Introduction to Princely Armours and Weapons of Childhood*, Leeds, 2003

RUEL 1995
Malcolm Ruel, 'Lucian Freud and the Naked Self', *Cambridge Journal of Anthropology*, vol. 18, no. 3, 1995, pp. 15–24

SAINT LOUIS/LONDON 2012
Judith W. Mann and Babette Bonn, *Federico Barocci, Renaissance Master of Color and Line*, exh. cat. Saint Louis (Art Museum)/London (National Gallery), New Haven, 2012

SALFORD 2018
Olivia Laing, 'It Never Actually Is,' in *Chantal Joffe: Personal Feeling Is the Main Thing*, exh. cat. Salford (The Lowry), 2018, pp. 161–64

SAN FRANCISCO/BALTIMORE/LONDON 1997
Joaneth A Spicer and Lynn Federle Orr (eds.), *Masters of Light. Dutch Painters in Utrecht during the Golden Age*, exh. cat. San Francisco (Fine Arts Museum)/Baltimore (Walters Art Gallery)/London (National Gallery), New Haven, 1997

SCHAMA 1991
Simon Schama, *The Embarrassment of Riches. An Interpretation of Dutch Culture in the Golden Age*, London, 1991

SCOTT 2010
Jennifer Scott, *The Royal Portrait: Image and Impact*, London, 2010

SHAWE-TAYLOR 2009
Desmond Shawe-Taylor, *The Conversation Piece: Scenes of Fashionable Life*, London 2009

SMITH 1981
Graham Smith, 'Jan Steen and Raphael', *The Burlington Magazine*, vol. 123, no. 936, 1981, pp. 159–160

SOLKIN 2008
David H. Solkin, *Painting out of the Ordinary. Modernity and the Art of Everyday Life in Early Nineteenth-Century England*, New Haven/London, 2008

STRONG 1969
Roy Strong, *The English Icon: Elizabethan and Jacobean Portraiture*, London/New York, 1969

TEMPLE BLACK 1988
Shirley Temple Black, *Child Star. An Autobiography*, New York, 1988

WALPOLE 1782
Horace Walpole, *Anecdotes of Painting in England; with some Account of the principal Artists; And incidental Notes on other Arts*, 2nd edn., 4 vols., London, 1782

WARNER 1979
Marina Warner, *Queen Victoria's Sketchbook*, London, 1979

WASHINGTON/AMSTERDAM 1996
Jansen, (ed.) *Jan Steen: Painter and Storyteller*, exh. cat. Washington DC (National Gallery of Art)/Amsterdam (Rijksmuseum), New Haven, 1996

WEBSTER 1989
M. Webster 'An eighteenth-century family: Hogarth's portrait of the Graham children', *Apollo*, vol. 130, no. 31, 1989, pp. 171–77.

WHITLEY 1915
William T. Whitley, *Thomas Gainsborough*, London, 1915

WHITLEY 1928
W.T. Whitley, *Artists and Their Friends in England 1700–1799*, London, 1928

WINDELER 1978
Robert Windeler, *The Films of Shirley Temple*, New York, 1978

WOODALL 1997
Joanna Woodall, *Portraiture: Facing the Subject*, Manchester, 1997

ŽAKULA 2011
Tijana Žakula, 'The indecorous appeal of beggar boys: Murillo, de Lairesse and Gainsborough', *Simiolus: Netherlands Quarterly for the History of Art*, vol. 35, no. 3, 2011, pp. 165–73

PHOTOGRAPHIC CREDITS

Front cover, figs. 7, 12, 14, 16, 17, 18, 20, 21, 26, 27, 28, 29, 30, 31, 32, 34, 36, 37 Royal Collection Trust/© Her Majesty Queen Elizabeth II 2018; back cover, fig. 56 © Trustees of Winifred Nicholson; frontispiece, fig 63 Photography by Peter Mallet; page 6, fig. 40 © Ashmolean Museum, University of Oxford; figs. 1, 11, 15 © Compton Verney, photography by Prudence Cuming Assosiates Ltd; fig. 2 National Galleries of Scotland. Purchased by Private Treaty with the aid of the National Heritage Memorial Fund 1984; fig. 3 © The National Gallery, London. Bequeathed by C. F. Leach, 1943.; fig. 4 Reproduced with kind permission of Unilever from an original in Unilever Archives. Image supplied by National Museums Liverpool.; fig. 5 © Victoria and Albert Museum, London. Reproduced with kind permission of Unilever from an original in Unilever Archives; fig. 6 Dulwich Picture Gallery, London; fig. 8 National Gallery of Art, Washington; Samuel H. Kress Collection; figs. 9, 49, 51 © Tate, London 2019; figs. 10, 57, 58, 59, endpiece © Chantal Joffe. Courtesy of the artist and Victoria Miro, London/Venice. Photography by Jack Hems; fig. 13 National Gallery of Art, Washington; Andrew W. Mellon Collection; fig. 19 Licensed by the Ministero dei beni e delle attività culturali - Torino, Musei Reali - Galleria Sabauda; fig. 22 The Governing Body of Christ Church, Oxford; fig. 23 National Galleries of Scotland. Purchased with the aid of the Heritage Lottery Fund, the Scottish Office and the Art Fund 1996; fig. 24 National Galleries of Scotland. Purchased 1935; fig. 25 Copyright Royal Armouries Museum; fig. 33 © The National Gallery, London. Presented by Lord Duveen through The Art Fund, 1934.; figs. 35, 44 © The Trustees of the British Museum; fig. 38 The Trustees of the Christopher Tower Collection; fig. 39 National Galleries of Scotland. Presented by Lady Murray of Henderland as a memorial to her husband, Lord Murray of Henderland 1860; fig. 41 Wolverhampton Art Gallery, West Midlands UK / Bridgeman Images; fig. 42 Photo by ullstein bild/ullstein bild via Getty Images; fig. 43 National Galleries of Scotland. Purchased with the assistance of the Art Fund and the National Heritage Memorial Fund 1989; fig. 45 Historic England Archive; fig. 46 Wellcome Collection. CC BY https://wellcomecollection.org/works/ghgbsvf4; fig. 47 Photograph © 2019 Museum of Fine Arts, Boston; fig. 48 © Victoria and Albert Museum, London; fig. 50 © Manchester Art Gallery / Bridgeman Images; fig. 51 © Tate, London 2019; fig. 52 Private Collection / Bridgeman Images; fig. 53 © Royal Academy of Arts, London; photographer: John Hammond; figs. 54, 55 © The Easton Foundation/VAGA at ARS, NY and DACS, London 2018 / © Tate, London 2019; fig. 60 The New Art Gallery Walsall, Garman Ryan Collection; figs. 61, 62 Photography by Peter White, FXP Photograph; 64 © Southbank Centre

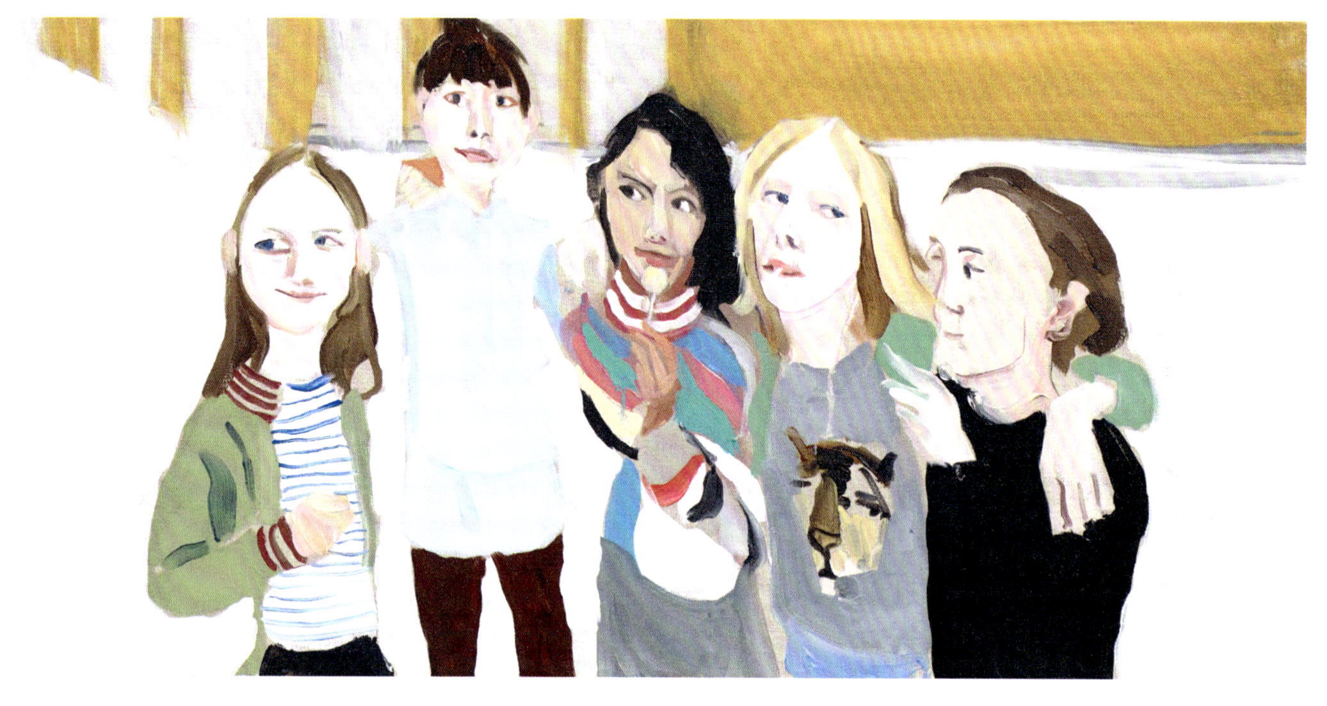

Chantal Joffe, *Poppy, Esme, Oleanna, Gracie and Kate*, 2014, oil on canvas, 40 x 80 cm